BBC
BOOKS

DELIA'S
VEGETARIAN
COLLECTION

Published by BBC Books, an imprint of Ebury Publishing
A Random House Group Company
The Random House Group Limited Reg. No. 954009

First published in hardback 2002
ISBN 978 0 563 48818 7
20 19 18 17 16 15 14 13 12

Paperback edition first published 2006
ISBN 978 0 563 49364 8
10 9 8 7 6

For photographic credits, see page 256

A proportion of these recipes have been previously published in *Delia's Winter Collection*, *Delia's Summer Collection*, *Delia's How to Cook* (three volumes), *Delia's Complete Illustrated Cookery Course* and *Delia Smith's Christmas*.

Edited for BBC Worldwide Ltd
by New Crane Publishing Ltd

Editor: Sarah Randell
Designer: Paul Webster
Sub-editor: Heather Cupit
Editorial Assistant: Diana Hughes
Recipe Testing: Pauline Curran
Commissioner for BBC Books: Vivien Bowler

Printed and bound by Butler Tanner & Dennis Ltd

BBC
BOOKS

DELIA'S
VEGETARIAN
COLLECTION

Conversion tables

All these are approximate conversions, which have either been rounded up or down. In a few recipes it has been necessary to modify them very slightly. Never mix metric and imperial measures in one recipe. Stick to one system or the other.

All spoon measurements used throughout this book are level, unless specified otherwise.

All butter is salted, unless specified otherwise.

Weights

½ oz	10 g
¾	20
1	25
1½	40
2	50
2½	60
3	75
4	110
4½	125
5	150
6	175
7	200
8	225
9	250
10	275
12	350
1 lb	450
1 lb 8 oz	700
2	900
3	1.35 kg

Volume

2 fl oz	55 ml
3	75
5 (¼ pint)	150
10 (½ pint)	275
1 pint	570
1¼	725
1¾	1 litre
2	1.2
2½	1.5
4	2.25

Dimensions

⅛ inch	3 mm
¼	5
½	1 cm
¾	2
1	2.5
1¼	3
1½	4
1¾	4.5
2	5
2½	6
3	7.5
3½	9
4	10
5	13
5¼	13.5
6	15
6½	16
7	18
7½	19
8	20
9	23
9½	24
10	25.5
11	28
12	30

Oven temperatures

Gas mark	1	275°F	140°C
	2	300	150
	3	325	170
	4	350	180
	5	375	190
	6	400	200
	7	425	220
	8	450	230
	9	475	240

Foreword

Look, there's no point me pretending I spend day in and day out julienning baby organic beetroot, tossing them in extra virgin avocado oil, teasing them with mortared rock salt and serving them wrapped in a buckwheat parcel with a tied-chive garnish. I'm a cheese-on-toast person, and my idea of fine dining is not eating it standing up.

My other confession must be that the only recipes of Delia's I've done are the Christmas Cake and the Chocolate Brownie with Fudge Topping (in fact the book falls open, embarrassingly, at that very page, rather like a 60s edition of *Lady Chatterley's Lover*). Much as I love Delia the person, you will never find me throwing a three-course Delia dinner, calling all pals with a merry cry of 'I'm doing page 53 and most of the last chapter!'

But I'm willing to give this a go. I'm that sad throwback, a 70s vegetarian. I scavenged for wholefood ingredients in warehouses where you brought your own scoop and everything was in its own dustbin. I made huge glutinous lentil stews, which were only thrown out when they started to fizz. I baked bread that could only be sliced by taking it to a timber yard. And don't get me started on the butter bean loaf. I'll just say that eating it in a room without adequate ventilation was tantamount to suicide.

So whoo hoo for this book, I say. I may never do more than the carrot soup and the bubble and squeak, but I know all you proper cooks out there will get stuck in, and that means my chances of being invited out and NOT given a plate of tired veg with a space where they've just hastily removed the chicken, have just shot up 100 per cent. Thanks, Delia.

Victoria Wood

Contents

Introduction

There are three reasons why this book has come into being. First, throughout the 38 years I've been writing recipes – although not a vegetarian myself – I have greatly enjoyed creating vegetarian recipes, and cooking and serving them at home. I have always included a selection of them in each of my books. Not unreasonably, many, many people have requested that I should bring them all together in one book, which would be exclusively for vegetarians.

There are also – and this is the second reason – a growing number of people who are not vegetarians but who find themselves entertaining vegetarians. They, too, have been making precisely the same request.

Lastly, this book is for me and my team of chefs at Norwich City Football Club. Since we started running an enormous full-time catering operation, we have been cooking for vegetarians on a daily basis. This means we have to search constantly through all my books for ideas and recipes, all of which can be very time-consuming.

So here for all of you (and me) is the best of Delia, vegetarian-wise, a collection that spans my entire cookery career, plus a whole batch of brand-new recipes, too. But, whatever your reasons for wanting this book, I hope it fits the bill.

Delia

Delia Smith

Chapter One
Soups

Chickpea, Chilli and Coriander Soup
Serves 6

Slow-cooked Celery and Celeriac Soup
Serves 6

This has decidedly Mexican overtones. It isn't too hot and spicy but the presence of the chilli does give it a nice kick, and the flavour and texture of chickpeas is perfect for soup.

8 oz (225 g) chickpeas, soaked overnight in twice their volume of cold water

2 small red chillies, halved, deseeded and chopped

1 tablespoon coriander seeds

½ oz (10 g) fresh coriander, leaves and stalks separated (reserve the leaves as garnish)

1 tablespoon cumin seeds

2 oz (50 g) butter

6 fat cloves garlic, peeled and finely chopped

1 teaspoon ground turmeric

grated zest 1 lemon, plus 2-3 tablespoons lemon juice, to serve

7 fl oz (200 ml) crème fraîche

salt and freshly milled black pepper

To garnish:
1 mild, fat red or green chilli, deseeded and cut into very fine hair-like shreds
reserved coriander leaves (see above)

You will also need a large saucepan with a capacity of 6 pints (3.5 litres).

First of all, drain the chickpeas in a colander, rinse them under the cold tap, then place them in the saucepan with 2¾ pints (1.75 litres) of boiling water. Bring them up to simmering point, put a lid on and cook them very gently for about 1 hour or until the chickpeas are absolutely tender and squashy.

While they're cooking, prepare the rest of the soup ingredients. The coriander and cumin seeds should be dry-roasted in a small pre-heated frying pan for 2-3 minutes, then

crushed in a pestle and mortar. After that, melt the butter in the frying pan, add the crushed spices, along with the chopped garlic and chillies, and cook over a low heat for about 5 minutes. Now add the turmeric, stir and heat that gently before removing from the heat.

As soon as the chickpeas are tender, drain them in a colander placed over a bowl to reserve the cooking water. Transfer the chickpeas to a blender, together with a couple of ladles of cooking water, and purée them until fine and smooth. Now add the lemon zest, coriander stalks and spices from the frying pan, along with another ladleful of cooking water and blend once more until fine and smooth.

Next, the whole lot needs to go back into the saucepan with the rest of the reserved cooking water. Bring it all up to a gentle simmer, give it a good stir, season, then let it simmer gently for a further 30 minutes. All this can be done in advance, then when you're ready to serve the soup, re-heat very gently without letting it come to the boil. Stir in half the crème fraîche and the lemon juice, taste to check the seasoning, then serve in hot soup bowls with the rest of the crème fraîche swirled in and scatter with the shredded chilli and coriander leaves ■

Because the vegetables are very slowly cooked, this soup has lots of lovely flavour, and it's quite satisfying and filling, particularly with some Celeriac and Lancashire Cheese Bread (see page 225).

1 lb (450 g) celery stalks, trimmed and leaves reserved

1 lb 4 oz (570 g) celeriac

1 medium onion, peeled

2½ pints (1.5 litres) hot stock made with Marigold Swiss vegetable bouillon powder

3 bay leaves

salt and freshly milled black pepper

To garnish:
2 tablespoons natural yoghurt or crème fraîche
2 teaspoons celery salt
a few celery leaves (see above)

You will also need a blender, and a lidded, flameproof casserole with a capacity of 6 pints (3.5 litres).

Pre-heat the oven to gas mark 1, 275°F (140°C).

Just a word first about preparing the vegetables. You need to use a potato peeler to pare off any really stringy bits from the outside stalks of the celery. The nice thing is that the outside stalks are fine for soups – so if you're using a whole head of celery, once you've weighed out the amount you need, you can keep the tender inside stalks for munching on.

Peeling the celeriac may mean you lose quite a bit of the outside, as it's very fibrous. Once that's done, weigh it (you need 1 lb/450 g) and cut it into large chunks. The celery should also be cut into large chunks, and the same with the onion. All you do now is pop

the whole lot into the casserole, then add the stock and bay leaves, along with some salt and freshly milled black pepper. Bring it all up to simmering point on the hob, then put the lid on and transfer it to the oven to simmer very gently and slowly for 3 hours. After that, remove the bay leaves, allow the soup to cool a little, then blend in batches until smooth. (A large bowl to put each batch in is helpful here.)

Then, return the soup to the casserole and bring it back to a gentle simmer, tasting to check seasoning before serving. Serve in hot bowls with the yoghurt (or crème fraîche) spooned on top and the celery salt sprinkled over, garnished with a few celery leaves ■

Slow-cooked Celery and Celeriac Soup with Celeriac and Lancashire Cheese Bread

Left: Carrot and Artichoke Soup
Top right: Roasted Tomato Soup with a Purée of Basil and Olive Croutons

Roasted Tomato Soup with a Purée of Basil and Olive Croutons
Serves 4

Carrot and Artichoke Soup
Serves 6-8

At first you're going to think, 'Why bother to roast tomatoes just for soup?', but I promise you that once you've tasted the difference you'll know it's worth it – and roasting really isn't any trouble, it just means time in the oven.

1 lb 8 oz (700 g) medium ripe red tomatoes

1 small bunch fresh basil leaves, ¾ oz/20 g

3-4 tablespoons extra virgin olive oil

1 fat clove garlic, peeled and chopped

4 oz (110 g) potato

1 heaped teaspoon tomato purée

1 teaspoon balsamic vinegar

salt and freshly milled black pepper

For the olive croutons:

4 medium slices ciabatta bread, cubed

1 tablespoon olive oil

1 dessertspoon olive paste

You will also need a solid, shallow roasting tray, about 13 x 13 inches (33 x 33 cm).

Pre-heat the oven to gas mark 5, 375°F (190°C).

First of all, skin the tomatoes by pouring boiling water over them, then leave them for 1 minute exactly before draining them and slipping off the skins (protect your hands with a cloth if necessary). Now slice each tomato in half, arrange the halves on the roasting tray, cut side uppermost, and season with salt and pepper. Sprinkle a few droplets of olive oil on to each one, followed by the chopped garlic, and finally, top each one with a piece of basil leaf (dipping the basil in oil first to get a good coating).

Now pop the whole lot into the oven and roast the tomatoes for 50 minutes-1 hour or until the edges are slightly blackened – what happens in this process is that the

liquid in the tomatoes evaporates and concentrates their flavour, as do the toasted edges. About 20 minutes before the end of the roasting time, peel and chop the potato, place it in a saucepan with some salt, 15 fl oz (425 ml) boiling water and the tomato purée and simmer for 20 minutes.

For the croutons, place the bread cubes in a bowl, together with the olive oil and olive paste, and stir them around to get a good coating of both. Then arrange the croutons on a small baking sheet and bake in the oven for 8-10 minutes (remember to put a timer on). Leave to cool on the baking sheet.

When the tomatoes are ready, remove them from the oven and scrape them with all their juices and crusty bits into a food processor (a spatula is best for this), then add the contents of the potato saucepan and whiz everything to a not-too-uniform purée. If you want to, you can now sieve out the seeds but I prefer to leave them in, as I like the texture.

Just before serving the soup – which should be re-heated very gently, make the basil purée by stripping the remaining leaves into a mortar, sprinkling with ¼ teaspoon of salt, then bashing the leaves down with the pestle. It takes a minute or two for the leaves to collapse down and become a purée, at which point add 2 tablespoons of olive oil and the balsamic vinegar and stir well. Serve each bowl of soup, garnished with a swirl of purée and a few croutons ◼

This is one of my most favourite soups ever. Firstly, it has an extremely rich, beautiful colour – almost saffron-like, I would say. And secondly, the combination is so unique that people can never quite guess what it is. Jerusalem artichokes don't look user-friendly, but once you've cut off and discarded all the knobbly bits, the flavour is quite outstanding.

1 lb (450 g) carrots

1 lb 8 oz (700 g) Jerusalem artichokes

3 celery stalks

3 oz (75 g) butter

1 medium onion, peeled and roughly chopped

2½ pints (1.5 litres) hot stock made with Marigold Swiss vegetable bouillon powder

salt and freshly milled black pepper

To garnish:

2-3 tablespoons crème fraîche

fresh flat-leaf parsley leaves

You will also need a large saucepan with a capacity of about 6 pints (3.5 litres).

Start by peeling and de-knobbling the artichokes and, as you peel them, cut them into rough chunks and place them in a bowl of cold, salted water to prevent them from discolouring. Then scrape the carrots and slice them into largish chunks. Next, use a potato peeler to pare off any stringy bits from the celery and then roughly chop it.

Now melt the butter in the saucepan and soften the onion and celery in it for 5 minutes, keeping the heat fairly low. Then drain the artichokes and add them to the pan, along with the carrots. Add some salt and keeping the heat very low, put a lid on and let the vegetables sweat for 10 minutes to release their juices. After

that, pour in the stock, stir well, put the lid back on and simmer very gently for a further 20 minutes, or until the vegetables are soft. Now allow the soup to cool a little, then blend it in batches (a large bowl to put each batch in is helpful here). Taste to check the seasoning and re-heat the soup very gently until it just comes to simmering point.

Serve it in hot bowls, garnishing each one with a swirl of crème fraîche and a few parsley leaves ◼

Chilled Spanish Gazpacho
Serves 6

This is a truly beautiful soup for serving ice-cold in summer and particularly refreshing if we're lucky enough to have hot weather. However, please don't attempt to make it in the winter, as the flavourless imported salad vegetables will not do it justice.

1 lb 8 oz (700 g) firm ripe tomatoes

4 inch (10 cm), piece of cucumber, peeled and chopped

2 or 3 spring onions, peeled and chopped

2 cloves garlic, peeled and crushed

½ large red or green pepper, deseeded and chopped

1 heaped teaspoon chopped fresh basil, marjoram or thyme (whatever is available)

4 tablespoons olive oil

1½ tablespoons wine vinegar

salt and freshly milled black pepper

For the garnish:

½ large red or green pepper, deseeded and very finely chopped

4 inch (10 cm), piece of cucumber, peeled and finely chopped

2 spring onions, finely chopped

1 hard-boiled egg, finely chopped

1 heaped tablespoon chopped fresh parsley

salt and freshly milled black pepper

To serve:

4 ice cubes

small croutons

Begin by placing the tomatoes in a bowl and pouring boiling water over them; after a minute, the skins will loosen and you can slip them off very easily (use a cloth to protect your hands if you need to). Halve the tomatoes, scoop out and discard the seeds and roughly chop the flesh.

Now place the tomatoes, cucumber, spring onions, crushed garlic and chopped pepper in a blender, adding a seasoning of salt and pepper, the herbs, oil and wine vinegar. Then blend everything at top speed until the soup is absolutely smooth. (If your blender is very small, combine all the ingredients first, then blend in 2 or 3 batches.) Taste to check the seasoning and pour the soup into a bowl. Stir in a little cold water to thin it slightly — anything from 5 to 10 fl oz (150 to 275 ml) — cover the bowl with foil and chill thoroughly.

To make the garnish, simply combine all the ingredients, together with a seasoning of salt and freshly milled black pepper, and hand it round at the table, together with small croutons of bread fried till crisp in olive oil, well drained and cooled. Serve the soup with 4 ice cubes floating in it ■

Gardener's Soup
Serves 6-8

This is a soup for autumn when there's nearly always a glut of tomatoes and the over-ripe ones are sold cheaply; or, as the title suggests, it's helpful for the gardeners whose tomato and cucumber crops threaten to overwhelm them.

12 oz (350 g) ripe tomatoes, skinned

12 oz (350 g) cucumber, peeled and chopped

1 oz (25 g) butter

1 tablespoon oil

1 small onion, peeled and finely chopped

1 clove garlic, peeled and crushed

the outside leaves of a lettuce, shredded

1 medium potato, peeled and chopped

1 dessertspoon lemon juice

1 pint (570 ml) hot water, mixed with 1 teaspoon tomato purée

1 tablespoon shredded fresh basil

2 teaspoons chopped fresh parsley

salt and freshly milled black pepper

First, in a thick-based saucepan melt the butter with the oil and soften the onion in it for 5 minutes. Next, add the garlic, lettuce, cucumber, tomatoes and potato. Stir everything around, add seasoning and lemon juice, then pop the lid on and, keeping the heat low, let the vegetables sweat for a good 15 minutes. Add the hot water mixed with tomato purée, bring it up to simmering point, cover and simmer gently for a further 20 minutes or until the vegetables are soft.

Now pour the soup into a blender but only blend it for 6-8 seconds (the vegetables should be in very fine bits). Stir in the basil and sprinkle with the parsley. Serve hot with some fresh, crusty bread ■

Slow-cooked Root Vegetable Soup
Serves 6

Something happens to vegetables when they're cooked very slowly for a long time: their flavour becomes mellow but at the same time more intense. This soup is also virtually fat free.

8 oz (225 g) peeled carrots, cut into 2 inch (5 cm) lengths

8 oz (225 g) peeled celeriac, cut into 2 inch (5 cm) pieces

8 oz (225 g), trimmed and washed leeks, halved and cut into 2 inch (5 cm) lengths

8 oz (225 g) peeled swede, cut into 2 inch (5 cm) pieces

1 small onion, peeled and roughly chopped

2½ pints (1.5 litres) hot stock made with Marigold Swiss vegetable bouillon powder

3 bay leaves

salt and freshly milled black pepper

To garnish:

3 tablespoons fat-free Greek yoghurt

a few fresh chives, snipped

You will also need a 6 pint (3.5 litre) lidded, flameproof casserole.

Pre-heat the oven to gas mark 1, 275°F (140°C).

There's not much to do here once everything is peeled and chopped. All you do is place everything in the casserole and bring it up to a gentle simmer, then put the lid on, place it in the lowest part of the oven and leave it there for 3 hours, by which time the vegetables will be meltingly tender. Next, remove the bay leaves and process or blend the soup in several batches to a purée, then gently re-heat, and serve the soup in bowls with a teaspoon of Greek yoghurt swirled in each and garnished with the chives ■

Slow-cooked Root Vegetable Soup

Left: Watercress Soup. Top right: Pumpkin Soup with Toasted Sweetcorn

Pumpkin Soup with Toasted Sweetcorn
Serves 6

Watercress Soup
Serves 8

Cream of Celery Soup
Serves 4

This is a very fine combination: the soft, velvety texture of the pumpkin makes the soup deliciously creamy and the toasted sweetcorn provides contrasting flavour and some crunch.

1 lb 8 oz (700 g) pumpkin or butternut squash, peeled, deseeded and chopped into 1 inch (2.5 cm) dice

1 lb 4 oz (570 g) sweetcorn (off the cob weight, from 5-6 cobs)

1 oz (25 g) butter, plus 1 extra teaspoon, for the sweetcorn

1 medium onion, peeled and finely chopped

10 fl oz (275 ml) whole milk

1¼ pints (725 ml) hot stock made with Marigold Swiss vegetable bouillon powder

salt and freshly milled black pepper

Begin by melting 1 oz (25 g) of the butter in a large saucepan, then add the onion and soften it for about 8 minutes. After that, add the chopped pumpkin (or butternut squash), along with half the sweetcorn, then give everything a good stir and season with salt and pepper. Put the lid on and, keeping the heat low, allow the vegetables to sweat gently and release their juices – this should take about 10 minutes. Next, pour in the milk and stock and simmer gently for about 20 minutes. Put the lid on for this but leave a little gap (so it's not quite on) because, with the presence of the milk, it could boil over. Keep a close eye on it, anyway.

While that's happening, pre-heat the grill to its highest setting for 10 minutes. Melt the extra teaspoon of butter, mix the rest of the sweetcorn with it and spread it out on a baking tray, season with salt and pepper and pop it under the hot grill, about 3 inches (7.5 cm) from the heat – it will take about

8 minutes to become nicely toasted and golden, but remember to move the sweetcorn around on the baking tray halfway through.

When the soup is ready, pour it into a food processor or blender and blend it to a purée, leaving a little bit of texture – it doesn't need to be absolutely smooth. You will probably need to do this in 2 batches. Serve the soup in hot bowls with the toasted sweetcorn sprinkled over ■

Watercress is a star performer in so many ways. I love the fat, green leaves in salads, sprinkled with sea salt in sandwiches, in a sauce and perfect most of all, in this soup, which is always a joy to make and eat.

9 oz (250 g) watercress, de-stalked and chopped, a few leaves reserved for garnishing

4 oz (110 g) butter

the white part of 5 leeks (weighing about 14 oz/400 g), cleaned and roughly chopped

4 potatoes (about 1 lb 8 oz/700 g), peeled and roughly chopped

3 pints (1.75 litres) hot stock made with Marigold Swiss vegetable bouillon powder

4 heaped tablespoons crème fraîche

salt and freshly milled black pepper

First of all, melt the butter in a large, heavy-based saucepan, then add the chopped leeks, potatoes and watercress and stir them around so they are coated in butter.

Next, sprinkle in some salt, then cover with a lid and let the vegetables sweat over a very gentle heat for about 20 minutes, giving the mixture a good stir about halfway through.

After that, add the stock, bring everything up to simmering point and simmer, covered, for 10-15 minutes, or until the vegetables are quite tender. Then remove the pan from the heat and when the soup has cooled a little, blend it in batches, then return it to the saucepan. Now stir in 3 tablespoons of crème fraîche, season to taste and re-heat the soup very gently, without letting it boil.

Serve it in hot bowls and garnish each one with the reserved watercress leaves and an extra swirl of crème fraîche. Or, cool the soup and serve, chilled, garnished in the same way ■

Originally, the older varieties of so-called 'dirty' celery from the flat, black-earthed Fenlands of East Anglia had a short season – from October to January. If you're lucky enough to find some to use in this soup, there is much washing to do, but the flavour is exceptional, particularly after a light frost, when it's sweetest of all.

12 oz (350 g), celery stalks, trimmed and leaves reserved

1 oz (25 g) butter

4 oz (110 g), potatoes, peeled and cut into chunks

the white parts of 2 medium leeks, cleaned and sliced

1 pint (570 ml) hot stock made with Marigold Swiss vegetable bouillon powder

¼ teaspoon celery seeds

5 fl oz (150 ml) single cream

5 fl oz (150 ml) milk

salt and freshly milled black pepper

In a largish pan melt the butter over a low heat. Then chop the celery and add it to the pan with the potatoes and prepared leeks. Stir well, coating the vegetables with butter, cover and cook for about 15 minutes.

Then add the stock with the celery seeds and some salt. Bring to simmering point, cover once more and cook very gently for 20-25 minutes or until the vegetables are really tender. Purée the soup by blending it in batches, then return to the pan, stirring in the cream and milk.

Bring the soup back to the boil, check the seasoning, adding more salt and some pepper, if necessary. Then just before serving, chop the reserved celery leaves and stir them into the soup to give it extra colour ■

Cauliflower Soup with Roquefort
Serves 4-6

This is a truly sublime soup, as the cauliflower and Roquefort seem to meld together so well but I have also tried it with mature Cheddar and I'm sure it would be good with any cheese you happen to have handy. More good news – it takes little more than 40 minutes to make.

1 medium, good-sized cauliflower, about 1 lb 4 oz/570 g
2 oz (50 g) Roquefort, crumbled, or mature Cheddar, grated
2 bay leaves
1 oz (25 g) butter
1 medium onion, peeled and chopped
2 sticks celery, chopped
1 large leek, trimmed, washed and chopped
4 oz (110 g) potato, peeled and chopped into dice
2 tablespoons half-fat crème fraîche
1 tablespoon snipped fresh chives, to garnish
salt and freshly milled black pepper

The stock for this is very simply made with all the cauliflower trimmings. All you do is trim the cauliflower into small florets and then take the stalk bits, including the green stems, and place these trimmings in a medium-sized saucepan. Then add 2½ pints (1.5 litres) water, the bay leaves and some salt, bring it up to the boil and simmer for 20 minutes with a lid.

Meanwhile, take another large saucepan with a well-fitting lid, melt the butter in it over a gentle heat, then add the onion, celery, leek and potato, cover and let the vegetables gently sweat for 15 minutes. Keep the heat very low, then when the stock is ready, strain it into the pan to join the vegetables, adding the bay leaves as well but throwing out the rest. Now add the cauliflower florets, bring it all back up to simmering point and simmer very gently for 20-25 minutes, until the cauliflower is completely tender, this time without a lid.

After that, remove the bay leaves, then place the contents of the saucepan in a food processor or blender and process until the soup is smooth and creamy. Next, return it to the saucepan, stir in the crème fraîche and cheese and keep stirring until the cheese has melted and the soup is hot but not boiling. Check the seasoning, then serve in hot bowls, garnished with the chives ■

Curried Parsnip and Apple Soup with Parsnip Crisps
Serves 6

This is such a lovely soup. The sweetness of the parsnips is sharpened by the presence of the apple, and the subtle flavour of the spices comes through beautifully. You can make the parsnip crisps in advance, as they will stay crisp for a couple of hours.

For the soup:
1 lb 8 oz (700 g) young parsnips
1 medium Bramley apple, 6 oz/175 g
1 heaped teaspoon coriander seeds
1 heaped teaspoon cumin seeds
6 whole cardamom pods, seeds only
1½ oz (40 g) butter
1 tablespoon groundnut or other flavourless oil
2 medium onions, peeled and chopped
2 cloves garlic, peeled and chopped
1 heaped teaspoon turmeric
1 heaped teaspoon ground ginger
2 pints (1.2 litres) hot stock made with Marigold Swiss vegetable bouillon powder
salt and freshly milled black pepper

For the parsnip crisps:
1 medium to large parsnip, 10-12 oz/275-350 g
6 tablespoons groundnut or other flavourless oil
salt

You will also need a large saucepan with a capacity of about 6 pints (3.5 litres).

First, heat a small frying pan and dry-roast the coriander, cumin and cardamom seeds – this is to toast them and draw out their flavour. After 2-3 minutes they will change colour and start to jump in the pan. Now crush them finely with a pestle and mortar.

Next, heat the butter and oil in the saucepan until the butter begins to foam, then add the onions and gently soften for about 5 minutes before adding the garlic. Let that cook, along with the onions, for another 2 minutes, then add all the crushed spices, along with the turmeric and ginger, stir and let it all continue to cook gently for a few more minutes while you peel and chop the parsnips into 1 inch (2.5 cm) dice. Add these to the saucepan, stirring well, then pour in the stock, add some seasoning and let the soup simmer as gently as possible for 1 hour without putting on a lid.

While the soup is cooking, you can make the parsnip crisps. First, peel the parsnip and then slice it into rounds as thinly as you possibly can, using a sharp knife. Now heat the oil in a 10 inch (25.5 cm) frying pan until it is very hot, almost smoking, then fry the parsnip slices in batches until they are golden brown, about 2-3 minutes (they will not stay flat or colour evenly but will twist into lovely shapes). As they're cooked, remove them with a slotted spoon and spread them out on kitchen paper to drain. Sprinkle lightly with salt.

When the soup is ready, remove it from the heat, then blend it, if possible; if not, use a food processor and then a sieve, squashing the ingredients through, using the bowl of a ladle. After the soup has been puréed, return it to the saucepan, taste to check the seasoning, then when you're ready to serve, re-heat very gently. While that's happening, peel the apple and as the soup just reaches simmering point, grate the apple into it. Be careful to let the soup barely simmer for only 3-4 minutes. Serve in hot soup bowls, garnished with the parsnip crisps ■

Chilled Lemon Grass and Coriander Vichyssoise
Serves 4

In summer, if the weather is really hot, nothing could be more refreshing than a chilled soup. Leeks are not in season in summer, but this alternative is made using fresh lemon grass, available at oriental shops and supermarkets. Remember to serve the soup well chilled.

4 thick stems lemon grass

2 oz (50 g) fresh coriander

4 spring onions

2 oz (50 g) butter

2 medium onions, peeled and chopped

10 oz (275 g) new potatoes, scraped and chopped small

1½ pints (850 ml) stock (see below)

5 fl oz (150 ml) milk

salt and freshly milled black pepper

To serve:

thin lemon slices and ice cubes

First of all, strip the coriander leaves from the stalks and reserve the stalks. Lemon grass is dealt with in exactly the same way as leeks: that is, you trim the root and the tough top away, leaving approximately 6 inches (15 cm) of stem, remove the outer skin and chop the lemon grass quite finely. Then do the same with the spring onions.

Next, gather up all the trimmings from both, wash them and pop them into a saucepan, together with the coriander stalks, some salt and 1½ pints (850 ml) of water and simmer, covered, for about 30 minutes to make a stock.

To make the soup, melt the butter in a large saucepan, then add the chopped lemon grass, onions (reserve the spring onions till later) and potatoes and, keeping the heat low, let the vegetables sweat gently, covered, for about 10 minutes. After that, pour in the stock through a strainer, discard

the debris, then add the milk and about three-quarters of the coriander leaves. Season with salt and pepper, bring the soup up to simmering point and simmer very gently for about 25 minutes.

Allow the soup to cool a little before pouring it into a food processor or blender, whiz it up, then pour it through a strainer into a bowl. When it's cold, cover and chill thoroughly till you're ready to serve.

I think it's a good idea to serve the soup in glass bowls that have already been chilled. Add a cube of ice to each bowl and sprinkle in the rest of the coriander (finely chopped) and the spring onions as a garnish. Finally, float some lemon slices on top and serve straightaway ▣

Ajo Blanco (chilled almond soup)
Serves 4

My friend Neville, who has a house in Andalucia surrounded by almond trees, gave me this supremely wonderful recipe for chilled almond soup, generously laced with garlic, which is made by the locals. You can make it up to five days ahead – as Neville says, it goes on improving in flavour.

7 oz (200 g) unblanched almonds (preferably Spanish almonds – never ready-blanched for this recipe)

7 fl oz (200 ml) Spanish olive oil

3 cloves garlic, peeled

1 dessertspoon sherry vinegar

2 teaspoons salt, or more, to taste

To serve:

8 ice cubes

4 oz (110 g) black grapes, deseeded and halved

1 dessert apple, peeled, cored and thinly sliced

First, you need to blanch the almonds. To do this, place them in a bowl, pour in enough boiling water to cover and leave them aside for 3-4 minutes. Drain them in a colander and squeeze the nuts out of their skins.

After that, put the almonds in a blender and pour in the olive oil. (The oil should just cover the almonds – if it doesn't, add a little more.) Then, add the peeled garlic, vinegar and salt and blend until smooth. Now, with the motor still running, slowly add about 12 fl oz (340 ml) cold water. Pour the soup into a large bowl and if it seems too thick, add a little more water. Cover the bowl with clingfilm and keep it well chilled.

Just before serving, stir in the ice cubes and ladle the soup into 4 chilled bowls. Garnish with the grapes and apple slices ▣

Stilton Soup with Parmesan Croutons
Serves 4-6

Not simply a recipe for leftover bits of Stilton, this one, but a delicious creamy soup that can enhance any dinner or supper party.

4 oz (110 g) Stilton cheese, crumbled

2 oz (50 g) butter

1 onion, peeled and finely chopped

1 leek, cleaned and chopped

1 large potato, peeled and diced small

1 heaped tablespoon plain flour

5 fl oz (150 ml) dry cider

1 pint (570 ml) hot stock made with Marigold Swiss vegetable bouillon powder

10 fl oz (275 ml) milk

1 tablespoon double cream

salt and freshly milled black pepper

For the parmesan croutons:

2 oz (50 g) bread, cubed

1 tablespoon olive oil

1 dessertspoon parmesan

Pre-heat the oven gas mark 4, 350°F (180°C).

Start off by melting the butter in a thick-based saucepan, then add the vegetables and some salt, and cook gently with the lid on for 5-10 minutes. Next, stir in the flour and when smooth, gradually pour in the cider – still stirring. Then add the stock, cover the pan and simmer gently for 30 minutes.

Next, make the croutons: place the bread cubes in a bowl with the oil, stirring until the oil is soaked up. Sprinkle in the parmesan, stir and bake for 8-10 minutes. Now add the milk and Stilton to the soup and re-heat, stirring, until the cheese has melted. Taste and season with salt and pepper, then stir in the cream. Purée the soup in blender, or if you like the texture of the vegetables, keep it as it is. Be careful not to boil the soup when re-heating ▣

French Onion Soup
Serves 6

There are few things more comforting than French Onion Soup – slowly cooked caramelised onions that turn mellow and sweet in a broth laced with white wine and Cognac. The whole thing is finished off with crunchy baked croutons of crusty bread topped with melted, toasted cheese.

1 lb 8 oz (700 g) onions, peeled
and thinly sliced
2 tablespoons olive oil
2 oz (50 g) butter
2 cloves garlic, peeled and crushed
½ teaspoon golden caster
or granulated sugar
2 pints (1.2 litres) hot stock made with
Marigold Swiss vegetable bouillon powder
10 fl oz (275 ml) dry white wine
2 tablespoons Cognac (optional)
salt and freshly milled black pepper

For the croutons:
1 small stick of French bread or
1 baguettine, cut into six 1 inch (2.5 cm)
diagonal slices
1 tablespoon olive oil
1-2 cloves garlic, peeled and crushed

To serve:
6 large croutons (see below)
8 oz (225 g) Gruyère or Emmental, grated

You will also need a wide-bottomed saucepan or flameproof casserole with a capacity of 6 pints (3.5 litres) and a heatproof tureen or soup bowls.

Pre-heat the oven to gas mark 4, 350°F (180°C).

First make the croutons – begin by drizzling the olive oil on a large, solid baking sheet, add the crushed garlic and then, using your hands, spread the oil and garlic all over the baking sheet. Now place the bread slices on top of the oil, then turn over each one so that both sides have been lightly coated with the oil. Bake for 20-25 minutes till crisp and crunchy.

Next, place the wide-bottomed saucepan or casserole on a high heat and melt the oil and butter together. When this is very hot, add the onions, garlic and sugar, and keep turning them from time to time until the edges of the onions have turned dark – this will take about 6 minutes. Then reduce the heat to its lowest setting and leave the onions to carry on cooking very slowly, uncovered, for about 30 minutes, by which time the base of the pan will be covered with a rich, nut brown, caramelised film.

After that pour in the stock and white wine, season, then stir with a wooden spoon, scraping the base of the pan well. As soon as it all comes up to simmering point, turn down the heat to its lowest setting, then go away and leave it to cook very gently, still without a lid, for about 1 hour.

All this can be done in advance, but when you're ready to serve the soup, bring it back up to simmering point, taste to check for seasoning – and if it's extra-cold outside, add a couple of tablespoons of Cognac! Warm the tureen or soup bowls in a low oven and pre-heat the grill to its highest setting. Then ladle in the hot soup and top with the croutons, allowing them to float on the surface of the soup.

Now sprinkle the grated Gruyère (or Emmental) thickly over the croutons and place the whole lot under the grill until the cheese is golden brown and bubbling. Serve immediately – and don't forget to warn your guests that everything is very hot! ▩

Wild Mushroom Soup
Serves 4-6

Although I have been told that Italians never put porcini into soup, some dried porcini added to a classic English mushroom soup really give it a depth of flavour that could only come from wild mushrooms.

1 oz (25 g) dried porcini mushrooms
8 oz (225 g) fresh, dark-gilled
mushrooms
8 oz (225 g) fresh chestnut mushrooms
3 oz (75 g) butter
1 large onion, peeled and finely chopped
2 fat cloves garlic, peeled
and finely chopped
2 teaspoons chopped fresh thyme
¼ whole nutmeg, grated
5 fl oz (150 ml) dry Madeira
5 fl oz (150 ml) milk
1 heaped tablespoon crème fraîche
salt and freshly milled black pepper

Begin by pouring 1½ pints (850 ml) of boiling water over the porcini mushrooms. Stir them around a bit and then leave them aside to soak for about 30 minutes.

Meanwhile, in a large saucepan melt 2 oz (50 g) of butter and gently cook the onion and garlic until soft, which takes about 6 minutes.

While that is happening, chop the fresh mushrooms into roughly ½ inch (1 cm) pieces, then when 30 minutes is up, place a sieve over a large bowl, lined with a sheet of kitchen paper, and allow the porcini mushrooms to drain, pressing them to extract all their soaking liquid. Reserve the liquid.

After that, chop them quite small and add them, along with the fresh mushrooms, to the onions and garlic. Add the thyme, nutmeg and another 1 oz (25 g) butter. Then carry on cooking everything gently for 4-5 minutes, stirring it all around in the buttery juices. Now pour in the porcini soaking liquid, along with the Madeira and the milk. Season with salt and freshly milled black pepper, bring everything up to a gentle simmer, then turn the heat down to its lowest setting and simmer very gently for about 30 minutes, without a lid, giving it a stir now and then.

Next, using a slotted draining spoon, remove about one-third of the mushrooms into a dish, then ladle the remainder of the mushrooms into a blender or processor with enough of the liquid to blend until smooth. Now pour the whole lot back into the pan, together with the reserved mushrooms. Taste and add a little more seasoning, if necessary, then continue to simmer the soup very gently for a further 20 minutes. To serve, add a marbling of crème fraîche stirred into each portion ▩

Tuscan Bean and Pasta Soup with Rosemary
Serves 4

This is Tuscany in a bowl, with all those lovely Italian flavours in a big hefty soup – it is perfect for winter months with a light main course to follow.

8 oz (225 g) dried borlotti beans

4 oz (110 g) short-cut macaroni

1 heaped tablespoon fresh rosemary, bruised in a mortar, then very finely chopped

2 tablespoons olive oil

1 large onion, peeled and finely chopped

2 cloves garlic, peeled and crushed

2¼ tablespoons tomato purée

parmesan, grated or shaved, to serve

salt and freshly milled black pepper

First, you need to soak the beans. You can either soak them overnight in 4 pints (2.25 litres) of cold water, or you can simply bring them up to the boil (using the same quantity of water), then boil for 10 minutes and leave them to soak for 2 hours.

Next, drain the beans, reserving the soaking liquid. Heat the oil in a large saucepan, add the onion and cook gently for about 10 minutes without colouring. Then add the garlic and cook for another minute. Now add the tomato purée and rosemary, stir for a minute, then pour in the beans, together with 3 pints (1.75 litres) of the reserved water (top up the liquid, if necessary) and some salt. Now simmer very gently, partially covered, for about an hour, or until the beans are tender.

Next, season with salt and freshly milled black pepper, then pour half the soup into a blender and blend until absolutely smooth. Now return the puréed half to the pan, bring to a gentle simmer, then add the macaroni and simmer for 10-12 minutes, stirring from time to time, until the pasta is cooked. Serve in hot soup bowls with lots of parmesan ■

Beetroot Soup with Orange and Mint
Serves 6

This is the best beetroot soup I've ever tasted and my thanks to London chef Colin Westal from restaurant Ransome's Dock (and now Parade), who kindly gave me this recipe. It can also be served chilled in the summer, with a teaspoon of crème fraîche to top each serving.

2 lb (900 g) fresh red beetroot

2 oranges

12 fresh mint sprigs, chopped, plus 6 small leaves, to garnish

2 oz (50 g) butter

1 medium red onion, peeled and thinly sliced

salt and freshly milled black pepper

First of all, melt the butter in a large, thick-based saucepan and then gently cook the onion in it until soft and translucent. Meanwhile, wash, top, tail and peel the beetroot and cut into ¾ inch (2 cm) cubes. Now add the beetroot to the onion, then cover with a lid and cook gently for 20 minutes, stirring now and then. Next, add 2 pints (1.2 litres) of cold water and season with salt and freshly milled black pepper. Now bring the soup to the boil before reducing the heat and simmering for 25-30 minutes or until the beetroot is cooked. Allow the soup to cool a little, then purée it in batches until smooth in a blender.

Next, finely grate the zest of the oranges, taking care not to remove any of the bitter white pith as you do so. Add the zest to the soup (you don't need the orange juice for this recipe). Now taste the soup to check the seasoning, adding more salt or pepper if you think it needs it. Finally, put a little chopped mint into the bottom of each hot soup bowl, ladle on the hot soup and finish each bowl with a small sprig of mint ■

Eliza Acton's Vegetable Mulligatawny
Serves 8

Eliza Acton is one of my favourite cookery writers and this is a recipe I adapted from her cookery book, published in 1840.

3 large onions, peeled and chopped

1 lb 8 oz (700 g) peeled marrow or unpeeled courgettes, cut into 1 inch (2.5 cm) cubes

1 large potato, peeled and cut into 1 inch (2.5 cm) cubes

8 oz (225 g) tomatoes, skinned and chopped

4 oz (110 g) butter

3 whole cardamom pods, seeds only

1 teaspoon each cumin and fennel seeds

1 dessertspoon coriander seeds

3 fl oz (75 ml) white basmati rice, cooked in 6 fl oz/175 ml boiling water (see page 122)

1½ pints (850 ml) hot stock made with Marigold Swiss vegetable bouillon powder

small croutons, to serve

salt and freshly milled black pepper

You will also need a 6 pint (3.5 litre) saucepan.

First, melt the butter in a large saucepan, then add the onions and cook until they're a golden brown colour. Now place the cardamom, cumin, fennel and coriander seeds in a small frying pan to dry-roast – this will take 2-3 minutes. As soon as the seeds start to jump, tip them into a mortar and crush them finely, then add them to the onions. Next, add the marrow (or courgettes), potato and tomatoes. Season well, then let the vegetables cook gently, covered, until soft – about 20 minutes.

Next, when the vegetables are cooked, put them into a blender and reduce to a purée. Then pour the purée back into the saucepan and stir in the cooked rice, together with the stock. Re-heat gently, cook for about 5 minutes more, then serve with some crisp croutons sprinkled in each bowl ■

Leek, Onion and Potato Soup
Serves 4-6

This has to be one of my own favourites and has proven to be one of my most popular recipes over the years.

4 large leeks

1 medium onion, peeled and chopped small

2 medium potatoes, peeled and diced

2 oz (50 g) butter

1½ pints (850 ml) hot stock made with Marigold Swiss vegetable bouillon powder

10 fl oz (275 ml) milk

salt and freshly milled black pepper

To serve:

1½ tablespoons snipped fresh chives or chopped fresh parsley

2 tablespoons cream or crème fraîche

Begin by trimming the leeks, discarding the tough outer layer. Now split them in half lengthways and slice them quite finely, then wash them thoroughly in 2 or 3 changes of water. Drain well.

In a large, thick-based saucepan, gently melt the butter, then add the leeks, onion and potatoes, stirring them all around with a wooden spoon so they get a nice coating of butter. Season with salt and pepper, then cover and let the vegetables sweat over a very low heat for about 15 minutes.

After that, add the stock and milk, bring to simmering point, cover and let the soup simmer very gently for a further 20 minutes or until the vegetables are soft – if you have the heat too high the milk in it may cause it to boil over. Now you can put the whole lot into a blender and blend to a purée. Return the soup to the saucepan and re-heat gently, tasting to check the seasoning. Stir in the snipped chives (or parsley) and add a swirl of cream or crème fraîche before serving ■

Chapter Two
Starters and
Salads

Asparagus
with Lemon Butter Crumbs
Serves 4

Marinated Cucumber
and Sesame Salad
Serves 2

Globe Artichokes
with Shallot Vinaigrette
Serves 2

This is just to ring the changes from plain melted butter and the crumbs add a lovely crunchy texture.

1 lb 4 oz (570 g) fresh asparagus
finely grated zest 1 lemon, plus
1 tablespoon lemon juice for sprinkling
2 oz (50 g) butter
1½ oz (40 g) fresh fine white breadcrumbs, about 2 slices bread, crusts removed
salt and freshly milled black pepper

You will also need a steamer.

First, wash the asparagus in cold water, then take each stalk in both hands and bend and snap off the woody end. Arrange the asparagus stalks in a steamer and steam over simmering water for 5-6 minutes, or until they feel tender when tested with a skewer, being careful not to overcook them.

While the asparagus is cooking, heat 1 oz (25 g) of the butter in a medium-sized frying pan. As soon as it is frothy, stir in the breadcrumbs and cook them, stirring constantly, until they're evenly browned and crispy. Then tip the crumbs on to a plate, stir in the lemon zest and season with salt and pepper.

Now put the pan back on to the heat and add the remaining butter. As soon as it is frothy, add the cooked asparagus and toss to coat them in the butter. Sprinkle with the lemon juice and season with salt and pepper. Divide the asparagus between warmed serving plates and sprinkle with the crumbs. Serve immediately ■

This very simple little salad makes a nice side dish. I like to serve it as a nibble before an oriental meal (see recipes on pages 103, 112 and 171).

½ cucumber
1 rounded tablespoon sesame seeds
1½ tablespoons Japanese soy sauce
1 teaspoon mirin
1 teaspoon saké or dry white wine
1 teaspoon rice vinegar
½ teaspoon sugar

Begin by toasting the sesame seeds. Do this by using a small, solid frying pan, pre-heat it over a medium heat, then add the sesame seeds and toast them, moving the around in the pan to brown them evenly. As soon as they begin to splutter and pop and turn golden, they're ready. This will take about 1-2 minutes. Then remove them from the frying pan to a plate.

Next, cut the cucumber in half lengthways, then in quarters and then in eighths. Remove the seeds, chop into small 1½ inch (4 cm) wedges, then place them in a bowl. After that, measure the soy sauce, mirin, saké, rice vinegar and sugar into a screw-top jar, shake them together thoroughly, then pour them over the cucumber and leave to marinate for about 1 hour, giving them one good stir at half-time.

Just before serving, lightly crush the toasted sesame seeds using a pestle and mortar and sprinkle them over the salad ■

An artichoke is, without doubt, a work of art – dark and pale green leaves with purple edges forming a perfectly shaped bud. There's something extremely satisfying about leisurely peeling off the leaves, dipping them into vinaigrette and biting into the fleshy part at the base of each leaf. Then, of course, the prize – the heart at the very centre, providing a kind of grand finale to the whole affair.

2 large globe artichokes, each weighing about 14 oz/400 g
1 tablespoon lemon juice (or white wine vinegar)
salt

For the vinaigrette:
1 shallot, peeled and finely chopped
1 rounded teaspoon sea salt
1 clove garlic, peeled
1 rounded teaspoon mustard powder
1 tablespoon good-quality red wine vinegar
5 tablespoons extra virgin olive oil
freshly milled black pepper

First, prepare the artichokes. Remove about 4 of the toughest outer leaves, then place the artichoke at the edge of a table so that the stalk overhangs the edge. Grasp the artichoke and snap away the stalk, removing some of the tough fibres running up into the base. Now with a large serrated knife, carefully slice off the top quarter of each artichoke and discard. Then, with a pair of scissors, trim away the tips of all the leaves.

Don't boil artichokes in iron or aluminium pans, as this can discolour them. Have your chosen large pan ready-filled with salted, boiling water, with the tablespoon of lemon juice (or white wine vinegar) added. Simmer the artichokes, uncovered, for 30-40 minutes, or until one of the outer leaves pulls away easily and the bases feel tender when tested with a skewer. Then drain upside down, shaking them to get rid of excess water.

Now remove the hairy 'choke': carefully spread the leaves until you come to the central cone of thinner, lightly coloured leaves – pull these out and underneath you'll find the choke. Pull it out in clumps – it will come away very easily.

Finally, make up the vinaigrette. Begin by crushing the salt quite coarsely in a mortar, then add the garlic. As it comes into contact with the salt, it will break down into a purée. Next, add the mustard powder and work it in with circular movements. After that, add some freshly milled black pepper. Now work in the vinegar in the same way. Then add the shallot and the oil, switch to a small whisk and whisk thoroughly.

Serve the vinaigrette in a bowl to dip the artichoke leaves into, and on the table, have a finger bowl, napkins, a separate plate for the discarded leaves, and a knife and fork each to eat the heart – wonderful! ■

Toasted Goats' Cheese with Blackened Sherry Vinegar Onions

Toasted Goats' Cheese with Blackened Sherry Vinegar Onions
Serves 4

Toasted goats' cheese became very fashionable in the 1990s, and not surprisingly, as it's still a supremely good way to enjoy good goats' cheese just on the point of melting. The blackened onions make a great accompaniment – lots of lovely gutsy flavour.

2 x 100 g soft-rind goats' cheeses, such as Welsh or Somerset (or 4 crottins)
3 fl oz (75 ml) sherry vinegar
1 lb (450 g) large, mild Spanish onions, about 3
1 oz (25 g) molasses sugar
2 tablespoons extra virgin olive oil
1 small curly lettuce
2 oz (50 g) rocket, stalks removed
salt and freshly milled black pepper

For the vinaigrette:
1 clove garlic, peeled
1 rounded teaspoon sea salt
1 rounded teaspoon mustard powder
1 dessertspoon balsamic vinegar
1 dessertspoon sherry vinegar
5 tablespoons extra virgin olive oil
freshly milled black pepper

You will also need a baking tray measuring 10 x 14 inches (25.5 x 35 cm) for the onions, and a smaller solid baking tray, lightly oiled, for the goats' cheese.

Pre-heat the oven to gas mark 8, 450°F (230°C).

Begin this by roasting the onions: first you need to mix the molasses sugar and sherry vinegar together in a large bowl and give it a good whisk, then leave it to one side for 10 minutes or so for the sugar to dissolve. Meanwhile, peel the onions, then, leaving the root intact, cut each one into 8 sections through the root, so in half first and then each half into 4. Then add the onions and oil to the vinegar and sugar mixture and toss them around so they get a good coating. After that, spread them out on the baking tray, pouring the rest of the dressing over and season well. Now place them on a high shelf in the oven and cook for 15 minutes. After that turn them over and give them another 15 minutes. Towards the end of the cooking time, check them and remove and set aside any that are in danger of over-blackening. Continue to cook the rest till they are all fairly dark, then remove them from the oven and set aside – they're not meant to be served hot.

When you are ready to serve the salad, pre-heat the grill to its highest setting for at least 10 minutes. Then make the vinaigrette dressing by first crushing the garlic and salt to a creamy paste in a pestle and mortar, then work in the mustard. Now switch to a whisk and add the vinegars and oil, then season with freshly milled black pepper. Next, slice each goats' cheese in half so you have 4 rounds, season these with freshly milled black pepper. Now place them on the oiled baking tray and grill them 3 inches (7.5 cm) from the heat for 5-7 minutes, until they are brown on top and soft (if you use the smaller crottins, these take only 3-4 minutes).

While they're grilling, arrange some lettuce leaves on each serving plate and divide and scatter the rocket between them. Then, when the cheese is ready, place one in the middle of each plate, scatter the onion all round and, finally, drizzle the vinaigrette dressing over each salad. Needless to say, lots of crusty bread should be available ■

Marinated Mushrooms with Garlic and Smoked Pimentón Mayonnaise
Serves 4

Serve these mushrooms with the pungent garlic and smoked pimentón mayonnaise and some bread for dipping – wonderful!

8 oz (225 g) mixed fresh mushrooms, wiped and thickly sliced
2 cloves garlic, peeled and very finely chopped
4 tablespoons olive oil
8 fl oz (225 ml) red wine
2 tablespoons chopped fresh parsley, plus a little extra, to sprinkle
8 crisp lettuce leaves, to serve
salt and freshly milled black pepper

For the garlic and smoked pimentón mayonnaise:
the basic mayonnaise recipe (see below), plus 3 extra cloves garlic, peeled
1 teaspoon smoked, sweet pimentón (mild, smoked paprika)

Heat the olive oil in a large frying pan, add the mushrooms, along with the garlic, and cook for a couple of minutes over a medium heat – shaking the pan and stirring from time to time. Now pour in the red wine, turn the heat up high and let it all bubble for a minute or two and reduce a little. Turn the heat down and cook for a further 4 minutes. Season to taste, stir in the chopped parsley and then transfer to a small serving dish. Allow the mushrooms to cool before covering them and popping them into the fridge to chill.

Now make the mayonnaise, following the recipe on page 46, but using 4 cloves of garlic instead of 1 and stir the smoked, sweet pimentón into the finished mayonnaise. Serve the mushrooms on crisp lettuce leaves with some chopped parsley sprinkled on top, and about a dessertspoon of mayonnaise per person. The leftover mayonnaise will keep for a week in the fridge ■

Feta Cheese, Spinach and Pine Nut Galettes
Serves 6

Galettes are very thin discs of pastry which, unlike conventional tarts, have no sides. You can serve them for a light lunch, as a first course, or on a picnic.

quick flaky pastry, made as on page 37
4½ oz (125 g) feta cheese, cubed
8 oz (225 g) young leaf spinach
1 oz (25 g) pine nuts
a little freshly grated nutmeg
1 oz (25 g) parmesan, finely grated

You will also need 2 solid baking trays measuring 14 x 10 inches (35 x 25.5 cm), lightly greased, and a 6 inch (15 cm) plain pastry cutter.

Pre-heat the oven to gas mark 7, 425°F (220°C).

While the pastry is chilling in the fridge, cook the spinach by placing it in a saucepan with a lid on, then place it over a medium heat. Just let it collapse down into its own juices, timing it for 2-3 minutes and turning it over halfway. Drain the spinach in a colander, pressing it with a saucer to extract every last bit of juice, then season with a little nutmeg.

Next, roll out the pastry on a lightly floured surface to ⅛ inch (3 mm), cut out six 6 inch (15 cm) discs and place these on the baking trays. Finely chop the spinach and divide it between the pastry circles, spreading it out towards the edges of the pastry, but leaving a small, uncovered rim around the edge. Next, scatter the feta over the spinach, then sprinkle over the pine nuts. Now cook the galettes for 10-12 minutes, one tray on the high shelf, the other on the next one down, until golden brown, swapping the baking sheets over halfway through. Remove from the oven, sprinkle the parmesan over and serve warm, or leave to cool on a cooling tray ■

Four Star Slaw
Serves 4-6

The four 'stars' in this case are celeriac, carrot, cabbage and spring onion. The result is a very crunchy, fresh-tasting salad that can be made the day before, if you cover it with clingfilm and keep it in the fridge until needed.

4 oz (110 g) celeriac, peeled and coarsely grated

4 oz (110 g) carrots, peeled and and coarsely grated

4 oz (110 g) white cabbage, finely shredded

3 spring onions, finely chopped (including the green parts)

poppy seeds, to garnish

For the dressing:

3 fl oz (75 ml) soured cream

1 clove garlic, peeled and crushed

1 tablespoon mayonnaise

1 tablespoon natural yoghurt

½ teaspoon mustard powder

1 tablespoon olive oil

1 dessertspoon white wine vinegar

1 dessertspoon lemon juice

salt and freshly milled black pepper

Begin by combining the soured cream with the garlic, mayonnaise, yoghurt and mustard powder. Then mix together the oil, vinegar and lemon juice, and gradually whisk these into the soured cream mixture. Finally, taste and season with salt and pepper.

Next, to prepare the salad, simply combine all the grated, shredded and chopped vegetables in a bowl, then pour over the dressing and toss with forks to mix thoroughly. Taste at this stage, as it may need more seasoning, then cover and chill. Toss again and sprinkle with poppy seeds just before serving ■

Roasted Red Peppers Stuffed with Fennel
Serves 4-6

This delightful combination of flavours makes a very attractive first course. The dish needs lots of really good bread, as there's always a profusion of fragrant juices. If you want to make the peppers ahead of time, cover with foil after cooling but don't refrigerate them, as this spoils the fragrant flavour.

4 large red peppers

2 small bulbs fennel

8 dessertspoons good-quality olive oil

14 oz (400 g) tin Italian plum tomatoes

1 rounded teaspoon mixed pepper berries

¾ teaspoon whole coriander seeds

½ teaspoon fennel seeds

juice ½ lemon

finely chopped spring onion, to garnish (optional)

sea salt

You will also need a shallow baking sheet (I use a Swiss-roll tin).

Pre-heat the oven to Gas Mark 4, 350°F (180°C).

Begin by slicing each pepper in half lengthways, cutting right through the green stalk end and leaving it intact; though it won't be eaten, it adds much to the look of the thing. Remove all the seeds. Now place the pepper halves on the baking sheet, then drain the tomatoes (you don't need the juice), and divide them into 8 equal portions, placing each portion inside a pepper half.

Next, pare off any brownish bits of fennel with your sharpest knife and cut the bulbs first into quarters and then again into eighths, carefully keeping the layers attached to the root ends. Now put them in a saucepan with a little salt, pour boiling water on them and blanch them for 5 minutes. Then drain them in a colander and, as soon

as they're cool enough to handle, arrange 2 slices in each pepper half. Sprinkle 1 dessertspoon olive oil over each one, using a brush to spread the oil round the edges and sides of the peppers. Next, lightly crush the pepper berries, coriander and fennel seeds with a pestle and mortar, or rolling pin and bowl, sprinkle these evenly all over the fennel and peppers and finish off with a grinding of sea salt.

Then bake the peppers for approximately 1 hour on a high shelf in the oven until they are soft and the skin wrinkled and nicely tinged with brown. After removing them from the oven, sprinkle the lemon juice all over, cool and serve, garnished with a little finely chopped spring onion, or as they are ■

Roasted Tomato Salad
Serves 4-6

If you are a tomato addict, like me, and you think that good bread dipped into fruity olive oil and tomato juices is the food of the gods, then roast the tomatoes first and you'll agree that the gods have excelled themselves.

12 large tomatoes, skinned

24 large fresh basil leaves

2 fat cloves garlic, peeled and finely chopped

4 tablespoons extra virgin olive oil

2 tablespoons balsamic vinegar

24 black olives

salt and freshly milled black pepper

You will also need a shallow roasting tin about 16 x 12 inches (40 x 30 cm), oiled.

Pre-heat the oven to gas mark 6, 400°F (200°C).

First, cut each tomato in half and place the halves in the roasting tin, cut side uppermost, and season with salt and freshly milled pepper. After that, sprinkle on the chopped garlic, distributing it evenly between the tomatoes. Follow this with a few droplets of olive oil on each one, then top each one with half a basil leaf, turning each piece of leaf over to get a coating of oil.

Now place the roasting tin in the top half of the oven and roast the tomatoes for 50 minutes-1 hour or until the edges are slightly blackened. Then remove the tin from the oven and allow the tomatoes to cool. All this can be done several hours ahead.

To serve, transfer the tomatoes to individual serving plates, place half a basil leaf on top of each one, then whisk the remaining oil with the vinegar and drizzle this over. Finally, top each one with an olive. Lots of crusty bread is an essential accompaniment to this ■

Right: Roasted Tomato Salad
Top left: Roasted Red Peppers Stuffed with Fennel

Pesto Rice Salad

Pesto Rice Salad
Serves 4-6

Just as home-made pesto does such wonders for pasta, so it does for rice, too. This salad can be served warm as a first course. Served cold, it makes a lovely addition to a selection of salads for a buffet.

For the pesto sauce:
2 oz (50 g) fresh basil leaves
1 large clove garlic, peeled and crushed
1 tablespoon pine nuts
6 tablespoons extra virgin olive oil
1 oz (25 g) parmesan, grated
salt

For the salad:
Italian arborio rice measured to the
8 fl oz (225 ml) level in a glass
measuring jug
16 fl oz (450 ml) hot stock made with
Marigold Swiss vegetable bouillon powder
juice 1 lemon
2 tablespoons extra virgin olive oil
salt and freshly milled black pepper

To garnish:
a few torn fresh basil leaves
4 spring onions, finely chopped
1 oz (25 g) parmesan shavings,
made with a potato peeler

**You will also need a frying pan
with a 10 inch (25.5 cm) base
and a tight-fitting lid.**

First of all, make the pesto sauce. If you have a blender, put the basil, garlic, pine nuts and olive oil, together with some salt, in the goblet and blend until you have a smooth purée. Then transfer the purée to a bowl and stir in the grated parmesan. If you don't have a blender, use a large pestle and mortar to pound the basil, garlic and pine nuts to a paste. Slowly add the salt and cheese, then very gradually add the oil until you have obtained a smooth purée.

Next, measure the rice into a glass measuring jug, then add about one quarter of the pesto sauce to it and stir it around to coat all the grains. Tip the mixture into the frying pan and pour the hot stock into the jug, then pour this over the rice. Now turn on the heat and stir with a wooden spoon, adding 1 teaspoon of salt. Then, when it begins to boil, put a lid on, turn the heat down to low and let the rice cook for exactly 20 minutes.

As soon as it's ready, tip all the rice into a serving bowl, then simply pour in the lemon juice, olive oil and the remaining pesto sauce. Combine all the ingredients together, stirring and tossing. At this stage, taste and season with salt and pepper. Finally, scatter some torn basil leaves, finely chopped spring onions and then some shavings of parmesan over the surface of the salad as a garnish. If you want to serve the salad cold, add the basil, onion and parmesan just before serving ■

Tomato and Goats' Cheese Galettes
Serves 6

This is another version of the galette. I often freeze the pastry circles raw, interleaved with foil or baking parchment, so you can whip some out for an impromptu meal any old time.

For the quick flaky pastry:
4 oz (110 g) butter (see below)
6 oz (175 g) plain flour, plus a little extra
for dusting
pinch salt

For the topping:
12 medium ripe tomatoes
7 oz (200 g) firm goats' cheese
18 large fresh basil leaves, plus 6 sprigs,
to garnish
a little olive oil
salt and freshly milled black pepper

**You will also need 2 solid baking sheets
measuring 14 x 10 inches (35 x 25.5 cm),
lightly greased, and a 6 inch (15 cm)
plain pastry cutter.**

First of all, make the pastry. Remove a pack of butter from the fridge, weigh out 4 oz (110 g), then wrap it in a piece of foil and return it to the freezer or freezing compartment of the fridge for 30-45 minutes.

Then, when you are ready to make the pastry, sift the flour and pinch of salt into a large, roomy bowl. Take the butter out of the freezer, fold back the foil and hold it in the foil, which will protect it from your warm hands. Then, using the coarse side of a grater placed in the bowl over the flour, grate the butter, dipping the edge of the butter on to the flour several times to make it easier to grate. What you will end up with is a large pile of grated butter sitting in the middle of the flour. Now take a palette knife and start to distribute the gratings into the flour — don't use your hands yet, just keep trying to coat all the pieces of fat with flour. Then

sprinkle 2 tablespoons of cold water all over, continue to use the palette knife to bring the whole thing together, and finish off, using your hands. If you need a bit more moisture, that's fine — just remember that the dough should come together in such a way that it leaves the bowl fairly clean, with no bits of loose butter or flour anywhere. Now pop it into a polythene bag and chill for 30 minutes before using. Pre-heat the oven to gas mark 7, 425°F (220°C).

Meanwhile, you need to skin the tomatoes, so pour boiling water over them and leave for exactly 1 minute before draining and slipping off the skins (protect your hands with a cloth if they are too hot). Next, on a lightly floured surface, roll out the pastry very thinly to ⅛ inch (3 mm), cut out six 6 inch (15 cm) discs and place these on the baking sheets.

Now scatter the large basil leaves over the pastry, tearing them first if they're very large. Next, thinly slice the tomatoes and arrange them in circles overlapping each other on top of the basil. Peel the goats' cheese and crumble it over the tomatoes, then pour some olive oil on to a saucer and dip the 6 basil sprigs in it, placing one on each tart. Then season well and drizzle each one with a little olive oil. Now bake the galettes, one tray on a high shelf, the other on the next one down, for 10-12 minutes or until the tomatoes are tinged brown and the cheese is bubbling, swapping the baking sheets over halfway. Serve warm straight from the oven, or they're still excellent cold ■

Anya Potato Salad with Shallots and Vinaigrette

Anya Potato Salad
with Shallots and Vinaigrette
Serves 8

I love the consistently good flavour of Anya potatoes. If you can't get them, try to buy other good-flavoured salad potatoes for this.

2 lb (900 g) Anya or other new potatoes, washed

6 shallots, peeled and finely chopped

4 tablespoons freshly snipped chives

salt

For the vinaigrette:

1 rounded dessertspoon sea salt

2 cloves garlic, peeled

1 rounded dessertspoon mustard powder

1 tablespoon balsamic vinegar

1 tablespoon sherry vinegar

5 fl oz (150 ml) extra virgin olive oil

freshly milled black pepper

You will also need a steamer.

Steam the potatoes over a pan of boiling, salted water, covered with a lid, for about 20 minutes until they are tender. Meanwhile, make up the dressing. Begin by crushing the salt quite coarsely with a pestle and mortar, and then add the garlic. As you crush it and it comes into contact with the salt, it will quickly break down into a purée. Next, add the mustard powder and really work it in, giving it about 20 seconds of circular movements to get it well blended. After that, add some freshly milled black pepper. Now add the vinegars and work these in in the same way. Then add the oil, switch to a small whisk and give everything a really good whisking.

As soon as the potatoes are cooked, cool them in a mixing bowl for 10 minutes, then stir in the vinaigrette and shallots while the potatoes are still just warm. Now add the chives and give everything a good toss to distribute any dressing collected in the base of the bowl and transfer the salad to a serving bowl ▪

Pitta Bread Salad
Serves 6

A Middle Eastern salad, originally called *fattoush*, this may sound unlikely, but it really is good. It's robust and chunky with the fresh flavours of herbs and lemon – and dead simple to make.

2 standard-sized pitta breads

1 small Cos lettuce, cut into ½ inch (1 cm) strips

2 largish tomatoes, skinned and cut into ½ inch (1 cm) cubes

4 inches (10 cm) unpeeled cucumber, cut into ½ inch (1 cm) cubes

4 spring onions, thinly sliced (including the green parts)

1 smallish red onion, peeled and chopped small

1 red, yellow or green pepper, deseeded and chopped small

6 rounded tablespoons coarsely chopped fresh parsley

2 heaped tablespoons chopped fresh mint

For the lemon dressing:

5 fl oz (150 ml) olive oil

zest 1 lemon

4 tablespoons lemon juice

salt and freshly milled black pepper

Pre-heat the grill to its highest setting.

In a large, roomy salad bowl combine the salad vegetables and chopped herbs and toss lightly to mix them evenly together. Then, in another small bowl, combine the ingredients for the dressing, whisk and season liberally. Spoon the dressing over the salad and toss again.

Now toast the pitta breads, under the grill until they start to get really crisp. Cut them into postage-stamp-sized pieces, scatter them into the salad and toss once more. Taste for seasoning and serve immediately ▪

Grilled Spanish Onion
with Rocket-leaf Salad
Serves 4

I am constantly amazed after all my years of cooking at how there can be anything new – but there always is, again and again. This is an example, utterly simple, yet quite unlike any other salad. If rocket leaves are unavailable, flat-leaf parsley mixed with lamb's lettuce is a good substitute.

4 Spanish onions (the largest you can get)

6-7 tablespoons extra virgin olive oil

about 1 oz (25 g) rocket leaves, or flat-leaf parsley mixed with lamb's lettuce

3 oz (75 g) parmesan, in a piece

juice 1 large lemon

salt and freshly milled black pepper

You will also need a grill pan lined with foil, with a grill rack on top.

Pre-heat the grill to its highest setting.

First of all, don't peel the onions: simply trim off the root and top before cutting each one across into 4 slices about ¾ inch (2 cm) thick. Keeping the slices whole, transfer them to the grill rack (you might have to do this in 2 batches, depending on the size of your grill), then brush them with oil and season with salt and freshly milled pepper. Now position the grill pan so that the onion slices are about 4 inches (10 cm) from the heat and grill for 7 or 8 minutes until the onions are browned – indeed within a whisker of being blackened.

While that's happening, prepare the parmesan by shaving it into wafer-thin pieces with a potato peeler.

For the onions, the next stage needs a little care: use a palette knife to turn the slices over so that they don't break up into their constituent rings. Repeat the same oiling, seasoning and grilling on the other side, then remove from the heat and leave them on one side until they're cool enough to handle. Now discard the outside layers and any parts of the onion slices that are too blackened or chewy to eat, and separate the cold onion into rings. Put about a quarter of the rings in a layer on a serving dish and gradually build up the salad, intermingling onion rings with the torn rocket leaves and shavings of parmesan, sprinkling with more salt and pepper, lemon juice and about 3 tablespoons of olive oil as you go. This salad should not be tossed, so it relies on the cook to mingle the ingredients as the salad is put together. Serve at room temperature ▪

Warm Pear and Walnut Salad with Roquefort Dressing and Croutons
Serves 4

The combination of green leaves, crunchy walnuts, pears and creamy piquant dressing in this salad is a sensation – and just wait till you taste the croutons as well.

2 hard dessert pears
1½ oz (40 g) walnut pieces
1 tablespoon walnut oil
½ oz (10 g) butter
2 rounded tablespoons crème fraîche
5 oz (150 g) Roquefort, Shropshire Blue or Cashel Blue cheese
1 large egg yolk
4 oz (110 g) herb salad or equivalent

For the croutons:
2 oz (50 g) bread, cut into small cubes
1 dessertspoon olive oil

You will also need a solid baking sheet and a large frying pan.

Pre-heat the oven to gas mark 4, 350°F, (180°C).

Begin by making the croutons: first of all, place ½ oz (10 g) of the cheese (from the salad ingredients) in a bowl and, using a fork, blend it with the olive oil. Now add the cubes of bread and toss them around thoroughly to get an even coating. Then spread them out on the baking sheet and pop them into the oven for 10-12 minutes or until they are evenly brown. Best to put a timer on to remind you! The croutons can be made well in advance.

When you are ready to serve the salad, first cut the pears into quarters, remove the cores but leave the skins on, then cut each quarter into 4 slices. Next, heat the walnut oil in the large frying pan over a medium heat and lightly sauté the walnuts, tossing them around for about 1 minute. Now transfer them with a draining spoon to a plate. Add

the butter to the pan at the same heat, then add the pears and sauté them for about 2-3 minutes on each side until they are nicely brown. Next, drain the pears on kitchen paper, arrange them on a plate and keep them warm.

After that, make the sauce. To do this, place the crème fraîche in a small saucepan with the rest of the cheese, crumbling as you add it. Now whisk the two together over a gentle heat until the cheese begins to melt and form a sauce. Then drop in the egg yolk and continue to whisk until the sauce thickens; don't let it reach boiling point – it should be almost there but not quite.

Next, remove the pan from the heat and leave it on one side while you divide the salad leaves between 4 serving plates. Arrange the pears around the leaves, scatter with the walnuts, then pour the sauce over each salad. Finish off with a sprinkling of croutons and serve straightaway ■

Belarussian Carrot Salad
Serves 4-6

On a recent trip, I was privileged to be invited to a very special family meal in Minsk prepared by Sasha Shevchuk and her mother, Irina. Irina gave me her recipe for this simple, but oh-so-good carrot salad, which is perfect for winter when other salad ingredients are not at their best.

1 lb (450 g) carrots, peeled
2 tablespoons cider vinegar
1 teaspoon salt
1 dessertspoon coriander seeds
2 tablespoons groundnut or other flavourless oil
1 small onion, peeled and sliced
2 cloves garlic, peeled and finely chopped
pinch cayenne pepper

First of all, grate the carrots, using the fine grater blade on your food processor (or grate by hand). After that, transfer them to a bowl, pour over the vinegar and salt and mix to make sure everything is well coated. Cover and leave for at least 3 hours or, preferably, overnight in the fridge. If the carrots are very fresh, they develop too much juice, which should then be poured away.

Next, you need to dry-roast the coriander seeds. To do this, place them in a small frying pan over a medium heat and stir and toss them around for 1-2 minutes or until they begin to look toasted and start to jump in the pan. Now transfer them to a pestle and mortar and crush them lightly. After that, heat the oil in the same frying pan. Add the onion and fry until golden. Allow to cool a little, then drain the oil through a sieve on to the carrots and discard the onion, which was there just to give some flavour. Now add the coriander seeds to the carrots, along with the garlic and a pinch of cayenne pepper, and give everything a good stir. Covered, the salad will keep for a couple of days in the fridge ■

Roasted Figs with Gorgonzola and Honey Vinegar Sauce
Serves 4

This may sound like an unlikely combination but it's simply brilliant – a first course that's fast, unusual and absolutely no trouble at all to prepare.

12 ripe figs
6 oz (175 g) Gorgonzola Piccante, Shropshire Blue or Cashel Blue, chopped into ¼ inch (5 mm) dice
salt and freshly milled black pepper

For the sauce:
2 tablespoons Greek honey
2 tablespoons red wine vinegar

You will also need a baking tray, measuring 10 x 14 inches (25.5 x 35 cm), oiled.

Pre-heat the grill to its highest setting.

All you do is wipe and halve the figs, then place them, cut side up, on the baking tray. Season with salt and freshly milled black pepper, then pop them under the grill for 5-6 minutes, until they're soft and just bubbling slightly. When the figs are ready, remove the baking tray from the grill and divide the cheese equally between them, gently pressing it down to squash it in a bit. Then pop them back under the grill for about 2 minutes, until the cheese is bubbling and faintly golden brown.

Meanwhile, make the sauce by combining the honey and vinegar together, then serve the figs with the sauce poured over ■

Clockwise from top left: Belarussian Carrot Salad; Roasted Figs with Gorgonzola and Honey Vinegar Sauce; Warm Pear and Walnut Salad with Roquefort Dressing and Croutons

Fresh Asparagus with Foaming Hollandaise

Fresh Asparagus with Foaming Hollandaise
Serves 4

The marriage of asparagus and hollandaise was quite definitely made in heaven, and it seems sad to me that 'health' issues should bring about a divorce. Therefore, I now lighten the sauce somewhat by adding beaten egg whites and actually prefer the golden foam to the classic all butter and egg yolk sauce.

1 lb 4 oz (570 g) fresh asparagus, medium thick
salt

For the sauce:
2 large eggs, separated
1 dessertspoon lemon juice
1 dessertspoon white wine vinegar
4 oz (110 g) butter
salt and freshly milled black pepper

You will also need a steamer.

You can make the sauce at any time: we have tried it chilled overnight in the fridge, which makes a nice contrast with the hot asparagus, or you can serve it at room temperature or warm (heated in a bowl over a pan of barely simmering water, but make sure the bottom of the bowl does not actually touch the water).

Begin by placing the egg yolks in a food processor or blender, together with some salt and freshly milled black pepper, switch on and blend them thoroughly. In a small saucepan heat the lemon juice and vinegar till the mixture simmers, then switch the processor on again and pour the hot liquid on to the egg yolks in a steady stream.

Switch off, then in the same saucepan melt the butter – not too fiercely: it mustn't brown. When it is liquid and foaming, switch on the processor once more and pour in the butter, again in a steady thin stream, until it is all incorporated and the sauce has thickened. Next, in a clean, medium-sized bowl, whisk the egg whites until they form soft peaks and then fold the sauce, a tablespoon at a time, into the egg whites and taste to check the seasoning. When you've done that, it's ready to serve, or it can be left till later.

To cook the asparagus: take each stalk in both hands and bend and snap off the woody end, then trim with a knife to make it neater. Lay the asparagus stalks on an opened fan steamer (or an ordinary steamer will do) – they can be piled one on top of the other. Season with salt, place them in a frying pan or saucepan, pour in about 1 inch (2.5 cm) of boiling water from the kettle, then put a lid on and steam for 4-6 minutes.

Serve the hot asparagus with some sauce poured over the tips, and don't forget to have finger bowls and napkins at the ready ■

Note: This recipe contains raw eggs.

Brown and Wild Rice Salad with Dried Cranberries
Serves 6

This salad made with wild rice, looks very pretty with the jewelled colours of the dried cranberries and nuts. I like to serve it at buffet parties, just double the quantities to serve 12.

4 fl oz (120 ml) brown basmati rice (use a measuring jug)
2 fl oz (55 ml) wild rice (use a measuring jug)
1 oz (25 g) dried cranberries
1 dessertspoon groundnut or other flavourless oil
1 oz (25 g) walnuts, roughly chopped
2 medium-sized ripe, red tomatoes
1½ inch (4 cm) piece cucumber, cut into small dice (no need to peel)
½ small red (or yellow) pepper, deseeded and diced
1 small red-skinned dessert apple, washed, cored and finely chopped
2 spring onions, finely chopped (including the green parts)
salt and freshly milled black pepper

For the dressing:
1 small clove garlic, peeled
½ teaspoon sea salt
½ teaspoon mustard powder
1½ tablespoons Champagne vinegar (or good-quality white wine vinegar)
3 tablespoons extra virgin olive oil
freshly milled black pepper

You will also need 1 small and 1 medium-sized, heavy-based frying pan with tight-fitting lids.

Pre-heat the oven to gas mark 4, 350°F (180°C).

Begin by heating half the groundnut oil in the smaller frying pan, then add the wild rice and toss it around to coat the grains. Now pour over 4 fl oz (120 ml) of boiling water and add a little salt. Give it one stir, put the lid on and cook over a gentle heat for 50 minutes. Meanwhile, repeat the process with the brown rice, in the larger frying pan, this time adding 8 fl oz (225 ml) of boiling water – it will take 40-45 minutes for the water to be absorbed and the rice to become tender.

While the rice is cooking, you can make the dressing. Pound the garlic and salt to a creamy paste with a pestle and mortar. Next, work in the mustard powder, then switch to a small whisk and add the vinegar and olive oil. Season with plenty of freshly milled black pepper.

Now you'll need to toast the walnuts, so spread them out on a baking tray and place them in the oven for 8 minutes, putting a timer on so you don't forget them. Meanwhile, place the tomatoes in a heatproof bowl and pour boiling water on to them. After exactly a minute, remove them from the water and slip off their skins (protecting your hands with a cloth if the tomatoes are hot), then halve them, squeeze out the seeds and chop them into small pieces.

When both amounts of rice are cooked, mix them together in a serving bowl and add 2-3 tablespoons of the dressing. Toss the rice around in the dressing and then leave it to cool. When it's cool, mix in the cucumber, tomatoes, diced pepper, apple, cranberries, two-thirds of the spring onions and two-thirds of the walnuts. Drizzle with the remaining dressing and mix again so that everything is thoroughly combined and coated in dressing. Finally, just scatter the remaining spring onions and walnuts over the surface of the salad or serve them separately ■

Warm Lentil Salad with Walnuts and Goats' Cheese
Serves 4

I think we should all be eating more pulses, so the more recipes that include them the better. In this warm salad, I've chosen the little tiny black-grey Puy lentils but the green or brown variety will work just as well, given slightly less cooking time.

8 oz (225 g) Puy lentils

1½ oz (40 g) walnuts, roughly chopped

4 oz (110 g) firm goats' cheese

1 small red onion, peeled
and finely chopped

1 tablespoon extra virgin olive oil

1 fat clove garlic, peeled and crushed

1 bay leaf

1 heaped teaspoon chopped fresh
thyme leaves

1 oz (25 g) rocket leaves

salt

For the dressing:

1 fat clove garlic, peeled

1 teaspoon sea salt

1 rounded teaspoon mustard powder

2 tablespoons balsamic vinegar

2 tablespoons walnut oil

3 tablespoons extra virgin olive oil

freshly milled black pepper

First, you need to cook the lentils. To do this, heat the oil in a medium saucepan and when it's hot, lightly fry the chopped walnuts for about 1 minute. Then remove them with a draining spoon to a plate and keep them aside for later.

Now add the onion and crushed garlic to the oil left in the pan and let these cook and soften for about 5 minutes. After that, stir in the lentils, bay leaf and thyme and make sure they all get a good coating with oil. Next, add 10 fl oz (275 ml) of boiling water, put a lid on, turn the heat down to a gentle simmer and let the lentils cook for 30-40 minutes or until they're tender and all the liquid has been absorbed. You really need to bite one to test if they're done.

While the lentils are cooking you can prepare the dressing. Use a pestle and mortar and crush the garlic with the salt until it's creamy, then add the mustard and work that into the garlic paste. After that, whisk in the balsamic vinegar, followed by the oils. Then season well with freshly milled black pepper.

As soon as the lentils are cooked, add salt to taste. Empty them into a warm serving bowl and while they're still hot, pour the dressing over. Give everything a good toss, and stir, then crumble the goats' cheese all over and add the rocket leaves, torn in half. Give everything one more toss and stir, and serve straightaway with the walnuts scattered over ■

Eggs Mayonnaise
Serves 6

Not the kind you get in help-yourself salad bars and cafés – this is the real thing. Eggs, boiled – not hard, but with a bit of squidge at the centre – anointed with a shimmering, golden emulsion laced with a little garlic. I have to admit this is probably my most favourite starter. I like to serve it with sliced cornichons or pickled cucumbers and tiny black Provençal olives.

9 large eggs

18 medium cornichons (baby gherkins),
sliced lengthways

about 18 small black olives

For the mayonnaise:

2 large egg yolks

10 fl oz (275 ml) groundnut or other
flavourless oil

1 clove garlic, peeled and crushed

1 heaped teaspoon mustard powder

1 teaspoon salt, plus a little extra, if needed

1 teaspoon white wine vinegar

freshly milled black pepper

First, place a medium-sized mixing bowl on a damp tea cloth so it will remain steady and leave you both hands free to make the mayonnaise – one to drip the oil, the other to hold an electric hand whisk.

Next, measure out the oil into a jug. Now put the egg yolks into the bowl, adding the garlic, mustard powder, salt and a little freshly milled black pepper and mix all of these together well. Then, holding the jug of oil in one hand and the whisk in the other, add just a drop of oil to the egg mixture and whisk this in. However stupid it may sound, the key to a successful mayonnaise is making sure each drop of oil is thoroughly whisked in before adding the next drop. It won't take all day, because after a few minutes – once you've added several drops of oil, the mixture will begin to thicken and go very stiff and lumpy. When it gets to this stage, you need to add the vinegar, which will thin it.

Now the critical point has passed, you can begin pouring in the oil in large drops, keeping the whisk going all the time. When all the oil has been added, taste and add more salt and freshly milled black pepper, if it needs it. If you'd like the mayonnaise to be a bit lighter, add 2 tablespoons of boiling water and whisk it in.

Mayonnaise only curdles when you add the oil too quickly at the beginning. If that happens, don't despair. All you need to do is put a fresh egg yolk into a clean basin, add the curdled mixture to it drop by drop, then continue adding the rest of the oil as though nothing had happened.

Now place the 9 eggs in a pan of cold water. Bring them up to the boil and boil for 6 minutes, then cool them rapidly under cold, running water and leave them in the cold water for about 2 minutes. Next, remove them from the water, peel off the shells, cover the eggs with clingfilm, and leave them in a cool place until needed.

Now cut the eggs in half, arranging 3 halves on each plate, top with a heaped tablespoon of the mayonnaise and garnish with the cornichons and olives.

Any leftover mayonnaise should be stored in a screw-top jar in the fridge, but for no longer than a week ■

Note: This recipe contains raw eggs.

Tunisian Aubergine Salad

Tunisian Aubergine Salad
Serves 4

This is my adaptation of an Elizabeth David recipe. I never actually made it from her book, but one of my favourite restaurants, Chez Bruce, in Wandsworth, London, often serves it as a first course. It's so wonderful I never have anything else if it's on the menu. This salad is best made the day before you want to eat it.

1 lb 8 oz (700 g) aubergine, chopped into ½ inch (1 cm) cubes

1 lb 8 oz (700 g) ripe red tomatoes

about 3 tablespoons olive oil, plus a little extra for greasing

1 heaped teaspoon cumin seeds

1 teaspoon allspice berries

1 large onion, weighing about 10 oz (275 g), peeled and finely chopped

1 large red chilli, deseeded and finely chopped

4 cloves garlic, peeled and finely chopped

2 rounded tablespoons chopped fresh coriander

2 rounded tablespoons chopped fresh mint

sea salt and freshly milled black pepper

To serve:

4 tablespoons Greek yoghurt

8 pitta breads, warmed

1 tablespoon olive oil

1 rounded tablespoon chopped fresh coriander

1 rounded tablespoon chopped fresh mint

You will also need 2 baking trays, one measuring 11 x 16 inches (28 x 40 cm), the other measuring 10 x 14 inches (25.5 x 35 cm).

You'll need to start this recipe the day before you want to serve it. First, salt and drain the aubergines: place them in a large colander and, as you add them, sprinkle with 1 tablespoon of salt, then cover with a plate and weigh it down with a few scale weights or a similarly heavy object. Now place the colander on a plate and leave the aubergine to drain for 1 hour. When it has been draining for 30 minutes, pre-heat the oven to gas mark 8, 450°F (230°C).

Meanwhile, skin the tomatoes. To do this, pour boiling water over them and leave for exactly 1 minute before draining them (or 15 to 30 seconds if they are small), then slip off their skins (protecting your hands with a cloth if they are too hot). Cut them in half and place them, cut-side up, on the smaller baking tray, which should be lightly oiled, and brush the tomatoes with a little olive oil as well. Set to one side.

Now you need to dry-roast the cumin seeds and allspice berries, and to do this place them in a small frying pan or saucepan over a medium heat and stir and toss them around for 1-2 minutes, or until they begin to look toasted and start to jump in the pan. Now transfer them to a pestle and mortar and crush them to a powder.

When the aubergines are ready, squeeze them to get rid of any excess juices, dry them in a clean tea cloth, then place them in a bowl, add 1 tablespoon of the oil and toss them around so they get a good coating. After that, spread them out on the larger baking tray and place both baking trays in the oven, with the aubergines on the top shelf and the tomatoes on the next one down. Give them about 25 minutes, by which time the aubergines should be tinged golden brown at the edges and the tomatoes soft. Remove the vegetables from the oven and, when the tomatoes are cool enough, chop them into quite small pieces.

Meanwhile, heat 2 more tablespoons of the oil in a large frying pan over a medium to high heat and fry the onions until soft and pale gold – about 5 minutes – then add the chilli and garlic and fry for 1 more minute. Next, add the chopped tomatoes, aubergines and crushed spices, stir well, add the herbs and season with salt and freshly milled black pepper. Bring everything up to a gentle simmer, then remove the pan from the heat and pile everything into a serving dish. Leave for 24 hours, or longer if possible, covered, in the fridge.

Serve the salad at room temperature, drizzled with the olive oil. Serve with the warm pitta breads, about a tablespoon of Greek yoghurt with each serving and the fresh herbs scattered over ■

Chinese Beansprout Salad with Soy Dressing
Serves 4-6

This is a very bright and beautiful salad to look at and the unusual dressing makes it really different.

8 oz (225 g) fresh beansprouts

1 small red pepper, deseeded and chopped

about 6 inches (15 cm), cucumber, unpeeled and diced

1 small onion, thinly sliced and separated into rings

2-3 oz (50-75 g) watercress

For the dressing:

½ teaspoon ground ginger

½ small onion, finely chopped

6 fl oz (175 ml) olive oil or groundnut oil

2 fl oz (55 ml) red wine vinegar

2 tablespoons Japanese soy sauce

1 small celery stalk, chopped

2 teaspoons tomato purée

2 teaspoons lemon juice

salt and freshly milled black pepper

In a good, roomy bowl, combine the beansprouts, chopped pepper, diced cucumber and sliced onion. Pick over the watercress, selecting the best leaves and add them to the salad. Cover the bowl with clingfilm and chill in the fridge while you make up the dressing. For this, all you do is simply place all the dressing ingredients, together with 2 fl oz (55 ml) water, in a blender, and blend until smooth. If you don't have a blender, then combine the dressing ingredients by shaking them together in a screw-top jar. Taste, and season the dressing, as required.

For this salad, I would suggest you serve the dressing separately in a jug, for people to help themselves ■

Asparagus, Cheese and Egg Tartlets
Serves 6

These delightful tartlets contain a combination of melted cheese, lightly sautéed asparagus tips and whole, lightly baked eggs. They are simple to prepare and just need popping into the oven 12-15 minutes before they are served.

For the cheese pastry:

1½ oz (40 g) mature Cheddar, finely grated

2 oz (50 g) soft butter, at room temperature

4 oz (110 g) plain flour

½ teaspoon mustard powder

pinch cayenne pepper

1 beaten egg for the glaze

For the filling:

7 oz (200 g) asparagus tips

5 oz (150 g) Gruyère or Emmental, finely grated

6 large eggs

2 oz (50 g) parmesan, finely grated

1 dessertspoon olive oil

salt and freshly milled black pepper

You will also need six 4 inch (10 cm) quiche tins and a 5½ inch (14 cm) plain cutter or saucer.

First of all, make the pastry by rubbing the butter into the flour, then add the cheese, mustard and cayenne. Mix with just enough cold water to make a smooth dough. Now place the dough in a plastic bag and rest in the fridge for 20 minutes.

Next, pre-heat the oven to gas mark 4, 350°F (180°C). Then roll out the pastry as thinly as possible, and stamp or cut out 6 rounds. Line the tins with pastry, pushing the pastry into the tins, taking care not to stretch it – this will stop it shrinking during cooking. Bake the pastry cases for 15 minutes until lightly cooked. Remove them from the oven and brush the base and sides of each with beaten egg. Return to the oven and cook for 5 more minutes.

Meanwhile, prepare the filling. Wash the asparagus tips and cut them into 1 inch (2.5 cm) diagonal pieces, heat up the dessertspoon of oil in a medium-sized frying pan and gently sauté them for 5 minutes, keeping them on the move.

Now divide the grated Gruyère (or Emmental) cheese between the tartlet cases, spreading it out over the base and then place the asparagus pieces around the edge of each one, keeping the tips turned up to make a nice pattern on the top.

Next, break an egg into a saucer or small bowl, then slip one into the centre of each tartlet. Season with salt and pepper and sprinkle the tops with parmesan. Now bake the tartlets in the oven for 12-15 minutes, depending on how you like your eggs cooked – the whites should be set and the yolks still soft and creamy. Serve immediately because if they wait around, the eggs will go on cooking ■

Bruschetta with Tomato and Basil
Serves 4-6 (makes 12)

Good bread, good olive oil – what more could you want? Just two things: very red, ripe plum tomatoes and basil leaves. It's perhaps the best bruschetta of all, and perfect for serving with drinks before a meal instead of serving a starter.

1 ciabatta loaf, cut in 12 thin slices

6 red, ripe plum tomatoes

a few torn fresh basil leaves

1 clove garlic, peeled and rubbed in a little salt

about 8 tablespoons extra virgin olive oil

sea salt and freshly milled black pepper

You will also need a cast-iron, ridged griddle (or grill, see below).

First, pre-heat the ridged griddle over a high heat for about 10 minutes. Now you can prepare the tomatoes. All you do is place them in a bowl, pour boiling water over them and leave for exactly 1 minute before draining them and slipping off the skins (protect your hands with a cloth if they are too hot). Then chop them finely.

When the griddle is really hot, place the slices of bread – on the diagonal – and grill them for about 1 minute on each side, until they're golden and crisp and have charred strips across each side. (Alternatively, toast them under a conventional grill.) Then, as they are ready, take a sharp knife and quickly make about three little slashes across each one, rub the garlic in and drizzle about half a tablespoon of olive oil over each one.

Now top the bruschetta with the tomatoes and basil leaves, season with salt and freshly milled black pepper and sprinkle a few more drops of olive oil over before serving. It's hard to believe that something so simple can be so wonderful ■

Mexican Guacamole
Serves 4

The first time I ever used Tabasco (hot chilli sauce) was when I made my first guacamole. This spicy Mexican purée, made with fresh avocados, chillies and ripe tomatoes, is still a great favourite. Serve it as a first course with good crusty bread or as a dip with raw vegetable strips. Don't make guacamole more than three hours ahead, though, or it will discolour.

2 ripe avocados

2 large, red, ripe tomatoes

2 small cloves garlic, peeled and sliced

½ red onion, peeled and cut into quarters

2 small red chillies, halved and deseeded

juice 2 limes

a few drops Tabasco

2 tablespoons fresh coriander leaves, to garnish

salt and freshly milled black pepper

First, it's important to have ripe avocados. All you do is halve them, remove the stones, then cut them into quarters, remove the flesh from the skin and place it in the bowl of a food processor. Now, using a teaspoon, scrape away any green part of the avocado flesh that has adhered to the skin and add this, as this will help to give lots of green colour.

Next, skin the tomatoes by pouring boiling water over them, then leave them for exactly 1 minute before draining and slipping off their skins (protect your hands with a cloth). Then halve them and pop them in to join the avocado, followed by the garlic, onion and chillies, and then add the lime juice, a few drops of Tabasco and some salt and pepper. Now whiz it all to a smooth purée, pile it into a serving bowl and cover with clingfilm. Chill till you need it and serve it sprinkled with the fresh coriander leaves ■

Clockwise from top left: Asparagus, Cheese and Egg Tartlets;
Bruschetta with Tomato and Basil; Mexican Guacamole

Mushrooms in Hot Garlic Butter
Serves 4

Japanese-style Salad
with a Sesame Dressing
Serves 4

This recipe is for people who, like me, love sizzling garlic butter. The mushrooms can be cooked in one large, ovenproof baking dish or four individual gratin dishes.

1 lb (450 g) mushrooms
2-3 large cloves garlic, peeled and crushed
6 oz (175 g) butter, at room temperature
1-2 tablespoons chopped fresh parsley
1 tablespoon lemon juice
salt and freshly milled black pepper

Pre-heat the oven to gas mark 7, 425°F (220°C).

Begin by preparing the mushrooms simply by wiping them with kitchen paper, then pull off the stalks – but don't discard them. Now, in a small basin, combine the crushed garlic with the butter, and stir in the parsley and lemon juice. Season the mixture with salt and black pepper.

Next, arrange the mushroom caps, skin side down (in one large dish or divide them between 4 individual gratin dishes), with the stalks arranged amongst them. Place a little of the garlic butter mixture on each cap, and spread whatever remains on the stalks as well.

Now place the dish (or dishes) on the top shelf of the pre-heated oven and cook for 10-15 minutes or until the butter is sizzling away and the mushrooms look slightly toasted. Serve straight from the oven with lashings of crusty bread to mop up the garlicky juices ▪

This brilliant recipe comes from Lindsey Greensted-Benech at Norwich City Football Club. The tofu is coated with crunchy sesame seeds and served with a creamy dressing.

For the tofu:
1 x 285 g pack firm tofu
3 oz (75 g) sesame seeds
1 teaspoon caster sugar
2 tablespoons saké or dry white wine
1 dessertspoon Japanese soy sauce
juice 1 lime
1 teaspoon freshly grated ginger
1 dessertspoon cornflour
1 small egg white, lightly beaten with a fork
2 tablespoons vegetable oil
1 tablespoon sesame oil
salt

For the salad:
14 oz (400 g) head Chinese leaves, leaves separated and washed
4 oz (110 g) fine asparagus, stalks trimmed diagonally
3 oz (75 g) small mangetout, trimmed
½ cucumber
4 oz (110 g) enoki or shiitake mushrooms, sliced
1 large carrot, 8 inches/20 cm long, peeled (only needed if using enoki mushrooms)
4 spring onions, trimmed and cut into diagonal slices
1 small red chilli, deseeded and finely diced

For the dressing:
1 tablespoon saké or dry white wine
1½ tablespoons Japanese soy sauce
1 tablespoon groundnut or other flavourless oil
1 tablespoon sesame oil
salt and freshly ground black pepper

You will also need four 8 inch (20 cm) long wooden skewers, and a frying pan with a diameter of 10 inches (25.5 cm).

Half-fill a medium-sized saucepan with water and bring it to the boil. Cook the tofu in the simmering water for 2 minutes, then remove it from the pan and leave it to drain on several layers of kitchen towel. Allow to cool, then pat the surface with more kitchen towel.

Trim the tofu into a 3 in (7.5 cm) square and reserve the trimmings. Split the tofu in half horizontally, cut each piece into 3 fingers, then cut each finger in half widthways. Leave to drain on plenty of kitchen towel.

Meanwhile, toast 2 tablespoons of the sesame seeds in the frying pan over a high heat for 2-3 minutes, shaking them constantly until at least half have turned deep golden brown. Tip the seeds into a blender, then add the tofu trimmings, sugar, saké (or wine), soy sauce, lime juice, ginger and ½ teaspoon of salt. Whiz until it forms a smooth and creamy sauce, speckled with sesame seeds.

Lightly dust the remaining tofu pieces with the cornflour, dip into the egg white, ensuring they are evenly coated, then dip them into the remaining sesame seeds. Push a skewer through 3 pieces of tofu with their long sides touching, then repeat with the rest of the tofu. Heat the vegetable and sesame oils in the frying pan over a medium-high heat and slide the skewers of tofu into the oil. Fry for 3 minutes on each side, until crisp and golden, but be careful, as the sesame seeds tend to spit. Remove the skewers from the pan and drain on kitchen paper. This can all be done the day before and chilled. Preheat the oven to gas mark 5, 375°F (190°C).

Now to prepare the salad, put a medium-sized pan of salted water on to boil. Cut away the stalk from the Chinese leaves and discard, then cut each leaf into ½ inch (1 cm) ribbons. Cut the asparagus into 3 diagonally and cook in the boiling water for 2 minutes. Remove, refresh in cold water and drain, then cook the mangetout in the same boiling water for 1 minute, refresh and drain. Thinly slice the cucumber, then layer it in stacks and cut into ¼ inch (5 mm) strips. If you are using enoki mushrooms, use a peeler to cut 4 long ribbons from the carrot and trim them diagonally at each end. Divide the enoki into 4 bundles and cut 1 inch (2.5 cm) off the ends. Then make each bundle into a bouquet by wrapping a carrot ribbon around it.

Put the tofu skewers on a baking tray and place in the oven for 7-8 minutes. Whisk the dressing ingredients together and season.

To serve, toss together the Chinese leaves, asparagus, mangetout, the sliced cucumber, spring onions and chilli and place in the centre of each salad, put a mushroom bouquet (or the shiitake mushrooms) on top. Finally, remove the tofu skewers from the oven and put a skewer across each salad, then drizzle the dressing around and serve immediately ▪

Potato Salad with Roquefort
Serves 6-8

This potato salad, with creamy, piquant cheese and the added crunch of celery and shallots, is good to eat all by itself, but I also like to serve it as part of a buffet lunch.

2 lb (900 g) small new potatoes or salad potatoes

1 oz (25 g) Roquefort, Shropshire Blue or Cashel Blue, crumbled

4 shallots, peeled and finely chopped

2 celery sticks, trimmed and chopped into ¼ inch (5 mm) pieces

4 spring onions, trimmed and finely chopped

salt

For the dressing:

1½ oz (40 g) Roquefort, Shropshire Blue or Cashel Blue, crumbled

1 clove garlic, peeled

1 teaspoon sea salt

1 heaped teaspoon grain mustard

1 tablespoon lemon juice

2 tablespoons balsamic vinegar

2 tablespoons olive oil

5 fl oz (150 ml) half-fat crème fraîche

2 tablespoons mayonnaise

freshly milled black pepper

You will also need a steamer.

Place the potatoes in a steamer over boiling water and sprinkle them with a dessertspoon of salt, then put a lid on and let them steam for 20-25 minutes.

Meanwhile, make the dressing. To do this, place the garlic, along with the teaspoon of salt, into a mortar and crush it to a creamy mass, then add the mustard and work that in. Next add the lemon juice, vinegar and, after that, the oil, then whisk everything together thoroughly. Now, in a medium-sized bowl, first combine the crème fraîche and mayonnaise, then gradually whisk in the dressing. When it's thoroughly blended, add the cheese and season with freshly milled black pepper.

When the potatoes are cooked, remove the steamer and place a cloth over them for about 4 minutes to absorb the steam. Then cut any larger potatoes in half, transfer them to a large bowl and, while they are still warm, pour the dressing over them, along with the shallots and celery. Give everything a good gentle mixing, then, just before serving, sprinkle over the rest of the crumbled cheese and the spring onions ■

Char-grilled Aubergine and Roasted Tomato Salad with Feta Cheese
Serves 4

I am indebted to Chris Payne, who very generously gave me this splendid recipe. If you don't possess a ridged griddle pan, you could grill the aubergine slices till nicely browned and tender. Either way, this is a truly delicious combination of textures and flavours.

2 medium aubergines

8 small, ripe plum tomatoes

7 oz (200 g) feta cheese, cut into thin slices

8 tablespoons extra virgin olive oil, plus a little extra, for brushing the griddle

1 heaped tablespoon torn fresh basil leaves

2 tablespoons balsamic vinegar

4 oz (110 g) assorted salad leaves

7 fl oz (200 ml) half-fat crème fraîche

a little paprika

sea salt and freshly milled black pepper

You will also need a baking tray measuring 10 x 14 inches (25.5 x 35 cm), and a cast-iron ridged griddle.

Pre-heat the oven to gas mark 6, 400°F (200°C).

First of all, skin the tomatoes by covering them with boiling water for 15-30 seconds, then drain them and slip off their skins (protect your hands, if necessary). Cut them in half and place them on the baking tray, cut-side up, then season well, drizzle 1 tablespoon of the olive oil over and place them on the top shelf of the oven to roast for 50-60 minutes. After this time, leave them aside to cool.

While they're cooling, cut the aubergines across into ½ inch (1 cm) slices, lay the slices on a board and lightly sprinkle them with salt on both sides. Leave them for 20 minutes to draw out some of the excess moisture, then blot them dry with kitchen paper. Next, brush them on both sides using 1 tablespoon of the olive oil and season with freshly milled black pepper. Brush the griddle lightly with olive oil and place it over a high heat, then, when it is very hot, cook the aubergines in batches for about 2½ minutes on each side (this should take about 20 minutes in all).

Now pour the remaining 6 tablespoons of olive oil into a large bowl, add the basil and balsamic vinegar, then toss the cooked aubergines in this marinade and leave them in a cool place until you are ready to serve.

Divide the salad leaves between 4 plates and arrange the tomatoes and aubergines alternately all around. Then place equal quantities of the feta slices in the middle of each salad and drizzle with the remaining marinade. Finally, put 1 tablespoon of crème fraîche on top of each salad and sprinkle a little paprika over ■

Chapter Three
Eggs

Alpine Eggs with Lancashire Cheese and Asparagus
Serves 2

Egg and Lentil Curry with Coconut and Pickled Lime
Serves 2

This recipe never fails to please and is one of the quickest supper dishes. Serve with crusty fresh bread and a crisp green salad.

4 large eggs

4 oz (110 g) Lancashire cheese, crumbled

10-12 oz (275-350 g) fresh asparagus, trimmed

1 oz (25 g) butter

1 dessertspoon snipped fresh chives, to garnish

salt and freshly milled black pepper

Pre-heat the oven to gas mark 4, 350°F (180°C).

You will also need a steamer, and a baking dish measuring 8 x 6 x 2 inches (20 x 15 x 5 cm), generously buttered.

First of all, lay the spears of asparagus in an opened fan steamer (they can be piled one on top of the other) and place it in a frying pan or saucepan. Now add 1 inch (2.5 cm) of boiling water, then cover with a lid and steam the asparagus for just 3 minutes.

Next, lay the asparagus in the base of the dish and scatter with half the grated cheese. Now carefully break the eggs on to the cheese and season with salt and freshly milled black pepper. Then sprinkle the rest of the cheese over the eggs, covering them completely.

Dot with a few flecks of butter here and there, then bake in the centre of the oven for 12-15 minutes, by which time the cheese will be melted and bubbling, and the eggs just set. Just before serving, sprinkle with the snipped chives ■

This is one of my very favourite store-cupboard recipes. If you always keep a stock of spices and lentils handy and a pack of creamed coconut stashed away in the fridge, you can whip this one up in no time at all. It also happens to be inexpensive.

4 large eggs

3 oz (75 g) green-brown lentils

3 oz (75 g) creamed coconut

1 rounded teaspoon lime pickle

juice and grated zest ½ fresh lime

1 large onion

1 small red chilli (preferably bird eye)

2 fat cloves garlic

1 inch (2.5 cm) piece fresh root ginger

3 cardamom pods, crushed

1 teaspoon cumin seeds

1 teaspoon fennel seeds

1 dessertspoon coriander seeds

2 tablespoons groundnut or other flavourless oil

1 rounded teaspoon turmeric powder

1 teaspoon fenugreek powder

a few sprigs fresh flat-leaf parsley or coriander, to garnish

salt

To serve:

5 fl oz (150 ml) rice, cooked in 10 fl oz (275 ml) boiling water (see page 122)

a little extra lime pickle, and some mango chutney (optional)

You will also need a medium frying pan with a lid.

Start off by getting everything prepared and ready to go. First, peel the onion, cut it in half and then into thin slices. Next, deseed and finely chop the chilli, peel and chop the garlic as well, then measure out the lime pickle and chop that quite finely. Now peel and grate the ginger – you need a good heaped teaspoonful.

The creamed coconut should be shredded with a sharp knife and placed in a heatproof measuring jug. At this stage put the kettle on to boil.

Now place the frying pan over a medium heat and, as soon as it gets hot, measure the whole spices (cardamom, cumin, fennel and coriander) straight into it. What they need to do now is dry-roast, and this will take 2-3 minutes. Shake the pan from time to time to toss them around a bit and, as soon as they start to jump, remove them from the heat and tip them straight into a mortar.

Now place the pan back over the heat, turn it up high and add the oil. As soon as it is really hot, add the onions and, keeping the heat highish, let them sizzle and brown and become quite dark at the edges, which will take about 4 minutes. After that, turn the heat back down to medium and add the chilli, garlic, ginger and lime pickle, along with the turmeric and fenugreek. Now crush the roasted spices finely with a pestle, add these to the pan as well, then stir everything together.

See to the coconut next: all you need to do here is pour boiling water up to the 1 pint (570 ml) level in the jug containing the coconut, then whisk it all together.

Now stir the lentils in to join the rest of the ingredients, add the grated lime zest and the coconut liquid, stir again and, as soon as it reaches simmering point, turn the heat down. Put the lid on and let the mixture simmer as gently as possible for 45 minutes, stirring it now and then (don't add any salt at this stage).

About 10 minutes before the end of the cooking time, place the eggs in a saucepan of cold water, bring them up to a gentle simmer and time them for 6-7 minutes,

depending on how you like them. When they're ready, let the cold tap run on them until they're cool enough to handle. When the sauce is ready, season it well with salt and add the lime juice. Now peel the eggs under cold running water, slice them in half and pop them on top of the sauce, giving everything a couple more minutes' cooking with the lid on. Garnish with parsley or coriander sprigs and serve the egg curry with rice, some more lime pickle, and perhaps some mango chutney to add a touch of sweetness ■

Eggs en Cocotte with Morel or Porcini Mushrooms

Eggs en Cocotte with Morel or Porcini Mushrooms
Serves 4

I love to make this with dried morels, which are available from specialist food shops, but dried porcini will also be excellent.

4 large eggs

½ oz (10 g) dried morels or porcini

3 shallots, peeled and chopped

4 oz (110 g) dark-gilled, flat mushrooms, roughly chopped

¼ whole nutmeg, grated

1 oz (25 g) butter

3 rounded tablespoons crème fraîche, half-fat crème fraîche or Greek yoghurt

salt and freshly milled black pepper

You will also need four 1½ inch (4 cm) deep ramekins with a base diameter of 3 inches (7.5 cm), well buttered, and a baking tin measuring 11 x 8 x 2 inches (28 x 20 x 5 cm).

Start by soaking the morels or porcini about 30 minutes ahead of time. Place them in a bowl with 5 fl oz (150 ml) boiling water and leave them aside to soak. After that, strain them in a sieve and squeeze them to get rid of any surplus water. (You can reserve the soaking water, which can be frozen and is great for soups and sauces.) Set aside 4 pieces of the morels or porcini and put the rest in a food processor, along with the shallots, flat mushrooms, nutmeg and a seasoning of salt and freshly milled black pepper. Process until finely chopped.

Heat the butter in a small saucepan. When it starts to foam, add the chopped mushroom mixture and, keeping the heat low, let it cook very gently, without a lid, for 25-30 minutes; the idea is that any excess liquid will evaporate and leave a lovely, dark, concentrated mixture.

All this can be prepared in advance, but when you're ready to cook the eggs, start by pre-heating the oven to gas mark 4, 350°F (180° C) and boil a kettle. Gently re-heat the

mixture and, stirring in 1 rounded tablespoon of the crème fraîche or yoghurt, divide it between the ramekins, making a small indentation where the egg will be placed.

Now break an egg into each one and season. Stir the rest of the crème fraîche or yoghurt around to loosen it, divide between the dishes, then spread it gently over the eggs, using the back of the spoon or a small palette knife. Place a piece of the reserved morels or porcini on top of each ramekin, then place the ramekins in the baking tin, pop the tin on the centre shelf of the oven and add enough boiling water to the tin to come halfway up the sides of the dishes.

Bake for 15-18 minutes. These are lovely served with slices of wholemeal bread and butter ■

Gratinée of Eggs Basque
Serves 2

An ingenious little supper dish with plenty of colour and flavour. If you're less hungry, just use one egg for each person.

4 large eggs

4 red ripe tomatoes, skinned and chopped or 4 tablespoons tinned chopped tomatoes

2 tablespoon olive oil

a medium onion, peeled and chopped small

1 small green or red pepper, chopped into ½ inch (1 cm) squares

2 medium-sized courgettes, sliced thinly

1 large clove garlic, peeled and crushed

3 oz (75 g) Gruyère or Emmental, grated

2 teaspoons fresh chopped parsley

salt and freshly milled black pepper

You will also need two individual gratin dishes with a base diameter of 5 inches (13 cm), buttered.

First of all, pre-heat the grill to its highest setting. Now in a medium, thick-based frying pan heat the oil and fry the onion and pepper over a medium heat for about 10 minutes until golden and almost cooked. Then draw them to one side of the pan and add the courgette slices: brown these on both sides, then add the garlic and stir everything together.

Next, add the chopped tomatoes and a good seasoning of salt and pepper and let it all cook for 1 minute more. Now spoon the mixture into the gratin dishes and spread it out evenly, making two little spaces in each one for the eggs. Break 2 eggs into these, season them, then sprinkle the cheese all over. Place the dishes about 4 inches (10 cm) away from the grill, and cook for 10-15 minutes, depending on how you like your eggs. Serve, sprinkled with chopped parsley and with lots of crusty French bread ■

Pipérade with Roasted Peppers
Serves 2

This lovely, fluffy combination of scrambled eggs and peppers came originally from the Basque region of France. This is a variation of the classic recipe, leaving out the bacon but with the addition of pre-roasted peppers.

4 large fresh eggs

4 oz (110 g) roasted peppers in oil, drained (reserving a dessertspoon of the oil) and cut into ½ inch (1 cm) strips

½ oz (10 g) butter

2 medium onions, peeled and chopped small

1 or 2 cloves garlic, peeled and crushed (how much is up to you)

1 lb (450 g) firm tomatoes, peeled deseeded and chopped in ¼ inch (5 mm) cubes

½ tablespoon chopped fresh basil

salt and freshly milled black pepper

You will also need a heavy-based, medium-sized saucepan or frying pan.

Melt the butter and heat with the reserved oil from the peppers in the pan and add the onions, cooking them very gently for 10 minutes without browning. Now add the crushed garlic and tomatoes, stir everything around a little, season with salt and pepper and basil, and cook without covering for another 20 minutes or so, then stir in the strips of roasted pepper.

Now beat the eggs thoroughly, pour them into the pan and, using a wooden spoon, stir just as you would for scrambled eggs. When the mixture starts to thicken and the eggs are almost cooked, remove the pan from the heat, continuing to stir, and serve immediately (as with scrambled eggs, do be very careful not to overcook) ■

Eggs Florentine
Serves 2

This is a very quick and easy supper or lunch dish for two people.

4 large fresh eggs
1 lb (450 g) young leaf spinach,
cooked in its own juices for 2-3 minutes,
then well drained
freshly grated nutmeg
1 tablespoon double cream
salt and freshly milled black pepper

For the sauce:
1½ oz (40 g) butter, plus a little extra
10 fl oz (275 ml) milk
1 oz (25 g) plain flour
3 oz (75 g) Lancashire cheese, grated
1 tablespoon double cream
1 oz (25 g) parmesan, grated

Pre-heat the oven to gas mark 5, 375°F (190°C).

You will also need a shallow baking dish generously buttered.

First, arrange the cooked spinach over the base of the dish, then season with salt, pepper and freshly grated nutmeg. Next, sprinkle the cream over and pop the dish in the lower part of the oven to heat through.

Now, for the sauce, place the butter, milk and flour in a saucepan and whisk over heat to make a smooth sauce. Then stir in the grated Lancashire cheese and cook the sauce over a gentle heat for 3 minutes.

Next, take the dish out of the oven, make four depressions in the spinach and gently break an egg into each one. Lightly season the yolks and stir the tablespoon of cream into the sauce and pour it over the eggs to cover everything. Sprinkle with parmesan, add a few flecks of butter here and there and bake on a high shelf for 15-20 minutes ■

Melted Cheese Frittata with Four Kinds of Mushroom
Serves 4

I like to use Fontina cheese for this, but Gruyère and Emmental are also good melting cheeses, so you could use either of those instead. The mushrooms can be whatever is available, though I love the contrasting textures and colours of a mixture of oyster, shiitake, black dark-gilled mushrooms and the vibrant pied de mouton. However, none of this is vital: if you use only one type of mushroom it will still be extremely good.

8 large eggs
4 oz (110 g) Fontina, Gruyère or Emmental
12 oz (350 g) mixed mushrooms
or 3 oz (75 g) of each variety
1 tablespoon olive oil
salt and freshly milled black pepper

You will also need a 10 inch (25.5 cm) frying pan.

Pre-heat the oven to its lowest setting.

First of all, chop the mushrooms into roughly 1 inch (2.5 cm) chunks – it's going to look an enormous quantity at this stage, but they will lose approximately half their volume in the initial cooking. Now heat a teaspoon of the olive oil in the frying pan and, when it's hot, throw in the mushrooms and toss them around by shaking the pan. Don't worry that there is so little oil, because the mushrooms give off masses of juice once the heat gets to them. Season with salt and pepper, then turn the heat down to very low and just let the mushrooms cook gently, uncovered, so that all the juice evaporates and the flavour of the mushrooms becomes more concentrated. Leave them like that for 30 minutes, stirring them around once or twice.

While they are cooking, cut two-thirds of the cheese into ¼ inch (5 mm) cubes and grate the other third on the coarse blade of the grater. After that, break the eggs into a large bowl, whisk lightly with a fork and season well with salt and pepper. Then add three-quarters of the cooked mushrooms to the eggs, together with the cubed cheese. Place the rest of the mushrooms in a bowl covered with foil and keep them warm in the oven.

Now wipe the pan clean with some kitchen paper and put it back on a medium heat, add the rest of the olive oil and, when it's hot, swirl it around the pan. Turn the heat down to its lowest setting and pour the egg mixture into the pan, scattering the grated cheese all over the surface. Now all you have to do is leave it alone and put a timer on for 15 minutes.

When 15 minutes have passed, turn the grill on to its highest setting and see how the omelette is cooking – it will probably take about 20 minutes in total to cook, but there should still be about 10 per cent of liquid egg left on top. At that stage, transfer the pan to the grill – not too close – and cook briefly to allow the liquid egg to set. This will take 20-30 seconds. Scatter the remaining cooked mushrooms over the top of the frittata and cut it into 4 wedges.

Transfer the wedges to warm plates and serve immediately, because the egg will continue cooking, even though the frittata is no longer in contact with the heat. I like to serve this with 2 salads – a plain, green-lettuce salad and a tomato and basil salad ■

Eggs and Leeks en Cocotte
Serves 1

This provides something special for the bored dieter. You can ring the changes, too – instead of leeks, use steamed asparagus tips or cooked, chopped spinach. For a low-fat accompaniment, serve with wholemeal bread spread with a little Greek yoghurt.

1 large egg
2 oz (50 g) leeks (trimmed weight)
2 rounded tablespoons 5 per cent Greek yoghurt
½ teaspoon freshly grated parmesan
salt and freshly milled black pepper

You will also need a ramekin 1½ inches (4 cm) deep with a base diameter of 3 inches (7.5 cm), or a small, round, ovenproof dish, smeared with a trace of butter, and a small roasting tin.

Pre-heat the oven to gas mark 4, 350°F (180°C).

First of all, cut the leek vertically, fan it under cold, running water to get rid of any dirt, then chop it quite finely. Now place a small pan over a medium heat, add the leeks and some seasoning, stir, then turn the heat down to low. Cover and let them cook gently in their own juices for about 5 minutes, shaking the pan and stirring two or three times. After that, use a draining spoon to transfer the leeks to the ramekin (or dish).

Next, carefully break the egg in on top of the leeks and add some seasoning. Then gently spoon the yoghurt over, spreading it out so it covers the egg completely. Finally, sprinkle with the parmesan. Now pour about 1 inch (2.5 cm) of boiling water into the roasting tin, place the ramekin (or dish) in it and pop the whole lot in the oven to bake for 15-18 minutes, depending on how you like your egg cooked – bearing in mind it will go on cooking after it has been removed from the oven ■

Right: Melted Cheese Frittata with Four Kinds of Mushroom
Top left: Eggs and Leeks en Cocotte

Quails' Eggs
with Cracked Pepper and Salt
Serves 6

Broccoli Soufflé
with Three Cheeses
Serves 4

Peeling boiled quails' eggs is not my favourite job, so I usually rope in some help, but it's worth it because they look so pretty and taste wonderful dipped in cracked pepper and salt.

24 quails' eggs
1 tablespoon mixed peppercorns, crushed in a mortar
1 tablespoon sea salt

To cook the eggs, put them into plenty of boiling water, bring them quickly back to the boil and using a timer, give them 1 minute and 45 seconds.

Next, run cold water over them to stop them cooking and peel them while they are still slightly warm, reserving a few with the shell on, to garnish.

Then, to serve, arrange them on a platter with the unpeeled eggs and a little dipping pot containing the pepper and salt, which have been mixed together ■

The secret of a well-risen soufflé lies precisely in the size of the dish you use. If you want it to look amazing, use a small dish with a collar tied around – this way you can pile the mixture up high, then when it's cooked, remove the collar to reveal a spectacular height!

1 lb (450 g) broccoli, with the very thick stalks trimmed off
3 large eggs, plus 2 large egg whites
1 oz (25 g) butter, plus melted butter for the dish and collar
1¼ oz (30 g) plain flour
5 fl oz (150 ml) milk
¼ teaspoon cayenne pepper
¼ whole nutmeg, grated
1 oz (25 g) mature Cheddar, grated
1 oz (25g) Gruyère or Emmental, grated
2 tablespoons parmesan, grated
a slice of lemon
salt and freshly milled black pepper

You will also need baking parchment, string and a 1¾ pint (1 litre) soufflé dish measuring 5½ inches (14 cm) in diameter and 3 inches (7.5 cm) high.

Pre-heat the oven to gas mark 6, 400°F (200°C). Place the oven shelf in the lower third of the oven with no shelf above.

First of all, prepare the soufflé dish and its collar. To do this, cut a piece of baking parchment 20 x 12 inches (51 x 30 cm) in length. Fold in half along its length so that it now measures 20 x 6 inches (51 x 15 cm) doubled. Now turn up a 1 inch (2.5 cm) fold all along the length to stabilise the base of the collar. Next, butter the soufflé dish really well and sprinkle the inside with some of the parmesan, tipping the dish from side to side to give the base and sides a light

coating. Empty out the excess, then tie the paper collar around the dish with the 1 inch (2.5 cm) folded bit at the bottom. The paper will overlap around the circumference by 3 inches (7.5 cm) and stand 2 inches (5 cm) above the rim of the dish. Fix the collar in place with string and tie with a bow so that when it comes out of the oven you can remove it quickly and easily. Now butter the inside of the paper and that's it – the dish is now ready.

To make the soufflé, place the broccoli in a steamer, sprinkle with salt and steam over simmering water until tender – approximately 8-10 minutes. While the broccoli is cooking, prepare the eggs. Have ready a large bowl containing the extra egg whites and two small ones, separate the eggs into the small bowls, one at a time, transferring the whites from the small bowl into the larger bowl as you go. When the broccoli is tender, remove it and leave to cool until barely warm. Then pop it into the processor and whiz it almost to a purée.

Next, make the sauce. Place the butter, flour and milk in a small saucepan and whisk with a balloon whisk over a medium heat until you have a smooth, glossy paste. Season to taste with salt and pepper, then season with about the same amount again – this extra is really to season the large volume of eggs. Transfer to a mixing bowl and add the cayenne, nutmeg, Cheddar, Gruyère (or Emmental) and 1 tablespoon of the grated parmesan. Add the 3 egg yolks, plus the broccoli, and mix everything together.

Now the vital part – the beating of the egg whites. Make sure the bowl and whisk are spanking clean, then wipe them with the lemon to ensure they're absolutely grease free. If you're using an electric whisk, switch it on to low and beat the whites for

approximately 30 seconds or until they begin to start foaming. Then increase the speed of the whisk to medium and then to high, moving the whisk round and round the bowl while it's beating, until you get a smooth, glossy mixture that stands in stiff peaks when the whisk is removed from the bowl. It's better to underbeat than overbeat, so watch carefully.

Next, using a large metal spoon, stir 1 tablespoon of the egg whites into the broccoli to lighten the mixture, then empty the broccoli mixture into the egg whites and fold, using cutting and turning movements, until everything is well amalgamated. Don't be tempted to do any mixing – it must be careful folding done as quickly as possible. Now pour the mixture into the prepared dish, sprinkle the top with the remaining parmesan and place on a shelf in the lower third of the oven (with no shelf above) for 40-45 minutes. When it's done, it should be nicely browned on top, well risen and beginning to crack. It should feel springy in the centre but it's important not to overcook it, as it should be nice and moist, almost runny inside because, as you are taking it from the oven to the table, and even as you are serving it, it will go on cooking. Divide between warm serving plates and serve it absolutely immediately ■

Note: This soufflé can be made with other vegetable purées: parsnips, Jerusalem artichokes or courgettes would make lovely alternatives.

Swiss Baked Eggs
Serves 2

Scrambled Eggs with Gorgonzola
Serves 1

Twice-baked Roquefort Soufflés
Serves 6

This is a little gem of a supper dish and it's made in moments. Serve it with fingers of wholemeal toast.

4 large eggs

2 tablespoons double cream

2 oz (50 g) Gruyère or Emmental cheese, grated

salt and freshly milled black pepper

You will also need two ramekins with a 2½ inch (6 cm) base diameter, 2 inches (5 cm) deep, buttered, and a small baking tin and baking sheet.

Pre-heat the oven to gas mark 4, 350°F (180°C).

First, you need to boil some water. While you're waiting, pour a dessertspoon of cream into the base of each ramekin. Now break 2 eggs into each one, season them with salt and pepper and put the dishes in the baking tin, then pop the tin on the centre shelf of the oven and pour boiling water into the tin to come halfway up the sides of the dishes. Now let the eggs bake for 12 minutes if you like them soft and runny, or 15 minutes if you like them more set. Either way, bear in mind that they go on cooking as they leave the oven and reach the table. Meanwhile, pre-heat the grill to its highest setting.

Then when the eggs are ready, carefully remove the ramekins from the tin (using a cloth to protect your hands) and transfer them to the baking sheet. Spoon the rest of the cream over the eggs, then sprinkle with the grated cheese, and place the ramekins under the grill for a few minutes or until the cheese bubbles. Serve straightaway ■

For more people, just multiply the ingredients accordingly. The method remains the same, but more eggs will obviously take longer to cook. Serve on hot buttered toast or bagels.

2 large eggs

½ oz (10 g) butter

2 oz (50 g) creamy Gorgonzola or Cashel Blue, cubed

salt and freshly milled black pepper

First of all, break the eggs into a small bowl and use a fork to blend them lightly, whisking gently. Add a light seasoning of salt and some freshly milled black pepper. Now take a small, heavy-based saucepan and place it over a medium heat. Add half the butter to the pan and swirl it around.

Then, when the butter has melted and is just beginning to foam, pour in the beaten eggs. Using a wooden fork or spoon with a point, start stirring briskly, using backwards and forwards movements all through the liquid egg, getting into the corners of the pan to prevent it from sticking.

Keep on scrambling away until you calculate that three-quarters of the egg is now a creamy, solid mass and a quarter is still liquid. At this point, remove the pan from the heat, add the rest of the butter and the cheese and continue scrambling. The eggs will carry on cooking in the heat from the pan. As soon as there is no liquid egg left, serve the scrambled eggs absolutely immediately ■

The obvious advantage of twice-baked soufflés is that they can be done and dusted the day before you need them. Then they rise up again like a dream, with a brilliantly light texture and flavour.

4 large eggs, separated

6 oz (175 g) Roquefort or Cashel Blue

8 fl oz (225 ml) milk

¼ inch (5 mm) onion slice

1 bay leaf

grating of nutmeg

6 whole black peppercorns

1½ oz (40 g) butter

1½ oz (40 g) plain flour

5 fl oz (150 ml) double cream

6 sprigs watercress, to garnish

salt and freshly milled black pepper

You will also need six 1½ inch (4 cm) deep ramekins with a base diameter of 3 inches (7.5 cm), lightly buttered, a baking tin measuring 11 x 8 x 2 inches (28 x 20 x 5 cm) and a baking tray measuring 14 x 10 inches (35 x 25.5 cm).

Pre-heat the oven to gas mark 4, 350°F (180°C).

Begin by heating the milk, onion, bay leaf, nutmeg and peppercorns in a medium-sized saucepan till the milk reaches simmering point, then strain it into a jug, discarding the rest now. Rinse out the saucepan, then melt the butter in it. Add the flour and stir to a smooth, glossy paste, and cook this for 3 minutes, still stirring, until it turns a pale straw colour. Then gradually add the strained milk, whisking all the time, until the sauce is thick and cleanly leaves the sides of the pan. Then season lightly and cook the sauce on the gentlest heat possible for 2 minutes, stirring now and then. Next, remove the pan from the heat and let it cool

slightly, then beat in the egg yolks one at a time. Now crumble 4 oz (110 g) of the cheese into the mixture and stir until most of it has melted – don't worry if some cheese is still visible.

Put a kettle on to boil and, in a spanking clean, large bowl, whisk the egg whites to the soft-peak stage, then fold a spoonful of egg white into the cheese sauce to loosen it. Now fold the sauce into the egg white, using a large metal spoon and a cutting and folding motion.

Divide the mixture equally between the ramekins. Put them in the baking tin, place it on the centre shelf of the oven, then pour about ½ inch (1 cm) of boiling water into the tin. Bake the soufflés for 20 minutes, then transfer them to a cooling rack (using a fish slice) so they don't continue cooking. Don't worry if they sink a little as they cool, because they will rise up again in the second cooking.

When they are almost cold, run a small palette knife around the edge of each ramekin and carefully turn the soufflés out on to the palm of your hand, then place them the right way up on a lightly greased, shallow baking tray. They can now be stored in the fridge for up to 24 hours, lightly covered with clingfilm.

When you are ready to re-heat the soufflés, pre-heat the oven to gas mark 4, 350°F (180°C) and remove them from the fridge so they can return to room temperature. Dice the remaining cheese into ¼ inch (5 mm) pieces and sprinkle it on top of the soufflés, then place them in the oven, on the shelf above the centre, for 30 minutes. Then 2 or 3 minutes before serving, spoon a tablespoon of cream over each soufflé and return them to the oven while you seat your guests. Serve the soufflés immediately on warm plates and garnish each with a sprig of watercress ■

Twice-baked Roquefort Soufflés

Baked Eggs in Wild Mushroom Tartlets

Baked Eggs
in Wild Mushroom Tartlets
Serves 6

This not only tastes extremely good but looks very pretty. It's also a moveable feast in that quails' eggs make a lovely alternative, but the method is slightly different: use three eggs in each tartlet (poach them first for 1½ minutes), placing them on top of the warmed mushroom mixture. Then spoon over Foaming Hollandaise (see page 45) and grill for 30 seconds or until golden brown.

For the pastry:
3 oz (75 g) soft butter, plus a little extra for greasing
6 oz (175 g) plain flour, sifted
1½ oz (40 g) parmesan, finely grated

For the filling:
6 large eggs
1 oz (25 g) dried porcini
6 oz (175 g) chestnut mushrooms
6 oz (175 g) open-cap mushrooms
3 oz (75 g) butter
2 small red onions, peeled and finely chopped
2 cloves garlic, peeled and chopped
2 teaspoons lemon juice
1 heaped tablespoon chopped fresh parsley
1 oz (25 g) parmesan, finely grated,
salt and freshly milled black pepper

You will also need six ½ inch (1 cm) deep quiche tins with a base diameter of 4 inches (10 cm), lightly greased, a 5½ inch (14 cm) plain cutter, and a solid baking sheet.

Begin by placing the porcini in a bowl. Pour 7 fl oz (200 ml) boiling water over them and leave to soak for 30 minutes. Now make the pastry. This can be done in a processor, or by rubbing the butter into the flour and stirring in the grated parmesan and sufficient cold water (about 3 tablespoons) to mix to a soft but firm dough. Place it in a plastic bag and leave in the fridge for 30 minutes. This pastry will need a little more water than usual, as the cheese absorbs some of it. For the filling, heat 2 oz (50 g) of the butter in a heavy-based frying pan, add the onions and garlic and fry until they are soft and almost transparent, about 15 minutes. Meanwhile, finely chop the chestnut and open-cap mushrooms. When the porcini have had their soaking, place a sieve over a bowl and strain them into it, pressing to release the moisture. You can freeze the liquid for stocks or sauces. Then chop the porcini finely and transfer them with the other mushrooms to the pan containing the onions. Add the remaining butter, season and cook till the juices of the mushrooms run, then add the lemon juice and parsley. Raise the heat slightly and cook the mushrooms without a lid, stirring from time to time, until all the liquid has evaporated and the mixture is of a spreadable consistency. This will take about 25 minutes.

Meanwhile, pre-heat the oven to gas mark 6, 400°F (200°C). Now roll out the pastry to a thickness of ⅛ inch (3 mm) and cut out 6 rounds, re-rolling, if necessary. Line the tins with the pastry, pushing it down from the top so it will not shrink while cooking. Trim any surplus from the top and prick the base with a fork. Now leave them in the fridge for a few minutes until the oven is up to temperature.

Next, place the tins on the baking sheet and bake on the middle shelf of the oven for 15-20 minutes or until the pastry is golden. Remove them from the oven and reduce the temperature to gas mark 4, 350°F (180°C). Divide the filling between the tarts, making a well in the centre with the back of a spoon. Then break an egg into a saucer, slip it into a tart and scatter a little parmesan over. Repeat with the other 5 tarts and now return them to the oven for 12-15 minutes, until they are just set. Serve straightaway ▪

Tortilla (Spanish omelette)
Serves 2-3

I sometimes marvel how it is that three basic, very inexpensive ingredients – eggs, onions and potatoes – can be transformed into something so utterly sublime. Yet it's simply the way the Spanish make their omelettes. A Spanish omelette, or tortilla, is not better than a French one, and it certainly takes longer to make, but in this age of complicated, overstated, fussy food, it's a joy to know that simplicity can still win the day. A well-made tortilla served with a salad and a bottle of wine can give two or more people a luxury meal at any time and at a very low cost.

1 medium onion, about 4 oz (110 g)
10 oz (275 g) small Desirée potatoes
3 tablespoons olive oil
5 large eggs
salt and freshly milled black pepper

You will also need a frying pan with a lid and a base diameter of 8 inches (20 cm). Use a non-stick pan if you don't have a well-seasoned frying pan. An enormous asset here is a flat saucepan lid or large plate that fits the pan.

First of all, peel and cut the onion in half, then thinly slice each half and separate the layers into half-moon shapes. Now thinly pare the potatoes, using a potato peeler, and slice them into half-moon shapes – you have to work pretty quickly here as you don't want the slices to brown. When they are sliced, rub them in a clean tea cloth to get them as dry as possible.

Next, heat 2 tablespoons of the olive oil in the frying pan and, when it's smoking hot, add the potatoes and onions. Toss them around in the oil to get a good coating, then turn the heat right down to its lowest setting, add a generous sprinkling of salt and pepper, put a lid on the frying pan and let the onions and potatoes cook gently for 20 minutes, or until tender. Turn them over halfway through and shake the pan from time to time, as they are not supposed to brown very much but just gently stew in the oil.

Meanwhile, break the eggs into a large bowl and, using a fork, whisk them lightly – it's important not to overbeat them. Finally, add some seasoning. When the onions and potatoes are cooked, quickly transfer them to the eggs in the bowl. Put the frying pan back on the heat, add the rest of the oil and turn the heat back up to medium. Then mix the potato and eggs thoroughly before pouring the whole lot into the frying pan and turning the heat down to its lowest setting immediately.

Now forget all about French omelettes and be patient, because it's going to take 20-25 minutes to cook slowly, uncovered. Every now and then, draw the edge in gently with a palette knife, as this will give it a lovely rounded edge. When there is virtually no liquid egg left on the surface of the omelette, turn it over to cook the other side. To do this, place a flat lid or plate over the pan, carefully invert both so that the omelette is on the lid or plate. Put the pan back on the heat and use the palette knife to gently ease the omelette back in. Give it about 2 minutes more, then turn the heat off and leave it for a further 5 minutes to settle. It should then be cooked through but still moist in the centre. Serve hot or cold, cut in wedges, with a salad and a glass of Rioja – it's brilliant ▪

Slimmers' Scrambled Eggs with Morel Mushrooms
Serves 2

This recipe is devised for people on a diet or for those who have to cut down on fat. Nevertheless, it's extremely good.

4 large eggs
¼ oz (5 g) dried morel (or porcini mushrooms)
2 tablespoons milk
2 heaped dessertspoons quark or cottage cheese
2 tablespoons freshly snipped chives
salt and freshly milled black pepper

Start by soaking the mushrooms about 30 minutes before you want to make the scrambled eggs. Place them in a small deep bowl or ramekin with the milk, so that the mushrooms are submerged in the liquid, and leave aside to soak.

After that, strain the mushrooms in a sieve (reserving the soaking liquid), and chop them finely. Now beat the eggs in a bowl, together with a good seasoning of salt and pepper. Next, place a medium-sized saucepan over a gentle heat, then add the milk (the reserved soaking liquid) to moisten the pan, whirling it around the edges. Add the eggs and, using a wooden fork or pointed wooden spoon, briskly stir backwards and forwards through the liquid egg. Keep on scrambling until three-quarters of the egg is a creamy, solid mass and a quarter is still liquid.

Now add the chopped mushrooms, the quark, or cottage cheese, and the chives and continue to scramble, then remove the pan from the heat and continue scrambling until no liquid egg is left ■

Poached Quails' Egg Salad with Watercress and Tarragon Sauce
Serves 6

This may sound more difficult than it is but it's actually blissfully simple and can all be made well in advance.

18 quails' eggs

For the watercress and tarragon sauce:
2 oz (50 g) watercress
1 tablespoon fresh tarragon leaves
1 large egg
½ teaspoon salt
1 small clove garlic, peeled
1 teaspoon mustard powder
4 fl oz (120 ml) groundnut or other flavourless oil
1 fl oz (25 ml) olive oil
1 teaspoon white wine vinegar
½ teaspoon lemon juice
freshly milled black pepper

To serve:
2 oz (50 g) rocket leaves
4 oz (110 g) watercress
a few fresh chives, finely snipped

Begin by poaching the eggs: fill a medium-sized frying pan with water to a depth of approximately 1½ inches (4 cm), then heat it to a temperature just sufficient to keep the water at a bare simmer. Then break the eggs, 5 or 6 at a time, into the simmering water and let them cook, uncovered, for 2 minutes. If you find it hard to break the shells, carefully make a cut in the shell with a small serrated knife before you break them into the water. Then use a draining spoon and a wad of kitchen paper underneath to lift them from the water and transfer them to a bowl of cold water.

Now continue to cook the remaining eggs in the same way, and leave them in a bowl of cold water until you are ready to use them.

For the sauce, separate the watercress leaves and discard the stalks. Now break the egg into a food processor or blender, add the salt, garlic, mustard powder and a few twists of freshly milled black pepper, then switch on to blend these together. Now mix the oils in a jug and pour in a thin trickle through the hole in the top with the machine still switched on. When all the oil is in, add the vinegar, lemon juice, watercress and tarragon leaves, then blend again until the leaves are quite finely chopped.

To serve, arrange some rocket and watercress on each plate and arrange 3 poached quails' eggs in the centre of each one. Drizzle some of the sauce over the top of each salad, followed by a sprinkling of a few snipped chives. Serve with crusty bread ■

Note: This recipe contains raw eggs.

Stilton Soufflé Omelette
Serves 1

This is a great recipe for one person. It's quick and easy, yet special and different. If you want to make it for two people, use a 9 inch (23 cm) pan and double the ingredients. It is excellent served with a tomato and basil salad.

3 oz (75 g) Stilton, crumbled
3 large eggs, separated
½ oz (10 g) butter
1 tablespoon freshly snipped chives
salt and freshly milled black pepper

You will also need a 7 inch (18 cm) solid frying pan.

First, pre-heat the grill to its highest setting, then put the frying pan on to a medium heat. Whisk the egg whites to soft peaks and leave them on one side while you beat the egg yolks in a separate bowl and season them well. Now melt the butter in the hot pan, being careful not to let it burn, then quickly fold the egg yolks and half of the Stilton, plus the chives, into the egg whites.

When the butter is foaming, pour the mixture into the pan, shaking the pan to make sure the mixture is evenly distributed – don't be tempted to stir it, though, or you will knock the air out of it. Cook the omelette for about 1 minute and then slide a palette knife around the edge to loosen it from the pan. Now scatter the remaining cheese all over the surface, then place the pan under the grill, 4 inches (10 cm) from the heat, and let the surface cook for about 1 minute, until it is lightly tinged brown and the cheese is melting.

Then remove the pan from the grill and, using the palette knife, carefully loosen the edges, fold one half of the omelette over the other, slide it out on to a heated plate and serve immediately ■

Right: Stilton Soufflé Omelette. Top left: Poached Quails' Egg Salad with Watercress and Tarragon Sauce.

A Soufflé Omelette with Three Cheeses and Chives

A Soufflé Omelette with Three Cheeses and Chives and a Sweet and Sour Red Onion Salad
Serves 1

This soufflé omelette is a doddle. It takes no more than five minutes and honestly tastes every bit as good as the oven-baked variety.

3 large eggs
1 oz (25 g) mature Cheddar, finely grated
1 oz (25 g) parmesan, finely grated
1 oz (25 g) Gruyère or Emmental, finely grated
1 heaped tablespoon finely snipped chives
½ oz (10 g) butter
salt and freshly milled black pepper

For the sweet and sour red onion salad:
1 medium red onion, cut into 8 wedges through the root
1 tablespoon olive oil
1 rounded teaspoon light soft brown sugar
1 tablespoon red wine vinegar
1 rounded teaspoon grain mustard
salt and freshly milled black pepper

You will also need a medium, solid-based frying pan with a base diameter of 7 inches (18 cm).

Pre-heat the grill to its highest setting for 10 minutes and have a warm plate ready.

First of all, make the salad. All you do is heat the oil in a small saucepan, add the onion and turn the heat down to low and let it cook gently for 5 minutes, stirring now and then. Next, add the sugar and 1 tablespoon of water, stir well then pop the lid on and let it continue cooking gently for another 10 minutes. After that, add the vinegar and mustard and a seasoning of salt and pepper, give everything another really good stir and turn the heat off while you make the soufflé omelette.

For the omelette, first separate the eggs — yolks into a small bowl and whites into a squeaky-clean large bowl; it helps if you separate the whites singly into a cup first before adding them to the bowl, then if one breaks, it won't ruin the rest. Now beat the egg yolks with a fork, seasoning well with salt and pepper. Next, put the frying pan on to a low heat to warm through.

While that's happening, whisk the egg whites with either an electric hand whisk or a balloon whisk, until they form soft peaks. Next, add the butter to the pan and turn the heat up. Then, using a large metal spoon, quickly fold the egg yolks into the egg whites, adding the Cheddar, half the parmesan and the chives at the same time.

Then, when the butter is foaming, pile the whole lot into the pan, shaking the pan to even it out. Now let the omelette cook for 1 minute exactly. Then slide a palette knife round the edges to loosen it, sprinkle the grated Gruyère (or Emmental) all over the surface and whack the omelette under the grill, about 4 inches (10 cm) from the heat. Let it cook for 1 more minute, until the cheese is melted and tinged golden. Next, remove the pan from the heat, then slide the palette knife round the edge again.

Take the pan to the warmed plate, then ease one half of the omelette over the other and tilt the whole lot out. Scatter the rest of the parmesan all over and serve immediately with the sweet and sour red onion salad.

Note: If you want to make this omelette for 2, that's okay if you double everything. Just use a 9 or 10 inch (23 or 25.5 cm) diameter pan and give each stage more time, then divide the omelette in half ▨

Cheese Soufflé
Serves 2-3

The one and only secret of success in making this soufflé is to whisk the egg whites properly. But do remember it is in the nature of soufflés to start to shrink straightaway, so serve it absolutely immediately.

3 large eggs, separated
3 oz (75 g) mature Cheddar, grated (or another hard cheese)
5 fl oz (150 ml) milk
1 oz (25 g) butter
1 oz (25 g) plain flour
pinch cayenne pepper
¼ teaspoon dry mustard powder
a little freshly grated nutmeg
a slice of lemon
a little parmesan, to serve
salt and freshly milled black pepper

Pre-heat the oven to gas mark 5, 375°F (190°C).

You will also need a 1½ pint (850 ml) soufflé dish measuring 5 inches (13 cm) in diameter and 3 inches (7.5 cm) high, lightly buttered, and a small solid baking sheet.

Place the milk, butter and flour in a medium saucepan over a medium heat and whisk until blended and thickened. Continue to cook for 3 minutes with the heat at its lowest setting, still giving it an occasional stir. Then remove the pan from the heat and stir in the cayenne, mustard, nutmeg and a seasoning of salt and pepper, and leave the sauce to cool a little before stirring in the grated cheese. Now beat the egg yolks thoroughly and stir them in.

Next, using a spanking clean bowl and whisk (which you have wiped with the lemon), whisk the egg whites till they are stiff. If you're using an electric whisk, switch it on to low and beat the egg whites for about 30 seconds or until they are foaming, then increase the speed to medium and then to high, moving the whisk round and round the bowl, until you get a glossy mixture that stands in stiff peaks. Now, using a large metal spoon, stir one spoonful of the egg whites into the sauce and then carefully fold in the rest, being gentle so you don't lose all the precious air. Now transfer the mixture to the soufflé dish, place it on a baking sheet in the centre of the oven and bake for 30-35 minutes.

The soufflé is cooked when a skewer inserted into the centre comes out fairly clean and not too liquid. Be careful not to overcook: it does need to be soft, not dry, in the centre. Serve immediately with a little dish of parmesan and perhaps a sharp, lemon-dressed lettuce and watercress salad ▨

Chapter Four
Cheese

Marinated Mozzarella with Avocado
Serves 2

This is very pretty and very summery.

4 oz (110 g) mozzarella
1 medium, ripe avocado
strip of red pepper, 1 x 3 inches
(2.5 x 7.5 cm)
about 18 fresh basil leaves
2 spring onions, finely chopped

For the vinaigrette dressing:
1 small clove garlic, peeled
1 teaspoon sea salt
1 rounded teaspoon mustard powder
1 dessertspoon white wine vinegar
5 dessertspoons extra virgin olive oil
1 dessertspoon freshly snipped chives
freshly milled black pepper

Start to prepare the salad about 2 hours before you need it (but no longer, as the cheese then will soften too much). Cut the mozzarella into ¼ inch (5 mm) slices; then halve the avocado, remove and discard the stone and skin and thinly slice each half.

Now arrange the mozzarella and avocado on a serving plate with alternate, overlapping, slices. Next, cut the strip of red pepper into fine shreds, starting from the narrow 1 inch (2.5 cm) end, then pile the basil leaves on top of each other and slice these into similar shreds and scatter both basil and red pepper over the cheese and avocado.

Make up the dressing by crushing the garlic and salt together with a pestle and mortar, and work the mustard powder into the puréed garlic and salt, followed by plenty of freshly milled pepper. Stir in the vinegar, oil and chives, then pour the dressing into a screw-top jar and shake vigorously before pouring it over the other ingredients on the plate. Cover with some foil and leave to marinate for 2 hours. Serve with ciabatta ■

Leek and Goats' Cheese Tart
Serves 4, or 6 as a starter

This is what I call a wobbly tart – creamy and soft centred. Leeks and goats' cheese have turned out to be a wonderful combination, and the addition of goats' cheese to the pastry gives it a nice edge.

For the pastry:
1 oz (25 g) firm goats' cheese (rindless)
4 oz (110 g) plain flour, plus a little extra for dusting
1 oz (25 g) pure vegetable fat
1 oz (25 g) softened butter
salt

For the filling:
1 lb 6 oz (625 g) leeks, about 12 oz (350 g) trimmed weight (see below)
6 oz (175 g) firm goats' cheese (rindless)
½ oz (10 g) butter
3 large eggs, beaten
7 fl oz (220 ml) crème fraîche or double cream
4 spring onions, trimmed and finely sliced (including the green parts)
salt and freshly milled black pepper

You will also need a 7½ inch (19 cm) fluted quiche tin with a removable base, 1¼ inches (3 cm) deep, very lightly buttered, and a small, solid baking sheet.

First, for the pastry, sift the flour with the pinch of salt into a large bowl, holding the sieve up high to give it a good airing. Then add the vegetable fat and butter and, using only your fingertips, lightly rub the fat into the flour, again lifting the mixture up high all the time. When everything is crumbly, coarsely grate the goats' cheese in and then sprinkle in some cold water – about 1 tablespoon. Start to mix the pastry with a knife and then finish off with your hands, adding a few more drops of water, till you have a smooth dough that will leave the bowl clean. Then pop the pastry into a polythene bag and let it rest in the fridge for 30 minutes. Meanwhile, pre-heat the oven to gas mark 5, 375°F (190°C) and pop the baking sheet in to pre-heat on the centre shelf.

Now prepare the leeks. First, take the tough green ends off and throw them out, then make a vertical split about halfway down the centre of each one and clean them by running them under the cold-water tap while you fan out the layers – this will rid them of any hidden dust and grit. Then slice them in half lengthways and chop into ½ inch (1cm) slices.

Next, in a medium-sized frying pan, melt the butter over a gentle heat and add the leeks and some salt. Give it all a good stir and let them cook gently, without a lid, for 10-15 minutes or until the juice runs out of them. Then you need to transfer them to a sieve set over a bowl to drain off the excess juice. Place a saucer with a weight on top of them to press out every last drop.

By this time the pastry will have rested, so remove it from the fridge and roll it out into a circle on a lightly floured surface. As you roll, give it quarter turns to keep the round shape and roll it as thinly as possible. Now transfer it, rolling it over the pin, to the tin. Press it lightly and firmly over the base and sides of the tin, easing any overlapping pastry back down to the sides, as it is important not to stretch it. Now trim the edges and press the pastry up about ¼ inch (5 mm) above the rim of the tin all round, then prick the base all over with a fork. After that, paint some of the beaten egg for the filling over the base and sides. Now place the tin on the baking sheet and bake for 20-25 minutes or until the pastry is crisp and golden. Check halfway through the cooking time to make sure that the pastry isn't rising up in the centre. If it is,

just prick it a couple of times and press it back down with your hands.

While the pastry case is pre-baking, crumble the goats' cheese with your hands, then gently combine it with the leeks in the sieve. Now, in a jug, mix the beaten eggs with the crème fraîche or double cream, seasoning with just a little salt (there is some already in the leeks) and a good grinding of freshly milled black pepper.

As soon as the pastry case is ready, remove it from the oven, arrange the leeks and cheese all over the base and then sprinkle the spring onions over the top. Now gradually pour half the cream and egg mixture in to join them, then put the tart back on the baking sheet with the oven shelf half pulled out, then slowly pour in the rest of the mixture. Gently slide the shelf back in and bake the tart for 30-35 minutes, until it's firm in the centre and the surface has turned a lovely golden brown.

Next, remove it from the oven and allow it to settle for 10 minutes before serving. This 10 minutes is important, as the tart will be much easier to cut into portions. The best way to remove the tart from the tin is to ease the edges from the sides of the tin with a small knife, then place it on an upturned jar or tin, which will allow you to carefully ease the sides away. Next, slide a palette knife or wide fish slice underneath and ease the tart on to a plate or board, ready to serve, or simply cut it into portions straight from the tin base ■

Leek and Goats' Cheese Tart

Left: Crumpet Pizza. Top right: Mexican Enchiladas with Cheese

Crumpet Pizza
Serves 2, or 4 as a snack

Mexican Enchiladas with Cheese
Serves 2, or 4 as a starter

Toasted Cheese
and Chilli Relish Sandwich
Serves 1

Well, a crumpet pizza does make sense if you think about it – soft, squidgy bread that gets lightly toasted for just a bit of crunch, then all those wonderful holes so that the cheese and other ingredients can melt right down into it. And because crumpets are quite small, the fillings get piled up very high and it all becomes rather lovely.

4 crumpets

6 oz (175 g) Gorgonzola, Cashel Blue, or dolcelatte, cubed

2 oz (50 g) mozzarella, cubed

2 oz (50 g) chopped walnuts

12 medium-sized fresh sage leaves

1 tablespoon olive oil

Pre-heat the grill to its highest setting.

All you do is lightly toast the crumpets on each side (they can be quite close to the heat at this stage) – they need to be lightly golden, which takes about 1 minute on each side. Then remove them to a baking sheet and just pile up the Gorgonzola (or other cheese) and mozzarella on each crumpet, then sprinkle with the chopped walnuts and finally, place the sage leaves – first dipped in the olive oil – on top. Now back they go under the hot grill, but this time 5 inches (13 cm) from the heat source, for 5 minutes, by when the cheeses will have melted, the walnuts toasted and the sage become crisp. Then you serve them straightaway.

You can get really creative and make up loads more ideas of your own. Obviously, the whole thing can be very easily adapted to whatever happens to be available ■

What are enchiladas? Well, they're Mexican pancakes made with wheatflour that can be spread with some spicy salsa and stuffed with almost anything you have handy – in this case cheese – and then baked. An excellent light lunch dish served with a salad.

For the salsa:

1 x 14 oz (400 g) tin chopped tomatoes

1 medium green chilli (the fat, squat variety that isn't too fiery)

1 medium red onion, peeled and finely chopped

2 heaped tablespoons chopped fresh coriander leaves, plus a little extra, to garnish

juice 1 lime

salt and freshly milled black pepper

For the enchiladas:

4 large flour tortillas

4 oz (110 g) Wensleydale, grated

5 oz (150 g) mozzarella, grated – a block of mozzarella is best for this

7 fl oz (200 ml) half-fat crème fraîche

You will also need an ovenproof baking dish measuring 9 inches (23 cm) square and 2 inches (5 cm) deep, lightly oiled, and a frying pan.

Pre-heat the oven to gas mark 4, 350°F (180°C).

Begin by making the salsa: first tip the tomatoes into a sieve over a bowl to let the excess liquid drain away. Next, remove the stalk from the chilli, cut it in half, remove and discard the seeds, chop the flesh very finely and place it in a bowl. Then add half the chopped onion, the drained tomatoes, chopped coriander leaves and lime juice, and season well with salt and pepper. Now give everything a thorough mixing. Meanwhile, mix the 2 cheeses

together in a bowl. Next, put the frying pan over a high flame to pre-heat and, when it's hot, dry-fry each of the tortillas for 6 seconds on each side.

Place 1 tortilla on a flat surface and spread a tablespoon of salsa over it, but not quite to the edges, sprinkle over a heaped tablespoon of the cheese mixture, then follow this with a tablespoon of the crème fraîche. Then roll the tortilla up and place it in the baking dish with the sealed side down. Repeat this with the others, then spread the remaining crème fraîche on top of the tortillas in the dish and sprinkle the rest of the salsa over the top, followed by the remaining cheeses and red onion.

Now place the dish on a high shelf of the oven for 25-30 minutes, garnish with the extra coriander and serve absolutely immediately – if you keep them waiting they can become a bit soggy ■

This is a vegetarian version of Croque Monsieur. You can use ready-made relish or my own home-made version (see page 176).

2 large slices good-quality white bread, buttered

2 heaped teaspoons tomato chilli relish

2 oz (50 g) Gruyère or Emmental, finely grated

½ small onion, peeled and sliced into thin rings

½ oz (10 g) butter, melted

1 oz (25 g) parmesan, finely grated

salt and freshly milled black pepper

Pre-heat the grill to its highest setting.

Start off by spreading both slices of bread with a heaped teaspoon of relish each. Now sprinkle the Gruyère (or Emmental) on one of the slices, then sprinkle the onion rings over, season with salt and pepper and then place the other piece of bread on top.

Next, brush the top of the sandwich with half the melted butter and sprinkle over half the parmesan, lightly pressing it down. Then place the sandwich on the grill rack and grill it 2 inches (5 cm) from the heat until the top of the sandwich is golden brown – about 2 minutes. Now turn the sandwich over and brush the top with the rest of the melted butter and parmesan, and return the sandwich to the grill for another 2 minutes. Finally, cut it into quarters and eat it pretty quickly ■

Eggs and Leeks au Gratin
Serves 4

Eggs, leeks and cheese are a really delicious trio and all this simple lunchtime dish needs to accompany it is some crusty wholewheat bread and good butter.

8 large eggs

4 medium leeks

3 oz (75 g) mature Cheddar, grated

1 tablespoon grated parmesan

15 fl oz (425 ml) milk

1½ oz (40 g) plain flour

2 oz (50 g) butter

cayenne pepper

salt

chopped fresh parsley or watercress, to garnish

You will also need a shallow baking dish, approximately 10 inches (25.5 cm) in diameter, or the oval equivalent, generously buttered.

First of all, select a saucepan that will hold 8 eggs fairly snugly, then cover them with cold water, bring the water to a gentle simmer and put a timer on for 7 minutes exactly – then cool them under cold running water. Peel the eggs and slice them in half lengthways. While the eggs are cooking, prepare the leeks.

First, take the tough green ends off and throw them out, then make a vertical split about halfway down the centre of each one and clean them by running them under the cold-water tap while you fan out the layers – this will rid them of any hidden dust and grit. Then slice them in half lengthways and chop them.

Next, make up a sauce by putting the milk in a saucepan, then simply add the flour and 1 oz (25 g) of butter and bring everything gradually up to simmering point, whisking continuously with a balloon whisk, until the sauce has thickened and becomes smooth and glossy.

Next, turn the heat down to its lowest possible setting and let the sauce cook very gently for 5 minutes, stirring from time to time. Meanwhile, taste and season with a pinch of cayenne pepper and salt. Next, melt the other 1 oz (25 g) of butter in a saucepan, stir in the chopped leeks and let them sweat gently (with a lid on) for 5 minutes – they should have cooked in that time but still have a bit of 'bite' to them.

Now arrange the leeks over the base of the buttered baking dish and place the peeled halved hard-boiled eggs on top – round side up. Next, stir two-thirds of the Cheddar cheese and all the parmesan into the sauce. Season well and, as soon as the cheese has melted, pour the sauce all over the eggs. Sprinkle the remaining Cheddar on top with a dusting of cayenne, then place the dish under a medium grill until the sauce is bubbling hot and the cheese is nicely toasted. Sprinkle with chopped parsley or garnish with watercress before serving ■

Potted Cheese
Serves 8

This can be made with any mixture of cheese and is a great way to use up leftover pieces. Serve it with toasted Irish soda bread and mustard and cress, or with crackers or oat biscuits. It is also good spread on toast.

2 oz (50 g) Sage Derby

3 oz (75 g) Double Gloucester with chives

3 oz (75 g) Blue Wensleydale

4 oz (110 g) butter, softened

1½ fl oz (40 ml) dry sherry

¼ teaspoon ground mace

½ teaspoon mustard powder

salt and freshly milled black pepper

You will also need eight 1¼ inch (3 cm) deep ramekins with a base diameter of 2¼ inches (5.5 cm).

Grate or crumble the cheeses into a mixing bowl, then add the rest of the ingredients. Now beat it all together like mad until you have a very fluffy, smooth paste (an electric hand whisk will save you a lot of energy).

Taste and season, as required, with salt and pepper, then pack the mixture into the ramekins. Leave the potted cheese in a cool place (though not in the fridge) until ready to serve ■

Cheese and Herb Sausages
Serves 3-4 (makes 12)

This is adapted from a traditional Welsh recipe called Glamorgan sausages. They are really lovely with home-made chutney or relish.

4 oz (110 g) mature Cheddar, grated

2 teaspoons chopped fresh mixed herbs

5 oz (150 g) fresh white or wholemeal breadcrumbs

1 medium onion, peeled and grated

¾ teaspoon dry mustard powder

1 large egg yolk

salt and freshly milled black pepper

For coating and frying:

1 oz (25 g) fresh white or wholemeal breadcrumbs

1 oz (25 g) parmesan, grated

1 large egg white, lightly beaten

2 tablespoons groundnut or other flavourless oil for cooking

Begin by placing the breadcrumbs (5 oz/ 150 g) in a large mixing bowl, together with the grated onion, Cheddar and herbs. Then, add the mustard powder and a seasoning of salt and pepper. Now add the egg yolk and stir to bind the mixture together. Next divide it into 12 small portions and, using your hands, roll each piece into a sausage shape, squeezing it to hold it together.

Before frying the sausages, mix the breadcrumbs with the parmesan cheese and dip each sausage first into the egg white and then into the breadcrumb and cheese mixture and coat evenly.

To cook the sausages, heat a shallow layer of oil in a large frying pan and fry them in the hot fat for 5-6 minutes or till crisp and golden. Turn them as they cook so that they brown evenly. Drain on crumpled kitchen paper before serving ■

Left: Asparagus and Cheese Tart
Top right: Marinated Halloumi Cheese Kebabs with Herbs

Asparagus and Cheese Tart
Serves 6

Just to make the very most of the English asparagus during its very short season, I cook it which way and every way, hence this very simple but sublime tart.

12 oz (350 g) asparagus
1½ oz (40 g) Cheddar, finely grated
1 tablespoon freshly grated parmesan
2 large eggs, beaten
10 fl oz (275 ml) single cream
salt and freshly milled black pepper

For the pastry:
1 oz (25 g) butter
1 oz (25 g) pure vegetable fat
4 oz (110 g) plain flour
1 oz (25 g) Cheddar, finely grated
pinch salt

You will also need a 7½ inch (19 cm) fluted quiche tin with a removable base, 1¼ inches (3 cm) deep, lightly greased, and a 10 x 12 inch (25.5 x 30 cm) solid baking sheet.

Pre-heat the oven to gas mark 4, 350°F (180°C). Put the baking sheet in the oven to heat up.

First, make the pastry by rubbing the butter and vegetable fat lightly into the flour, then add the cheese and salt, plus enough cold water to make a smooth dough – about 1 tablespoon. Then place the dough in a polythene bag to rest in the fridge for 20 minutes.

Next, roll the pastry out and line the tin with it. Be careful to press the dough firmly into the tin. Prick the base all over with a fork, then pre-bake the tart on the baking sheet for 20 minutes. After that, paint the inside of it with a little of the beaten egg (from the filling ingredients) and let it cook in the oven for a further 5 minutes. Meanwhile, prepare the asparagus. Take each stalk in both hands and bend and snap off the woody end, then arrange the spears in a steamer and steam over simmering water for 4-5 minutes (just to half-cook them). Then chop the spears into 1½ inch (4 cm) lengths and arrange them over the base of the pre-baked pastry case.

Next, beat the eggs together with the cream and grated Cheddar cheese and season with salt and pepper, then pour this mixture over the asparagus. Finally, sprinkle the parmesan over the top. Place the tart on the baking sheet in the oven and cook for 30-40 minutes – until the centre feels firm and the filling is golden brown and puffy ■

Marinated Halloumi Cheese Kebabs with Herbs and Fresh Mexican Tomato Salsa
Serves 2

This is something for the vegetarian barbecue. It has all the fun and flavour – but without meat.

12 oz (350 g) halloumi, cut into 1 inch (2.5 cm) cubes
1 medium pepper (any colour)
1 medium red onion, peeled
4 medium chestnut mushrooms

For the marinade:
1 teaspoon each chopped fresh thyme, oregano, rosemary, mint and parsley (or similar combination of whatever herbs are available)
1 fat clove garlic, peeled
2 fl oz (55 ml) extra virgin olive oil
juice 1 lime
freshly milled black pepper

For the salsa:
4 large firm tomatoes
1 fresh green chilli (the fat, squat variety that isn't too fiery)
½ medium red onion, peeled and finely chopped
2 heaped tablespoons chopped fresh coriander
juice 1 lime
salt and freshly milled black pepper

You will also need two 12 inch (30 cm) flat metal skewers.

Begin by cutting the pepper and onion into even-sized pieces, about 1 inch (2.5 cm) square, to match the size of the cubes of cheese. Then chop the herbs and garlic quite finely and combine them with the oil, lime juice and some freshly milled pepper.

Now place the cheese, pepper, onion and mushrooms in a large, roomy bowl and pour the marinade over them, mixing very thoroughly. Cover and place in the fridge for 24 hours, and try to give them a stir round every now and then.

The next day, begin by making the salsa. Place the tomatoes in a bowl, pour boiling water over them, then after 1 minute drain them and slip off the skins (protecting your hands with a cloth if you need to). Now cut each tomato in half and hold each half in the palm of your hand, cut side up, then turn your hand over and squeeze gently until the seeds come out – it's best to do this over a plate or bowl to catch the seeds!

Now, using a sharp knife, chop the tomatoes into approximately ¼ inch (5 mm) dice straight into a serving bowl. Next de-stalk the chilli, cut it in half, remove the seeds and chop the flesh very finely before adding it to the tomatoes. Add the chopped onion, coriander and lime juice, and season with salt and pepper. Give everything a thorough mixing, then cover and leave on one side for about an hour before serving.

When you're ready to barbecue the kebabs, take the two skewers and thread a mushroom on first (pushing it right down), followed by a piece of onion, a piece of pepper and a cube of cheese. Repeat this with more onion, pepper and cheese, finishing with a mushroom at the end. Place the kebabs over the hot coals, turning frequently till they are tinged brown at the edges – about 10 minutes. Brush on any leftover marinade juices as you turn them. Serve with the salsa ■

Cheese and Herb Fritters with Tomato and Balsamic Jam

Cheese and Herb Fritters with Tomato and Balsamic Jam
Serves 4

This is a great recipe for using up odd bits of cheese, which can be varied as long as the total amount ends up being about 12 oz (350 g) for four people or 6 oz (175 g) for two. And the tomato jam? So-called as it cooks slowly without a lid until it takes a jam-like consistency and makes a perfect accompaniment to the cheese.

4 oz (110 g) feta, finely grated

4 oz (110 g) Gruyère or Emmental, finely grated

4 oz (110 g) mature Cheddar, finely grated

3 heaped tablespoons chopped mixed fresh herbs (such as basil, thyme, oregano and parsley)

2 oz (50 g) plain flour, plus 1 slightly rounded dessertspoon seasoned flour for dusting

2 good pinches cayenne pepper

2 large eggs

2 tablespoons milk

3 tablespoons olive oil

salt and freshly milled black pepper

For the tomato and balsamic jam:

1 lb (450 g) ripe tomatoes

1 tablespoon olive oil

1 small red onion, peeled and finely chopped

1 large clove garlic, peeled and crushed

1 tablespoon balsamic vinegar

1 teaspoon dark soft brown sugar

salt and freshly milled black pepper

Begin this by sifting the 2 oz (50 g) of flour and cayenne pepper into a large bowl and season with salt and black pepper, then make a well in the centre and break the eggs into it. Now gradually whisk in the eggs, incorporating any bits of flour from the edge of the bowl as you do so. Next, whisk in the milk until you have a smooth batter, then gently stir in the grated cheeses and herbs. Now cover the bowl and leave it to stand in a cool place for about an hour, as this allows all the flavours to develop.

Meanwhile, make the tomato and balsamic jam by first placing the tomatoes in a bowl and pouring boiling water over them. Then, after 1 minute (or 15-30 seconds if they are small), drain them, slip the skins off (protect your hands with a cloth if necessary) and chop the flesh roughly. Next, heat the olive oil in a saucepan and soften the onion and garlic in it for 5 minutes without browning. Now add the rest of the ingredients, give them a good stir, then simmer gently, uncovered, for 30-40 minutes, until all the liquid has evaporated and you are left with a thick, jammy sauce. Then taste to check the seasoning.

When you're ready to cook the fritters, take 1 tablespoon of the mixture at a time and make 12 rounds, flatten them gently to about 2½ inches (6 cm) in diameter, then lightly dust each one with the seasoned flour.

Next, heat the oil over a highish heat in the frying pan and, when it's shimmering hot, cook half the fritters over a medium heat for 45-60 seconds each side, or until golden brown and crispy. Then carefully lift them out of the pan to drain on crumpled greaseproof paper or kitchen paper. Keep the first batch warm while you cook the second, then serve with the tomato and balsamic jam. A green salad would make a good accompaniment ■

Vegetarian Sausage Rolls
Makes 36

These make delicious party snacks and go well with chutney. They can be frozen before cooking and then glazed and cooked from frozen for about 30-35 minutes.

For the quick flaky pastry:

8 oz (225 g) plain flour, plus a little extra for dusting

6 oz (175 g) butter, chilled (see below)

pinch salt

beaten egg, to glaze

For the filling:

10 oz (275 g) fresh breadcrumbs

8 oz (225 g) mature Cheddar, grated

1 large onion, peeled and grated

3 tablespoons thick double cream

1 tablespoon fresh chopped herbs (such as chives, parsley or thyme)

1½ teaspoons mustard powder

pinch cayenne pepper

salt and freshly milled black pepper

You will also need two 14 x 10 inch (35 x 25.5 cm) baking sheets, lightly greased.

Pre-heat the oven to gas mark 7, 425°F (220°C).

First of all, make the quick flaky pastry. The fat needs to be rock-hard, so weigh out the required amount, wrap it in a piece of foil, then return it to the freezing compartment for 30-45 minutes.

Meanwhile, sift the flour and salt into a mixing bowl. When you take the fat out of the freezer, open it up and use some of the foil to hold the end with. Then dip the fat in the flour and grate it on a coarse grater placed in the bowl over the flour. Keep dipping the fat down into the flour to make it easier to grate. At the end you will be left with a pile of grated fat in the middle of the flour, so take a palette knife and start to distribute it into the flour (don't use your hands), trying to coat all the pieces of fat with flour until the mixture is crumbly. Next, add enough water to form a dough that leaves the bowl clean, using your hands to bring it all gently together. Put the dough into a polythene bag and chill it for 30 minutes in the fridge.

For the filling, simply place all the filling ingredients in a mixing bowl, season well and mix very thoroughly. Then roll out the pastry on a lightly floured surface to form an 24 x 12 inch (60 x 30 cm) oblong. Cut this oblong into 3 strips and divide the filling also into 3, making 3 long rolls the same length as the strips of pasty (if it's sticky, sprinkle on some flour).

Place one roll of filling on to one strip of pastry. Brush the beaten egg along one edge, then fold the pastry over and seal it as carefully as possible. Lift the whole thing up and turn it so the sealed edge is underneath. Press lightly and cut into individual rolls each about 2 inches (5 cm) long. It's nice to cut the rolls obliquely so that they form little diamond shapes. Snip 3 'V' shapes in the top of each roll with scissors and brush with beaten egg. Repeat all this with the other portions of filling and pastry.

Bake, on the greased baking sheets, on the top shelf of the oven for 20-25 minutes. Then leave them to cool on a wire rack before storing in an airtight tin (that is, if they're not all eaten before you get the chance), but these do need to be eaten as fresh as possible ■

...Roquefort Cheesecake with ...in Balsamic Vinaigrette

Serves 8

This cheesecake includes a clever blend of three cheeses. Cheese and pears are always good partners but this particular combination is a marriage made in heaven.

For the base:

4 oz (110 g) white breadcrumbs

2 oz (50 g) parmesan

1 oz (25 g) melted butter

freshly milled black pepper

For the filling:

6 oz (175 g) Roquefort, Shropshire Blue or Cashel Blue

3 large eggs

8 oz (225 g) medium-fat curd cheese

4 oz (110 g) 8 per cent fat fromage frais

1 tablespoon freshly snipped chives

4 spring onions, finely sliced

freshly milled black pepper

For the pears in balsamic vinaigrette:

4 firm but ripe pears

1 tablespoon balsamic vinegar

1 fat clove garlic, peeled

1 teaspoon sea salt

1 rounded teaspoon mustard powder

4 tablespoons extra virgin olive oil

freshly milled black pepper

You will also need a springform cake tin, measuring 9 inches (23 cm) in diameter, lightly oiled.

Pre-heat the oven to gas mark 5, 375°F (190°C).

First of all, make the base of the cheesecake by mixing the breadcrumbs and cheese together, then pour in the butter, adding a good grinding of pepper. Press the crumb mixture firmly down over the base of the tin, then bake in the pre-heated oven for 12-15 minutes. (This time will vary slightly, so it does need careful watching – the aim is for the base to be crisp and toasted. If it is undercooked, it does not have the lovely crunchy texture so necessary to the finished cheesecake.) Then remove it from the oven and turn the heat down to gas mark 4, 350°F (180°C).

Now make the filling. First beat together the eggs, curd cheese, fromage frais and some freshly milled black pepper in a bowl. After that crumble the Roquefort (or other cheese) fairly coarsely and stir it in, together with the chives. Pour the mixture into the tin and scatter the sliced spring onions over the top, then place it on the high shelf of the oven and bake for 30-40 minutes or until the centre feels springy to the touch. Allow the cheesecake to cool and settle for about 20 minutes before serving.

The pears in balsamic vinaigrette can be prepared up to 2 hours before serving. Thinly pare off the skins of the pears, using a potato peeler, leaving the stalks intact. Now lay each pear on its side with the stalk flat on a board, then take a sharp knife and make an incision through the tip of the stalk. Turn the pear the right way up and gently cut it in half, first sliding the knife through the stalk and then through the pear. Now remove the core of each half, then, with the pear core-side downwards, slice it thinly but leave the slices joined at the top. Press gently and the slices will fan out.

Make the vinaigrette by crushing the garlic and salt together in a pestle and mortar to a creamy paste. Now add the mustard and several grinds of black pepper. Work these in, then, using a small whisk, add the vinegar and then the oil – whisking all the time to amalgamate. Serve one pear half with each slice of the cheesecake, with a little of the vinaigrette spooned over ■

Apple, Cider Salad with Melted Camembert Dressing

Serves 2, or 6 as a starter

This makes an absolutely brilliant starter, especially in the winter months. It does need ripe Camembert, but a supermarket Camembert will have a date stamp to show when it will have fully ripened, so you can gauge the best time to make the salad. The piquancy of the apple combined with cheese is absolutely superb. You can, if you want to prepare the dressing ahead, then just gently melt it again before serving.

For the salad:

4 oz (110 g) Cox's apple (1 medium)

1 Cos lettuce

1 oz (25 g) rocket leaves

For the dressing:

a round, ripe Camembert, chilled (8-9 oz/220-250 g)

2 rounded tablespoons crème fraîche

1 or 2 tablespoons dry cider (2 tablespoons if the Camembert isn't quite ripe)

For the garlic croutons:

2 oz (50 g) bread, cut into small cubes

1 tablespoon olive oil

1 clove garlic, peeled and crushed

Pre-heat the oven to gas mark 4, 350°F (180°C).

First, make the garlic croutons. Just place the cubes of bread in a bowl, together with the oil and garlic, and stir them around so that they get an even coating. Then arrange them on a baking sheet. Bake them on a high shelf in the oven for 10 minutes or until they are crisp and golden. One word of warning: do use a kitchen timer for this operation because it's actually very hard to bake something for just 10 minutes without forgetting all about it. I have baked more batches of charcoal-coloured croutons than I care to remember! Then allow them to cool.

Next, prepare the dressing – cut the cheese in half and use a small, sharp knife to peel it carefully like a potato, paring away the skin from the soft cheese. Place the cheese in a small saucepan. Now measure in the crème fraîche but don't heat it until just before you are going to serve the salad.

When you're ready, mix the salad leaves together, breaking up the larger ones into manageable pieces, and arrange the salad on the serving plates. Slice the apple, leaving the skin on, and put the slices in a small bowl, then sprinkle on a little cider – just enough to give the slices a covering. After that, pat them dry and arrange over the salad leaves.

Now place the saucepan over a gentle heat and blend the cheese and crème fraîche together for about 3-4 minutes – using a small balloon whisk – until the mixture is smooth. If the cheese is very ripe and runny, you may not need the extra dry cider, but if the centre is less ripe, you will need to add a little cider to keep the mixture smooth. The main thing is to melt the cheese just sufficiently for it to run off the whisk in ribbons, while still retaining its texture. Don't allow the cheese to overheat or it may go stringy – it needs to be melted rather than cooked.

Next, using a small ladle, pour the dressing equally over the salad and finish with a scattering of croutons. Alternatively, you can hand the dressing round the table and let everyone help themselves ■

Apple, Cider Salad with Melted Camembert Dressing

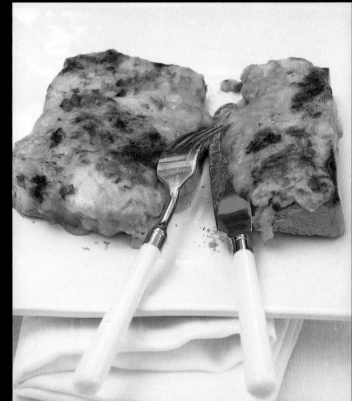

Welsh Rabbit
with Sage and Onions
Serves 2, or 4 as a starter

Rarebit or rabbit? I like the latter. Serve with Red Onion, Tomato and Chilli Relish (see page 176).

4 large, thick slices from a good-quality white sandwich loaf

1 dessertspoon chopped fresh sage

1 rounded dessertspoon grated onion

8 oz (225 g) mature Cheddar, grated

1 rounded teaspoon mustard powder

4 tablespoons brown ale

1 large egg, beaten

few drops Tabasco sauce

pinch cayenne pepper

You will also need a grill pan or baking tray lined with foil.

Pre-heat the grill to its highest setting.

Begin by mixing all the ingredients together, apart from the bread and cayenne pepper. Now place the bread under the grill and toast it on both sides till crisp and golden, then remove it to a toast rack for 3 minutes to get really crisp.

After that, divide the cheese mixture into 4, spread it over the toast – right to the edges so they don't get burnt – then sprinkle each one with a light dusting of cayenne pepper. Then back they go under the grill, 3 inches (7.5 cm) from the heat, until the cheese is golden brown and bubbling, which will take 4-5 minutes. Serve it just as it is or with some salad leaves and a sharp dressing ■

Fried Halloumi Cheese
with Lime and Caper Vinaigrette
Serves 2, or 4 as a starter

If you can get hold of some Greek olive oil for the dressing and eat this outside in the sunshine, the scent and the flavours will transport you to the Aegean in moments.

9 oz (250 g) halloumi cheese (in a block)

2 tablespoons olive oil

2 tablespoons well-seasoned flour

For the dressing:

juice and zest 1 lime

1 heaped tablespoon capers, drained

1 tablespoon white wine vinegar

1 clove garlic, peeled and finely chopped

1 heaped teaspoon grain mustard

1 heaped tablespoon chopped fresh coriander leaves

2 tablespoons extra virgin olive oil

a few sprigs coriander, to garnish

salt and freshly milled black pepper

First of all, unwrap the cheese and pat it dry with kitchen paper. Then, using a sharp knife, slice it into 8 slices, including the ends. Now prepare the dressing by simply whisking all the ingredients together in a small mixing bowl.

When you're ready to serve the halloumi, heat the oil in a frying pan over a medium heat. When the oil is really hot, press each slice of cheese into seasoned flour to coat it on both sides, then add them to the hot pan as they are done – they take 1 minute on each side to cook, so by the time the last one's in, it will almost be time to turn the first one over. They need to be a good golden colour on each side.

Serve them straightaway on warmed plates with the dressing poured over. This is good served with lightly toasted pitta bread or Greek bread with toasted sesame seeds ■

Caramelised Onion Tartlets
with Goats' Cheese and Thyme
Makes 24

When we first made these tartlets we couldn't stop eating them! Crisp, light pastry with such a luscious filling – lovely as part of a buffet or as a first course at a supper party.

For the pastry:

6 oz (175 g) plain flour

3 oz (75 g) butter, at room temperature, cut into smallish lumps

1½ oz (40 g) parmesan, finely grated

½ teaspoon mustard powder

pinch cayenne pepper

1 large egg, beaten

For the filling:

2 large Spanish onions, peeled and finely chopped

2 x 4 oz (110 g) firm goats' cheese logs

24 small sprigs fresh thyme, dipped in olive oil

1 oz (25 g) butter

1 large egg

4 fl oz (120 ml) single cream

¼ teaspoon mustard powder

cayenne pepper for sprinkling

salt and freshly milled black pepper

You will also need a 3¼ inch (8 cm) pastry cutter; and two 12-hole patty tins, with cups measuring 1¾ inches (4.5 cm) at the base, ¾ inch (2 cm) deep, well greased.

First, make the pastry. Sift the flour into a large bowl, then add the butter. Take a knife and begin to cut it into the flour until it looks fairly evenly blended, then add the parmesan, mustard and a pinch of cayenne pepper, plus just enough cold water to make a smooth dough (about 1½ tablespoons) before discarding the knife and bringing it together with your fingertips. Then place the dough in a plastic food bag and put it into the fridge to rest for 30 minutes. In the meantime, pre-heat the oven to gas mark 4, 350°F (180°C).

After that, roll it out as thinly as possible, use the cutter to stamp out 24 rounds and line the tins with them. (The pastry will stand proud of the rim of the cups to allow for shrinkage.) Then prick the bases and brush with the beaten egg.

Now bake on the middle and top shelves (swapping them over halfway through to ensure even browning) for about 10 minutes, or until the pastry is just cooked through, then cool them on a wire rack.

Meanwhile, for the filling, melt the butter in a large frying pan and cook the onions very gently, uncovered, stirring often, for about 30 minutes, or until they have turned a lovely golden brown caramel colour. Then leave them to cool and set aside until needed.

Now whisk the egg with the cream and mustard in a jug and add some seasoning. Next, spoon a little of the onion mixture into each pastry case, spread it out evenly and pour the egg mixture over. Cut each cheese log into 12 thin slices (wiping the knife between slices to cut more cleanly; the cheese is quite soft, so you may have to re-shape a few slices into rounds). Place a slice on the top of each tartlet, then top with a sprig of thyme and a sprinkling of cayenne pepper. Bake for 20 minutes, or until puffy and golden, swapping the tins again halfway through cooking ■

Camembert Croquettes with Fresh Date and Apple Chutney
Serves 6

Ideally, make the croquettes the day before you want to cook them. Ripe Camembert is essential for this recipe, so plan ahead and buy one which will be ready to use roughly on its sell-by date. I keep mine in the garage or in the boot of a car, which is cool enough in the winter, though you have to warn people about the smell!

For the croquettes:

a round, ripe Camembert, chilled, 8-9 oz (220-250 g)

1 small carrot

½ small onion

½ stick celery

10 fl oz (275 ml) whole milk

1 pinch ground or blade of mace

1 bay leaf

6 peppercorns

1½ oz (40 g) butter

2 oz (50 g) plain flour

groundnut or other flavourless oil for oiling and frying

6 flat-leaf parsley sprigs, to garnish

For the coating:

1 tablespoon seasoned flour

2 large eggs

2 tablespoons milk

6 oz (175 g) fine white breadcrumbs

For the chutney:

3 oz (75 g) fresh or dried stoned dates

2 small Granny Smith apples

⅓ teaspoon allspice berries

2 whole cloves

3 tablespoons balsamic vinegar

2 shallots, peeled and roughly chopped

pinch cayenne pepper

You will also need 6 ramekins with a 3 inch (7.5 cm) diameter, 1½ inches (4 cm) deep and some clingfilm.

First, make the chutney, which is best made a couple of hours in advance. Using a pestle and mortar, crush the spices to a fine powder. Quarter and core the apples, but leave the peel on, then cut each of the quarters into 8.

Place the apples, dates and all the rest of the ingredients in a food processor, give it all a good whiz to start, then use the pulse action to chop everything evenly. Transfer the whole lot into a serving bowl, cover with clingfilm and chill before serving.

To make the croquettes, first of all, peel and roughly chop the vegetables and place them in a saucepan with the milk, mace, bay leaf and peppercorns. Bring everything up to simmering point, then turn the heat off and leave to infuse for 30 minutes.

After that, strain the milk into a jug, using a sieve and pressing the vegetables with the back of a spoon to extract all the juices. Now rinse and dry the saucepan and, over a medium heat, melt the butter, then add the flour and, using a wooden spoon, stir until the mixture has turned a pale straw colour.

Next, add the milk a little at a time and switch to a balloon whisk, whisking vigorously after each addition until you have a very thick, glossy mixture. Then take the pan off the heat and allow it to cool slightly.

While the mixture is cooling you can deal with the cheese – although it needs to be ripe, it makes life a lot easier if it has been chilled. So all you do is cut the Camembert in half and, using a small sharp knife, peel it carefully, paring the skin away from the cheese. After that, add the cheese to the sauce in smallish pieces and give it all a really good mixing to combine it as thoroughly as possible. Then leave it aside

for 10 minutes or so to cool. Meanwhile, prepare the ramekins. The easiest way to do this is to lightly oil each one, then take pieces of clingfilm about 8 inches (20 cm) long and lay them across the centre of each ramekin. Next, using a clean pastry brush, push the clingfilm into the ramekins all round the edges – it doesn't matter if it creases.

Now divide the cheese mixture between each one and press it in evenly. Fold the surplus clingfilm over the top, smooth it out, then place ramekins in the fridge for several hours, but preferably overnight.

Sprinkle the seasoned flour on to a piece of greaseproof paper or baking parchment, then lightly beat the eggs and milk together and spread the breadcrumbs out on a plate. Also, have another flat plate to hand.

Then all you do is unfold the clingfilm and flip each croquette on to the flour and lightly coat it on all sides. Next, dip it in the beaten egg, then in the breadcrumbs, shaking off any surplus.

Now return it to the egg, and then back again to the breadcrumbs. This double coating gives good protection while the croquettes are cooking.

When the croquettes are coated, if you're not cooking them straightaway, put them on the flat plate and return them to the fridge, uncovered.

When you're ready to cook them, have some crumpled kitchen paper spread out on a plate and then heat up enough oil to just cover the base of a large solid frying pan. The oil needs to be really hot, so test it by dropping in a little cube of bread and if it turns golden in 30 seconds, the oil is ready. Now fry half the croquettes for about 2 minutes on each side and transfer them to

kitchen paper to drain while you fry the rest. You need to take some care here not to overcook them – it's okay for little bits to ooze out of the sides, but if you leave them in too long they tend to collapse.

Serve immediately, garnished with parsley and serve the chutney alongside ∎

Chapter Five
Pasta, Gnocchi
and Noodles

Roasted Tomato Sauce with Basil
Serves 2

Roasting the tomatoes gives this sauce a wonderfully intense tomato flavour. Serve it tossed into hot linguine or spaghetti.

1 lb 8 oz (700 g) ripe red tomatoes, skinned

¾ oz (20 g) fresh basil leaves, plus a few extra leaves to garnish

1 tablespoon extra virgin olive oil

1 fat clove garlic, peeled and chopped

1 tablespoon balsamic vinegar

8 oz (225 g) linguine or spaghetti

freshly grated parmesan, to serve

salt and freshly milled black pepper

You will also need a baking tray measuring 14 x 10 inches (35 x 25.5 cm).

Pre-heat the oven to gas mark 5, 375°F (190°C).

First of all, slice each tomato in half, arrange the halves on the baking tray, cut side uppermost, and season with salt and pepper. Sprinkle a few drops of olive oil on to each one, followed by the garlic, and finally, top each one with a piece of basil leaf (dipping the basil in oil first to get a good coating).

Now pop the whole lot into the oven and roast the tomatoes for 50 minutes-1 hour or until the edges are slightly blackened – what happens in this process is that the liquid in the tomatoes evaporates and concentrates their flavour, as do the toasted edges.

When the tomatoes are ready, remove them from the oven and scrape them with all their juices and crusty bits into a food processor. Then add the vinegar and whiz everything to a not-too-uniform purée. Gently re-heat the sauce while you cook the pasta, then toss the sauce with the hot, drained pasta. Garnish with the extra basil and serve with plenty of freshly grated parmesan ■

Gratin of Rigatoni with Roasted Vegetables
Serves 4

This recipe is a good choice for a supper dish with no meat. Oven-roasted vegetables have a magical, toasted, concentrated flavour, and they keep all their dazzling colours intact.

6 oz (175 g) rigatoni

1 heaped tablespoon grated parmesan, for the topping

For the roasted vegetables:

2 medium courgettes

1 small aubergine

1 lb (450 g) tomatoes, skinned

1 medium onion, peeled

1 small red pepper, deseeded

1 small yellow pepper, deseeded

3 tablespoons extra virgin olive oil

2 cloves garlic, peeled and chopped

2 oz (50 g) pitted black olives, chopped

1 heaped tablespoon salted capers or capers in vinegar, rinsed and drained

2 oz (50 g) mozzarella, grated

sea salt and freshly milled black pepper

For the cheese sauce:

1 pint (570 ml) milk

1½ oz (40 g) plain flour

1½ oz (40 g) butter

pinch cayenne pepper

2 oz (50 g) parmesan, finely grated

a little freshly grated nutmeg

salt and freshly milled black pepper

You will also need an ovenproof baking dish measuring 10 x 8 x 2 inches (25.5 x 20 x 5 cm), and a baking tray measuring 16 x 11 inches (40 x 28 cm).

Start off by preparing the courgettes and aubergine an hour ahead of time: chop them into 1½ inch (4 cm) chunks, leaving the skins on, and layer them in a colander with a sprinkling of salt between each layer. Then put a plate on top and weight it down with something heavy, which will draw out any excess moisture from the vegetables. After an hour, squeeze, then dry them in a clean tea cloth, then pre-heat the oven to gas mark 9, 475°F (240°C).

Now quarter the tomatoes and chop the onion and peppers into 1½ inch (4 cm) chunks. Next, arrange all the vegetables on the baking tray and sprinkle with the olive oil and chopped garlic. Give everything a good mix to coat all the pieces with the oil, then spread them out as much as possible. Season with salt and freshly milled black pepper, then roast on a high shelf in the oven for 30-40 minutes, until browned and charred at the edges.

Now make the cheese sauce – place the milk, flour, butter and cayenne pepper into a medium saucepan and place it over a gentle heat. Then, using a balloon whisk, begin to whisk while bringing it to a gentle simmer. Whisk continually until you have a smooth, glossy sauce, and simmer very gently for 5 minutes. Then add the 2 oz (50 g) parmesan and whisk again, allowing it to melt. Then season with salt, freshly milled black pepper and some freshly grated nutmeg.

Meanwhile, put a large pan of salted water on to boil for the pasta. About 5 minutes before the vegetables are ready, cook the rigatoni in the boiling water for exactly 6 minutes – no longer (remember to put a timer on for this). There's no need to put a lid on. Drain the pasta in a colander, transfer it to a large mixing bowl and combine it with the roasted vegetables, olives, capers and cheese sauce. At this point, turn the heat down to gas mark 6, 400°F (200°C), leaving the door open to let it cool down a bit quicker.

Now layer the mixture into the gratin dish, a third at a time, sprinkling the mozzarella over each layer and finishing with mozzarella. Finally, sprinkle the mixture with the heaped tablespoon of parmesan. Bake in the oven for another 6 minutes, and serve very hot with just a leafy salad and a sharp dressing to accompany it.

If you want to make this ahead of time, it will need 35-40 minutes in the oven at gas mark 6, 400°F (200°C) to heat it through from cold ■

Pesto alla Genovese (fresh basil sauce)

Pesto alla Genovese
(fresh basil sauce)
Serves 2

This is a sauce which, freshly made, will throw any pasta lover into transports of delight. The flavour of the fresh basil combined with olive oil and garlic is out of this world!

2 oz (50 g) fresh basil

1 fat clove garlic, peeled and crushed

1 tablespoon pine nuts

6 tablespoons olive oil

1 oz (25 g) parmesan, grated

salt

If you have a blender, put the basil, garlic, pine nuts and olive oil together with some salt in the goblet and blend until you have a smooth purée. Transfer the purée to a bowl and stir in the grated parmesan.

Alternatively, use a large pestle and mortar to pound the basil, garlic and pine kernels to a paste. Slowly add the salt and cheese, followed by the very gradual addition of the oil until you obtain a smooth purée.

The above quantities will make enough sauce for serving with 8-10 oz (225-275 g) of pasta, which is sufficient for two people ■

Spinach and Ricotta Lasagne
with Pine Nuts
Serves 4-6

This recipe is an absolute hit with everyone who eats it – even my husband, who professes not to like spinach!

For the sauce:

1½ pints (850 ml) milk

2 oz (50 g) butter

2 oz (50 g) plain flour

1 bay leaf

2½ oz (60 g) parmesan, freshly grated

salt and freshly milled black pepper

For the lasagne:

1 lb 5 oz (600 g) young leaf spinach

8 oz (225 g) ricotta

12 fresh lasagne sheets, weighing about 9 oz (250 g)

2 oz (50 g) pine nuts

knob of butter

¼ whole nutmeg, grated

7 oz (200 g) Gorgonzola, Shropshire Blue or Cashel Blue, crumbled

7 oz (200 g) mozzarella, coarsely grated

salt and freshly milled black pepper

You will also need an ovenproof dish measuring about 9 x 9 inches (23 x 23 cm), 2½ inches (6 cm) deep, well buttered.

Pre-heat the oven to gas mark 4, 350°F (180°C).

Begin this by making the sauce, which can be done using the all-in-one method. This means placing the milk, butter, flour and bay leaf together in a saucepan, giving it a good seasoning, then, over a medium heat, whisking the whole lot together continually until it comes to simmering point and has thickened. Now turn the heat down to its lowest possible setting and allow the sauce to cook gently for 5 minutes. After that, stir in 2 oz (50 g) of the parmesan, then remove it

from the heat, discard the bay leaf and place some clingfilm over the surface to prevent a skin from forming.

Now you need to deal with the spinach. First of all, remove and discard the stalks, then wash the leaves really thoroughly in 2 or 3 changes of cold water and shake them dry. Next, take your largest saucepan, pop the knob of butter in it, then pile the spinach leaves in on top, sprinkling them with a little salt as you go. Now place the pan over a medium heat, put a lid on and cook the spinach for about 2 minutes, turning the leaves over halfway through. After that, the leaves will have collapsed down and become tender.

Next, drain the spinach in a colander and, when it's cool enough to handle, squeeze it in your hands to get rid of every last drop of liquid. Then place it on a chopping board and chop it finely. Now put it into a bowl, add the ricotta, then approximately 5 fl oz (150 ml) of the sauce. Give it a good seasoning of salt and pepper and add the grated nutmeg. Then mix everything together really thoroughly and finally, fold in the crumbled Gorgonzola (or other cheese).

Now you need to place a small frying pan over a medium heat, add the pine nuts and dry-fry them for about 1 minute, tossing them around to get them nicely toasted but being careful that they don't burn. Then remove the pan from the heat and assemble the lasagne. To do this, spread a quarter of the sauce into the bottom of the dish and, on top of that, a third of the spinach mixture, followed by a scattering of toasted pine nuts. Next, place sheets of pasta on top of this – you may need to tear some of them in half with your hands to make them fit. Now repeat the whole process, this time adding a third of the grated mozzarella, along with the

pine nuts, then the lasagne sheets. Repeat again, finishing with a layer of pasta, the rest of the sauce and the remaining parmesan and mozzarella. When you are ready to cook the lasagne, place it on the middle shelf of the pre-heated oven and bake for 50-60 minutes, until the top is golden and bubbling. Then remove it from the oven and let it settle for about 10 minutes before serving ■

Pasta with Four Cheeses
Serves 2

There is a hidden cheese in this recipe because Torta Gorgonzola is in fact made from layers of two cheeses, Gorgonzola and mascarpone. Add to that ricotta and some pecorino and you have a five-star recipe – including the best-quality pasta, of course!

8 oz (225 g) dried pasta
(such as penne rigate)
2 oz (50 g) ricotta
3 oz (75 g) Torta Gorgonzola, or Torta di Dolcelatte, diced
1 oz (25 g) pecorino, or parmesan, finely grated, plus a little extra to serve
2 tablespoons freshly snipped chives
salt

You need to start this by measuring out the cheeses on a plate to have them at the ready, then cook the pasta in plenty of boiling, salted water for 1 minute less than the full cooking time. As soon as it's ready, drain the pasta in a colander and immediately return it to the saucepan so that it still has quite a bit of moisture clinging to it. Now quickly add the chives, ricotta, Torta Gorgonzola (or Torta di Dolcelatte) and pecorino (or parmesan) and stir till the cheese begins to melt. Serve it in hot bowls with the extra pecorino (or parmesan) on the table to sprinkle over ■

Spaghetti with Olive Oil, Garlic and Chilli
Serves 2

This one is pure pasta eaten and savoured for its own sake with the minimum amount of adornment – just a hint of garlic, chilli and olive oil.

8 oz (225 g) spaghetti or linguine
4 tablespoons Italian extra virgin olive oil
2 fat cloves garlic, peeled and finely chopped
1 fat red chilli, deseeded and finely chopped
salt and freshly milled black pepper

Begin by putting the pasta on to cook. To do this, place 4 pints (2.25 litres) of water with 1 tablespoon of salt in a very large saucepan and make sure the water is up to a good fierce boil before the pasta goes in. There's no need to put a lid on but use a timer and give it 10-12 minutes, tasting it after 8 minutes and every minute after this, to see if it's ready. Have a colander ready in the sink.

Then, just heat the olive oil in a small frying pan and, when it is hot, add the garlic, chilli and some freshly milled black pepper. Cook these very gently for about 2 minutes, which will be enough time for the flavourings to infuse the oil.

When the pasta is cooked, drain it in a colander, leaving a few drops of moisture still clinging to it, then return to the saucepan and pour in the hot oil. Mix well, then serve straight away on deep, warmed pasta plates ■

Semolina Gnocchi with Gorgonzola
Serves 3-4

This gnocchi is made with semolina instead of the usual potato. They are equally charming, with crisp, baked edges, and are light and fluffy on the inside. Remember, though, that the mixture needs to be prepared the day before you want to serve the gnocchi.

5 oz (150 g) coarse semolina
2 oz (50 g) Gorgonzola Piccante, Shropshire Blue or Cashel Blue, chopped into small dice
10 fl oz (275 ml) milk
freshly grated nutmeg
2½ oz (60 g) parmesan, finely grated
2 large eggs
2 oz (50 g) ricotta
salt and freshly milled black pepper

You will also need a non-stick baking tin measuring 6 x 10 inches (15 x 25.5 cm), 1 inch (2.5 cm) deep, lined with baking parchment, a 2 inch (5 cm) pastry cutter, and an ovenproof baking dish measuring 7½ inches (19 cm) square and 2 inches (5 cm) deep, lightly buttered.

First of all, you'll need a large saucepan, and into that put the milk and 10 fl oz (275 ml) water, along with a good grating of nutmeg, 1 teaspoon of salt and some freshly milled black pepper. Then sprinkle in the semolina and, over a medium heat and stirring constantly with a wooden spoon, bring it all up to the boil.

Let the mixture simmer gently for about 4 minutes, still stirring, until it is thick enough to stand the spoon up in, then remove the pan from the heat and beat in 2 oz (50 g) of the parmesan and the eggs.

Now adjust the seasoning, then pour the mixture into the prepared tin and spread it out evenly with a spatula. When it's

absolutely cold, cover the tin with clingfilm and leave it in the fridge overnight to firm up.

When you are ready to cook the gnocchi, pre-heat the oven to gas mark 6, 400°F (200°C). Turn the cheese and semolina mixture out on to a board and peel away the parchment paper, then cut the mixture into 2 inch (5 cm) rounds with the pastry cutter, re-shape the trimmings and cut out more rounds until the mixture is all used up. I quite like rounds, but if you prefer, you can cut out squares or triangles – it makes no difference. Place them, slightly overlapping, in the baking dish, then dot with the ricotta and sprinkle over the Gorgonzola (or other cheese), followed by the rest of the parmesan.

Bake on a high shelf of the oven for 30 minutes, until the gnocchi are golden brown and the cheese is bubbling ■

Right: Semolina Gnocchi with Gorgonzola
Top left: Spaghetti with Olive Oil, Garlic and Chilli

Penne Rigate with Fresh Tomato Sauce and Mozzarella

Penne Rigate with Fresh Tomato Sauce and Mozzarella
Serves 2-3

Roasted Mediterranean Vegetable Lasagne
Serves 4-6

Singapore Stir-fried N...
Serves 2

Although it's very simple, this classic tomato sauce reduces down to a very fresh concentrated tomato flavour, one of the best sauces ever invented. It even freezes well.

12 oz (350 g) penne rigate

5 oz (150 g) mozzarella, cubed

a little finely grated parmesan, to serve

a few whole basil leaves, to garnish

For the fresh tomato sauce:

2 lb 8 oz (1.15 kg) fresh, red, ripe tomatoes, skinned

1 tablespoon olive oil

1 medium onion, weighing about 4 oz (110 g), peeled and finely chopped

1 fat clove garlic, peeled and crushed

about 12 large leaves fresh basil

salt and freshly milled black pepper

Start by reserving 3 of the tomatoes for later and roughly chop the rest. Next, heat the oil in a medium saucepan, then add the onion and garlic and let them gently cook for 5-6 minutes, until they are softened and golden. Now add the chopped tomatoes with a third of the basil, torn into pieces. Add some salt and freshly milled black pepper, then all you do is let the tomatoes simmer on a very low heat, without a lid, for 1½ hours or until almost all the liquid has evaporated and the tomatoes are reduced to a thick, jam-like consistency, stirring now and then. Roughly chop the reserved tomatoes and stir them in, along with the rest of the torn basil leaves.

When you are ready to eat, gently re-heat the tomato sauce and put the pasta on to cook. Stir the mozzarella into the sauce and let it simmer for 2-3 minutes, by which time the cheese will have begun to melt. Serve the sauce spooned over the drained pasta, sprinkled with parmesan and add a few fresh basil leaves as a garnish ■

Baked lasagne is the most practical of dishes – it can be prepared well in advance and needs no more than a shove in the direction of the oven at the appropriate time. This recipe incorporates the smoky flavours of roasted Mediterranean vegetables and even if you make it on a dull day, its dazzling colours will still be sunny.

For the lasagne:

1 small aubergine

2 medium courgettes

1 lb (450 g) cherry tomatoes, skinned

1 small yellow or red pepper, deseeded and cut into 1 inch (2.5 cm) squares

9 sheets dried spinach lasagne (the kind that needs no pre-cooking)

1 large onion, peeled, sliced and cut into 1 inch (2.5 cm) squares

2 fat cloves garlic, peeled and crushed

2 tablespoons torn fresh basil leaves

3 tablespoons extra virgin olive oil

2 oz (50 g) pitted black olives, chopped

1 heaped tablespoon capers

3 oz (75 g) mozzarella, grated

sea salt and freshly milled black pepper

For the sauce:

1¼ oz (35 g) plain flour

1½ oz (40 g) butter

1 pint (570 ml) milk

1 bay leaf

grating of fresh nutmeg

3 tablespoons freshly grated parmesan, plus 1 tablespoon for the topping

salt and freshly milled black pepper

You will also need a large, shallow roasting tin and a heatproof baking dish measuring 9 x 9 x 2 inches (23 x 23 x 5 cm).

Pre-heat the oven to gas mark 9, 475°F (240°C).

Prepare the aubergine and courgettes ahead of time by cutting them into 1 inch (2.5 cm) dice, leaving the skins on. Then toss them in about 1 dessertspoon of salt and pack them into a colander with a plate on top and a heavy weight on top of the plate. Leave them on one side for an hour so that some of the bitter juices drain out. Next, squeeze out any juices left, and dry the aubergine and courgettes thoroughly in a clean cloth.

Now arrange the tomatoes, aubergine, courgettes, pepper and onion in the roasting tin, sprinkle with the crushed garlic, basil and olive oil, toss everything around in the oil to get a good coating, and season with salt and pepper. Then place the tin on the highest shelf of the oven for 30-40 minutes or until the vegetables are toasted brown at the edges.

Meanwhile, make the sauce by placing all the ingredients (except the cheese) in a small saucepan and whisking continuously over a medium heat until the sauce boils and thickens. Then turn the heat down to its lowest and let the sauce cook for 2 minutes. Now add the grated parmesan. When the vegetables are done, remove them from the oven and stir in the chopped olives and the capers. Turn the oven down to gas mark 4, 350°F (180°C).

Now, into the baking dish pour one-quarter of the sauce, followed by one-third of the vegetable mixture. Then sprinkle in a third of the mozzarella and follow this with a single layer of lasagne sheets. Repeat this process, ending up with a final layer of sauce, then sprinkle the remaining tablespoon of grated parmesan over the top. Now place the dish in the oven and bake for 25-30 minutes or until the top is crusty and golden. All this needs is a plain lettuce salad with a lemony dressing as an accompaniment ■

This is a brilliant combination of flavours, textures and colours.

4 oz (110 g) thin rice noodles

¾ oz (20 g) Chinese dried mushrooms

2 tablespoons groundnut or other oil

1 medium onion, peeled and chopped

1 large garlic clove, peeled and chopped

1 heaped teaspoon freshly grated ginger

3 oz (75 g) aubergine, chopped small

1 dessertspoon Madras curry powder

2 oz (50 g) small cauliflower florets

2 oz (50 g) small broccoli florets

half a red pepper, deseeded and sliced

4 oz (110 g) fresh sweetcorn (1 cob)

½ teaspoon salt

4 spring onions, finely chopped

1½ tablespoons Japanese soy sauce

2 tablespoons dry sherry

First of all, cover the mushrooms with boiling water and soak for 30 minutes, Then drain them, reserving 2 tablespoons of the liquid, give them a squeeze and chop them into fine shreds. Next, heat the oil in a wok or large frying pan and when it's very hot, add the mushrooms, onion, garlic, ginger and aubergine. Stir them round in the hot oil, then reduce the heat and let everything cook for 15 minutes; this slow cooking allows all the delicious flavours to permeate the oil. Now, place the noodles in a bowl, cover with warm water and soak for 10 minutes or less, according to the pack instructions.

Then, turn the heat to medium and add the curry powder, cauliflower, broccoli, pepper, sweetcorn and salt and cook, stirring, for 5 minutes. Drain the noodles and add with the spring onions, then toss everything around. Finally, sprinkle in the combined mushroom water, soy sauce and sherry, give everything a good stir and serve immediately ■

Rigatoni and Asparagus au Gratin
Serves 2

This is an excellent way to turn 8 oz (225 g) of asparagus into a substantial supper dish for two people.

5 oz (150 g) rigatoni
8 oz (225 g) asparagus (prepared weight)
10 fl oz (275 ml) milk
¾ oz (20 g) plain flour
¾ oz (20 g) butter
whole nutmeg
1½ oz (40 g) parmesan, finely grated
1½ tablespoons extra virgin olive oil
1 lb (450 g) ripe red tomatoes, skinned and chopped
1½ oz (40 g) pecorino or parmesan, pared into shavings with a potato peeler
salt and freshly milled black pepper

You will also need an ovenproof baking dish, 7 x 7 x 2 inches (18 x 18 x 5 cm), lightly buttered.

Pre-heat the oven to gas mark 6, 400°F (200°C).

First of all, place the milk, flour and butter in a saucepan and whisk together over a gentle heat until the sauce begins to simmer and thicken. Then season with salt and pepper and a good grating of nutmeg. After that, turn the heat down to its lowest setting and let the sauce cook for 3 minutes, then stir in the grated parmesan. Now remove from the heat, cover with a lid, and leave on one side while you prepare the other ingredients.

Next, cut the asparagus diagonally into pieces roughly the same size as the rigatoni. Then heat up the oil in a medium-sized frying pan and sauté the asparagus pieces for about 5 minutes, tossing them around the pan and keeping the heat fairly high so that they colour at the edges. Then add the tomatoes to the pan, and let them bubble and reduce for about 1 minute. Then turn the heat off.

Next, cook the pasta in plenty of boiling, salted water for 6 minutes only, then drain it in a colander. Return it to the saucepan, add the sauce and the asparagus mixture and mix thoroughly. Taste to check the seasoning, pour the whole lot into the baking dish, sprinkle with the shavings of pecorino (or parmesan) and bake in the oven for 8-10 minutes. Serve straightaway ▧

Sicilian Pasta with Roasted Tomatoes and Aubergines
Serves 2

Aubergines, tomatoes and mozzarella are the classic ingredients of any classic Sicilian sauce for pasta, and roasting the tomatoes and aubergines to get them slightly charred adds an extra flavour dimension.

8 oz (225 g) spaghetti
12 large tomatoes, roughly 2 lb (900 g)
1 large aubergine, cut into 1 inch (2.5 cm) cubes
2 large cloves garlic, peeled and finely chopped
about 4 tablespoons olive oil
12 large basil leaves, torn in half, plus a few extra for garnish
5 oz (150 g) mozzarella, cut into ½ inch (1 cm) cubes
sea salt and freshly milled black pepper

You will also need two baking trays measuring 14 x 10 inches (35 x 25.5 cm).

Pre-heat the oven to gas mark 6, 400°F (200°C).

First of all, place the aubergine cubes in a colander, sprinkle them with salt and leave them to stand for half an hour, weighed down with something heavy to squeeze out the excess juices.

Meanwhile, skin the tomatoes by pouring boiling water over them and leaving them for 1 minute, then drain off the water and, as soon as they are cool enough to handle, slip off the skins (protect your hands with a cloth, if necessary). Cut each tomato in half and place the halves on one of the baking trays, cut side uppermost, then season with salt and freshly milled black pepper. Sprinkle over the chopped garlic, distributing it evenly between the tomatoes, and follow this with a few drops of olive oil on each one. Top each tomato half with half a basil leaf, turning each piece of leaf over to give it a good coating of oil. Now place the baking tray on the middle shelf of the oven and roast the tomatoes for 50-60 minutes or until the edges are slightly blackened.

Meanwhile, drain the aubergines and squeeze out as much excess juice as possible, then dry them thoroughly with a clean cloth and place them in the other baking tray. Then drizzle 1 tablespoon of the olive oil all over them and place them on the top shelf of the oven, above the tomatoes, giving them half an hour.

Towards the end of the cooking time, cook the pasta in plenty of boiling, salted water. When the tomatoes and aubergines are ready, scrape them, along with all their lovely cooking juices, into a saucepan and place it over a low heat, then add the cubed mozzarella and stir gently.

Now drain the pasta, pile it into a warm bowl, spoon the tomato and aubergine mixture over the top and scatter over a few basil leaves ▧

Souffléed Macaroni Cheese

Spinach Gnocchi with Four Cheeses
Serves 2, or 4 as a starter

I dream about eating this recipe on a warm, sunny summer's day outside, but in winter, it's still an excellent lunch for two people, or as a first course for four. Make the gnocchi the day you are going to serve them, as they discolour if left overnight. If you are short of time, you can use 1 lb 2 oz (500 g) bought fresh *gnocchi di patate*.

8 oz (225 g) young leaf spinach

6 oz (175 g) ricotta

2 oz (50 g) creamy Gorgonzola, Cashel Blue or dolcelatte, roughly cubed

2 oz (50 g) Fontina, Gruyère or Emmental, cut into small cubes

2 oz (50 g) pecorino or parmesan, finely grated

1 medium King Edward potato, about 6 oz (175 g), unpeeled

a little freshly grated nutmeg

1 oz (25 g) plain flour, plus a little extra for rolling

1 large egg

2 oz (50 g) mascarpone

1 heaped tablespoon freshly snipped chives

salt and freshly milled black pepper

You will also need a shallow, ovenproof serving dish measuring about 10 x 7 inches (25.5 x 18 cm).

First, boil the potato, which will take about 25 minutes. Meanwhile, pick over the spinach, remove the stalks, then rinse the leaves. Place them in a large saucepan over a medium heat and cook briefly with a lid on for 1-2 minutes, until wilted and collapsed down. Then drain in a colander and, when cool enough to handle, squeeze all the moisture out and chop finely.

When the potato is cooked, drain and, holding it in a tea cloth, peel off the skin and sieve the potato into a bowl. Next, add the spinach, ricotta, nutmeg and flour to join the potato, then beat the egg and add half, together with some seasoning. Now, gently and lightly, using a fork, bring the mixture together. Finish off with your hands and knead the mixture lightly into a soft dough, adding a teaspoonful or more of the beaten egg if it is a little dry. Then transfer the mixture to a floured surface and divide it into 4. Roll each quarter into a sausage shape approximately ½ inch (1 cm) in diameter, then cut it on the diagonal into 1 inch (2.5 cm) pieces, placing them on a tray or plate as they are cut. Cover with clingfilm and chill for at least 30 minutes, but longer won't matter.

After that, using a fork with the prongs facing upwards, press the fork down on to each gnocchi, easing it into a crescent shape, so that it leaves a row of ridges on each one. Now cover and chill the gnocchi again until you are ready to cook them.

To cook the gnocchi, have all the cheeses ready. Pre-heat the grill to its highest setting, then bring a large, shallow pan of approximately 6 pints (3.5 litres) of water up to simmering point and put the serving dish near the grill to warm through. Now drop the gnocchi into the water and cook them for 3 minutes; they will start to float to the surface after about 2 minutes, but they need an extra minute. When they are ready, remove them with a draining spoon and transfer them straight to the serving dish.

When they are all in, quickly stir in first the mascarpone and chives, then sprinkle in the Gorgonzola and Fontina (or other cheeses), then season and cover the whole lot with the grated pecorino (or parmesan). Now pop it under the grill for 3-4 minutes, until golden brown and bubbling. Serve absolutely immediately ■

Souffléed Macaroni Cheese
Serves 2 generously

I've made many a macaroni cheese in my time, but this, I promise you, is the best ever.

6 oz (175 g) macaroni

3 oz (75 g) mascarpone

2 oz (50 g) Gruyère or Emmental, finely grated

2 oz (50 g) parmesan, finely grated

1 oz (25 g) butter

1 medium onion, about 4 oz (110 g), peeled and finely chopped

1 oz (25 g) plain flour

10 fl oz (275 ml) milk

¼ whole nutmeg, freshly grated

2 large egg yolks, lightly beaten and 2 large egg whites

salt and freshly milled black pepper

You will also need a shallow, ovenproof baking dish with a base measurement of 8 x 6 inches (20 x 15 cm), 2 inches (5 cm) deep, lightly buttered.

Pre-heat the oven to gas mark 6, 400°F (200°C).

Begin by having all your ingredients weighed out and the cheeses grated. Fill a large saucepan with 4 pints (2.25 litres) of water containing a dessertspoon of salt and put it on the heat to bring it up to the boil. Then, in a small saucepan, melt the butter over a gentle heat, add the onions and let them soften, without browning and uncovered, for 5 minutes. Then add the flour to the pan, stir it in to make a smooth paste, then gradually add the milk, a little at a time, stirring vigorously with a wooden spoon. Then switch to a balloon whisk and keep whisking so you have a smooth sauce. Then add some salt and freshly milled black pepper, as well as the nutmeg, and leave the sauce to cook gently for 5 minutes. After that, turn off the heat and whisk in the mascarpone and egg yolks, followed by the Gruyère and half the parmesan.

Next, place the baking dish in the oven to heat through, then drop the macaroni into the boiling water and, as soon as the water returns to a simmer, give it 4-6 minutes, until *al dente* (it's going to get a second cooking in the oven). When it has about 1 minute's cooking time left, whisk the egg whites to soft peaks. Drain the pasta in a colander, give it a quick shake to get rid of the water, then tip it back into the pan and stir in the cheese sauce, turning the pasta over in it so it is evenly coated. Then lightly fold in the egg whites, using a cutting and folding movement so as to retain as much air as possible.

Remove the warm dish from the oven, pour the pasta mixture into it, give it a gentle shake to even the top, then scatter the reserved parmesan over and return the dish to the oven on a high shelf for 12 minutes or until the top is puffy and lightly browned. Serve it, as they say in Italy, *presto pronto*.

To make this for 4 people, just double the ingredients and use a 10 x 8 x 2 inch (25.5 x 20 x 5 cm) dish, increasing the cooking time by 3-5 minutes ■

Left: Penne with Wild Mushrooms and Crème Fraîche
Top right: Gnocchi with Sage, Butter and Parmesan

Penne with Wild Mushrooms and Crème Fraîche
Serves 4-6

Gnocchi with Sage, Butter and Parmesan
Serves 2-3

Trofie Pasta Liguria (with pesto, green beans and potato)
Serves 2

Since writing my recipe for Oven-baked Wild Mushroom Risotto (see page 125), I've discovered all the lovely, concentrated mushroom flavour works well with pasta, too.

1 lb 2 oz (500 g) penne rigate

1 lb (450 g) mixed fresh mushrooms (such as flat, chestnut, shiitake or mixed wild mushrooms), finely chopped

½ oz (10 g) dried porcini mushrooms

9 fl oz (250 ml) crème fraîche

3 tablespoons milk

2 oz (50 g) butter

4 large shallots, peeled and finely chopped

2 tablespoons balsamic vinegar

¼ whole nutmeg, grated

lots of freshly grated parmesan, to serve

salt and freshly milled black pepper

First, pop the porcini in a small bowl, then heat the milk, pour it over the porcini and leave them to soak for 30 minutes. Then heat the butter in a medium frying pan, stir in the shallots and let them cook gently for 5 minutes. Next, strain the porcini into a sieve lined with kitchen paper, reserving the soaking liquid, and squeeze the porcini dry. Then chop them finely and add to the pan, along with the fresh mushrooms and the balsamic vinegar. Next, season with salt, pepper and nutmeg. Give it all a good stir, then cook gently, uncovered, for 30-40 minutes, until all the liquid has evaporated.

About 15 minutes before the mushrooms are ready, put the pasta on to cook. Then, 2 minutes before the pasta is cooked, mix the crème fraîche into the mushrooms with the soaking liquid, and warm through.

Drain the pasta, return it to the pan and mix in the mushroom mixture, then place back on a gentle heat for 1 more minute. Serve on warm plates, sprinkled with parmesan ■

This recipe is very simple, the gnocchi are served with just butter, sage and parmesan. Make them the day you're going to serve them, because they will discolour if left overnight.

10 oz (275 g) King Edward potatoes (about 2 medium-sized potatoes)

3½ oz (95 g) plain flour, sifted, plus a little extra for dusting

1 large egg, lightly beaten

3-4 tablespoons freshly grated parmesan, to serve

salt and freshly milled black pepper

For the sauce:

0 fresh sage leaves

2 oz (50 g) butter

1 large clove garlic, peeled and crushed

You will also need a shallow, ovenproof serving dish measuring about 10 x 7 inches (25.5 x 18 cm).

First, place the potatoes, with their skins on, in a suitably sized saucepan, almost cover with boiling water, add some salt, then put a lid on and simmer for 20-25 minutes, until tender. Then drain well and, holding them in your hand with a tea cloth, quickly pare off the skins using a potato peeler. Then place the potatoes in a large bowl and, using an electric hand whisk on a slow speed, start to break the potatoes up, then increase the speed and gradually whisk until smooth and fluffy. Now let them cool. Next, add the sifted flour to the potatoes, along with half the beaten egg, season lightly and, using a fork, bring the mixture together. Then, using your hands, knead the mixture lightly to a soft dough — you may need to add a teaspoonful or so more of the egg if it is a little dry. Now transfer the mixture to a lightly floured surface, flour your hands and divide it into quarters. Roll each quarter into a sausage

shape approximately ½ inch (1 cm) in diameter, then cut it, on the diagonal, into 1 inch (2.5 cm) pieces, placing them on a tray or plate as they are cut. Cover with clingfilm and chill for at least 30 minutes, but longer won't matter.

After that, using a fork with the prongs facing upwards, press the fork down on to one side of each gnocchi so that it leaves a row of ridges on each one; at the same time, ease them into crescent shapes. The ridges are there to absorb the sauce effectively. Now cover and chill the gnocchi again until you are ready to cook them.

To cook the gnocchi, firstly bring a large, shallow pan of approximately 6 pints (3.5 litres) of water to a simmer and put the serving dish in a low oven to warm through. Then drop the gnocchi into the water and cook for about 3 minutes; they will start to float to the surface after about 2 minutes, but they need 3 altogether. When they are ready, remove the gnocchi with a draining spoon and transfer them to the warm serving dish.

For the sauce, melt the butter with the garlic over a gentle heat until the garlic turns nut brown in colour — about 1 minute. Next, add the sage leaves and allow the butter to froth while the sage leaves turn crisp — about 30 seconds — then spoon the butter mixture over the warm gnocchi. Sprinkle half the parmesan over and serve the rest separately ■

I have given this dish this particular name because I have often eaten it in one of my favourite Italian restaurants in Portofino. To save time, use bought pesto sauce — the whole thing still tastes absolutely authentic.

6 oz (175 g) trofie pasta

1 x 120g tub bought fresh pesto (or same quantity home-made)

3 oz (75 g) dwarf or fine green beans, or fresh shelled peas

3 oz (75 g) Anya salad potatoes

2½ oz (60 g) freshly grated parmesan

salt

Begin this by heating some pasta bowls ready for serving. Then, in a large saucepan heat up 4 pints (2.25 litres) of water with a tablespoon of salt and bring it up to a good fierce boil. Add the pasta, stir once and let it boil briskly for 10 minutes.

Meanwhile, if you are using beans, trim and cut them into lengths, about 1½ inches (4 cm). Wash and slice the potatoes next, leaving the skins on; they need to be fractionally thicker than a 50p coin.

After the 10 minutes, throw the beans and potatoes in to join the pasta. (If using peas, give them slightly less cooking time.) Now give the ingredients another stir and bring the water back to the boil, then set a timer for 8 minutes.

After that, drain the pasta, potatoes and beans (or peas) in a colander, not completely, as it needs a little water still clinging to it. Then tip everything back into the saucepan, add the pesto sauce, and stir it pretty niftily to give everything a good coating. Finally, serve in the hot pasta bowls with the parmesan in a bowl to sprinkle over ■

Vegetarian Pad Thai Noodles
Serves 2-3

I first ate Pad Thai Noodles in a small street café in Ko Samui, an island off Thailand – this vegetarian version is every bit as good, I'm glad to say.

4 oz (110 g) rice noodles (medium width, about ⅛ inch/3 mm thick)

3 tablespoons groundnut or other flavourless oil

2 cloves garlic, peeled and crushed

2 medium red chillies, deseeded and finely chopped

2 spring onions, split lengthways and finely chopped

4 oz (110 g) broccoli, cut into small florets

1 small red pepper, deseeded, quartered and then each quarter cut into thin slices

4 oz (110 g) shiitake mushrooms, thickly sliced

4 oz (110 g) peas, fresh, or frozen and defrosted

juice 1 large lime (about 2 tablespoons)

2 large eggs, lightly beaten

salt

For the garnish:

2 heaped tablespoons fresh coriander leaves

3 oz (75 g) natural, roasted, unsalted peanuts, roughly chopped, or crushed in a pestle and mortar

2 spring onions, chopped, (including the green parts)

You will also need a deep frying pan with a diameter of 10 inches (25.5 cm), or a wok.

The way to tackle this is by having all the ingredients on the list prepared and assembled in front of you. First of all, place the noodles in a bowl and soak them in boiling water, making sure they're totally submerged. Soak them for 10 minutes or less according to the instructions given on the pack. After this time, drain the noodles in a colander, rinse them in cold water and then leave them to drain again.

When you're ready to start cooking, heat the oil in the frying pan or wok over a high heat until it is really hot. Then add the garlic, chillies and spring onions and fry for 1-1½ minutes, or until the onions are tender, then, keeping the heat high, add the broccoli florets, the strips of red pepper and the shiitake mushrooms and stir fry for 2 minutes. Now add the peas and lime juice, stirring them around for just a few seconds before adding the noodles. Now toss them around for 1-2 minutes, or until the noodles are heated through.

Next add the beaten egg by pouring it slowly and evenly all over. Let it begin to set for about 1 minute, then stir briefly once more until the egg is cooked into little shreds. Then mix in half a teaspoon of salt and half the garnish and give one final stir before serving absolutely immediately in hot bowls, with the rest of the garnish handed round to be sprinkled over ▦

Pasta With Pepper Relish
Serves 4

The great thing about this is that, because the flavour of the peppers and garlic is so intense, the pasta honestly doesn't need any cheese – making it a perfect recipe for waist watchers.

1 lb (450 g) pasta (such as rigatoni or spaghetti)

4 sprigs fresh basil, to garnish

For the relish:

1 lb (450 g) mixed red and yellow peppers, about 3 peppers in total, quartered, deseeded and cut into ¼ inch (5 mm) strips

1 rounded teaspoon cumin seeds, lightly crushed

1 dessertspoon olive oil

5 cloves garlic, peeled and chopped

2 medium-sized red chillies, deseeded and chopped

4 medium-sized ripe tomatoes

2 tablespoons sun-dried tomato paste

salt and freshly milled black pepper

You will also need a lidded frying pan with a 10 inch (25.5 cm) diameter.

First, dry-roast the cumin seeds in the frying pan for about a minute, until they become fragrant. Now add the oil and when it's hot, stir in the peppers, garlic and chillies and turn the heat down as low as possible. Then cover and cook slowly for about 40 minutes, stirring from time to time, until the peppers are really soft.

To skin the tomatoes, pour boiling water over them, leave them for 1 minute exactly, then drain and slip off the skins (protect your hands with a cloth, if necessary). Roughly chop the tomatoes.

After that, add the tomatoes and the sun-dried tomato paste to the softened peppers. Season and continue to cook, uncovered, over a highish heat, until the mixture is reduced and thickened slightly – about 5 minutes.

Next, keep the sauce warm and cook the pasta – for a minute less than the pack instructions advise. Then drain it and quickly return it to the hot pan, along with the sauce, and place it over a gentle heat. Stir, and continue to cook for about another minute to allow the pasta to absorb the sauce. Serve straightaway in hot bowls, garnished with the basil ▦

Pasta with Pepper Relish

Left: Lemon Pasta with Herbs and Cracked Pepper
Top right: Tagliatelle with Gorgonzola and Toasted Walnuts

Tagliatelle with Gorgonzola and Toasted Walnuts
Serves 2-3

Lemon Pasta with Herbs and Cracked Pepper
Serves 2

Soba Noodles with Soy and Citrus Dressing
Serves 2

This recipe comes from Annie South who was part of the *How To Cook* television production team. It is equally delicious made with fresh walnuts if you are lucky enough to have a walnut tree yourself or know a friend who does.

8 oz (225 g) tagliatelle

4 oz (110g) creamy Gorgonzola or Cashel Blue

4 oz (110 g) walnuts

2 oz (50g) butter

5 fl oz (150 ml) single cream

4 spring onions, trimmed

freshly grated parmesan, to serve

salt and freshly milled black pepper

Pre-heat the oven to gas mark 4, 350°F (180°C).

First of all, bring the water needed for the pasta to the boil. Use a large saucepan; you need at least 4 pints (2.25 litres) of water for this quantity of pasta and add a tablespoon of salt to it.

Meanwhile, place the walnuts on a baking tray in the oven and put a timer on for 6 minutes to toast them lightly. Over a low heat, melt the butter in a medium-sized saucepan. Then add the cheese, followed by the cream and leave to simmer very gently to become a creamy sauce. Once the pasta water is up to a fierce boil, put the pasta in and cook, without a lid, for 5-8 minutes or according to the pack instructions. Now chop the nuts into small pieces, finely slice the spring onions, then add them to the sauce and season it with salt and freshly milled black pepper. When the pasta is ready, drain it into a colander, then quickly return it to the saucepan. Add the sauce, toss it around thoroughly for 30 seconds or so, then serve in hot pasta bowls sprinkled with parmesan ■

This is a sauce that you can whiz together in moments and toss into any kind of pasta. I like it hot with linguine or tossed into cooked macaroni, then cooled and served as a salad.

6-8 oz (175-225 g) dried pasta (depending on how hungry you are)

1 tablespoon fresh lemon juice

1 tablespoon lemon zest, plus a little extra, to sprinkle at the end

6 whole peppercorns, lightly crushed in a pestle and mortar

¾ oz (20 g) fresh basil

½ oz (10 g) fresh mint

1 oz (25 g) fresh rocket leaves

3 spring onions, trimmed

1 clove garlic, peeled

2 tablespoons extra virgin olive oil

sea salt

Begin this by heating two pasta bowls ready for serving. Then, in a large saucepan heat up 4 pints (2.25 litres) of water with a tablespoon of salt and bring it up to a good fierce boil. Add the pasta to the boiling water and stir once, then let it boil briskly for 10 minutes.

All that happens now is that while the pasta is cooking, the rest of the ingredients are piled into a processor with a teaspoon of salt, then one big whiz till the herbs are chopped and that's it.

Now drain the pasta and return it quickly back to the saucepan with the sauce and toss the two together. Serve in the warm bowls with a little extra zest sprinkled over each one ■

Soba noodles are made with buckwheat and are traditionally served either hot in soups or cold in salads. The salad version is my favourite and you can, of course, use any green salad leaves in this recipe: rocket and young spinach leaves would be very good. This version is with watercress, which combines perfectly with the flavour of the seaweed. For a stockist of Japanese ingredients, see page 257.

3 oz (75 g) soba noodles

3 oz (75 g) beansprouts

1 tablespoon wakame (sea vegetable)

¼ oz (5 g) hijiki (dried seaweed)

1 teaspoon groundnut or other flavourless oil

1 tablespoon Japanese soy sauce, plus extra, to serve

1 bunch watercress, 2-3 oz/50-75 g, leaves only

2 spring onions, finely chopped

salt

For the dressing:

3 tablespoons Japanese soy sauce

3 tablespoons fresh lime juice

3 tablespoons groundnut or other flavourless oil

First, place the beansprouts in cold, salted water for 10 minutes, then drain them in a colander and dry them in a clean tea cloth. Wakame needs to be covered with cold water and soaked for 5 minutes, then drained and chopped, and the hijiki needs to be soaked in cold water for 15 minutes, then drained.

Now heat the oil in a frying pan, add the drained hijiki and toss it in the hot oil for about 1 minute. After that, pour in the tablespoon of soy sauce, then stir it around for another 5 minutes until all the soy has been absorbed. You'll find the little pieces

of hijiki will have reduced in size, but that's quite normal. Next, make up the dressing by shaking the ingredients together in a screw-top jar. Then, to cook the noodles, place them in boiling water with a little added salt and boil without a lid for 3 minutes exactly. Tip them into a colander and place under cold running water until they are completely cold. Then give the colander a good shake to get rid of any excess water.

Finally, mix all the salad ingredients together in a large bowl, tossing to coat thoroughly with the dressing. Serve with some extra soy sauce on the table ■

Chapter Six
Grains and
Pulses

Aduki Bean and Brown Rice Salad
Serves 6

Aduki beans go very well with brown rice, especially in a salad. If you forget to soak them overnight, use the same quantity of water but simply boil them for 10 minutes and then leave them to soak for two hours before cooking.

4 oz (110 g) dried aduki beans, soaked overnight in 2 pints (1.2 litres) cold water

10 fl oz (275 ml) brown basmati rice

1 large green pepper, deseeded and chopped

2 celery stalks, finely chopped

½ cucumber, diced – leave the peel on

6 spring onions, finely chopped (including the green parts)

2 tablespoons finely chopped celery leaves, to garnish

salt and freshly milled black pepper

For the dressing:

4 fl oz (120 ml) olive oil

1 tablespoon wine vinegar

1 fat clove garlic, peeled and crushed

1 teaspoon mustard powder

1 teaspoon salt

2 tablespoons finely chopped parsley

You will also need a medium-sized frying pan with a 10 inch (25.5 cm) base, and a tight-fitting lid.

Begin by putting the soaked beans in a medium-sized saucepan, together with the soaking water, bring to the boil, cover and cook for 45 minutes-1 hour or until the beans are tender.

Meantime, place the rice in the frying pan with some salt and add 1 pint (570 ml) boiling water. Bring to the boil, stir once, then cover and simmer gently for 40 minutes or until the rice is tender and all the water absorbed. Next, put all the ingredients for the dressing in a salad bowl and whisk together. Then while the cooked rice and the drained beans are still warm, empty them into the salad bowl and mix everything together lightly with a fork.

Leave the salad till cold, then add the chopped salad vegetables, mixing them in lightly. Taste, and season again, if it needs it. Serve, sprinkled with chopped celery leaves ■

Spiced Chickpea Cakes with Red Onion and Coriander Salad
Serves 4, or 6 as a starter

At Norwich City Football Club we're always trying out new ideas for vegetarians and this is a real winner. If you're serving it as a main course, it's nice with some nutty brown rice.

8 oz (225 g) chickpeas, soaked overnight in cold water and drained

1 heaped teaspoon coriander seeds

1 heaped teaspoon cumin seeds

2 oz (50 g) butter

1 small onion, peeled and finely chopped

1 small green pepper, deseeded and finely chopped

3 fat garlic cloves, peeled and finely chopped

2 small red chillies, deseeded and finely chopped

1 teaspoon turmeric

½ oz (10 g) fresh coriander, plus a few sprigs, to garnish

1 lb 2 oz (500 g) Greek yoghurt

grated zest ½ lemon

1 dessertspoon lemon juice

1 large egg, beaten

3 tablespoons wholemeal flour or chickpea flour (gram flour)

2 tablespoons groundnut or other flavourless oil

salt and freshly milled black pepper

For the red onion salad:

1 medium red onion, peeled and thinly sliced into half-moon shapes

1 teaspoon grated lemon zest

juice 1 lemon

3 tablespoons fresh coriander leaves

First of all, cover the drained chickpeas with fresh water and add a pinch of salt. Bring to a simmer and cook for 30 minutes. Then drain them thoroughly in a sieve. Now prepare the red onion salad – mix the onion with the lemon zest, juice and coriander in a small bowl and set aside to marinate for at least 30 minutes.

Next, you need to roast the coriander and cumin seeds in order to draw out their fragrance and flavour. To do this, place them in a small frying pan or saucepan over a medium heat and stir and toss them around for about 1-2 minutes or until they begin to look toasted and start to jump in the pan. Now transfer them to a pestle and mortar and crush them to a powder.

After that, put the butter in a saucepan and gently fry the onion and green pepper, along with the garlic and chillies, for 5 minutes until they have softened and begun to turn brown. Then stir in the toasted ground spices and turmeric and continue to cook for a further 30 seconds.

Next, tip the chickpeas into a food processor, along with the fresh coriander, and process until everything is evenly chopped, but not to a purée – the chickpeas should still have some of their texture. Transfer to a bowl now and stir in the softened onions, spices, 3 tablespoons of the Greek yoghurt and the lemon zest and juice. Now give it all a really good mix, taste, and add plenty of seasoning. As soon as the mixture is cool enough to handle, form it into 12 patties for a starter. They should be about 2 inches (5 cm) in diameter and ½ inch (1 cm) thick, or 8 larger patties if you are serving them for a main course. Now coat each one first with beaten egg, then toss them around in the wholemeal or chickpea flour. Next, heat the oil in a frying pan on a high heat and when it's really hot, fry the cakes in two batches to a golden brown colour, about 1 minute on each side. Drain well on kitchen paper and serve as soon as possible with the red onion salad and about 2 rounded tablespoons Greek yoghurt per person ■

Cauliflower and Broccoli Gratin with Blue Cheese
Serves 4

The cheese we used for the sauce in this recipe initially was Gorgonzola, but Roquefort and dolcelatte also taste extremely good here.

10 oz (275 g) cauliflower florets

10 oz (275 g) broccoli florets

1 tablespoon olive oil

2 medium onions, peeled and sliced into 8 through the root

10 fl oz (275 ml) brown basmati rice

1 pint (570 ml) hot stock made with Marigold Swiss vegetable bouillon powder

1 rounded teaspoon salt

For the blue cheese sauce:

4 oz (110 g) Roquefort, Gorgonzola or dolcelatte, cubed

1 pint (570 ml) milk

1½ oz (40 g) butter

1½ oz (40 g) plain flour

pinch cayenne pepper

a little freshly grated nutmeg

salt and freshly milled black pepper

For the topping:

1 oz (25 g) parmesan, finely grated

½ oz (10 g) fresh breadcrumbs

1 tablespoon finely chopped fresh parsley

You will also need an ovenproof baking dish with a base measurement of 8 x 6 inches (20 x 15 cm), 2 inches (5 cm) deep, and a 10 inch (25.5 cm) frying pan with a lid.

Begin by heating the oil in the frying pan over a medium heat, then add the onions and let them cook for 3-4 minutes, until lightly tinged brown. Next, stir in the rice – there's no need to wash it – and turn the grains over in the pan so they become lightly coated and glistening with oil. Now add the hot stock, along with the salt, stir once only, then cover with the lid, turn the heat to its very lowest setting and cook for 40-45 minutes. Don't remove the lid and don't stir the rice during cooking, because this is what will break the grains and release their starch, making the rice sticky.

While the rice is cooking, make the sauce, and all you do here is place the milk, butter, flour and cayenne pepper in a saucepan and, using a balloon whisk, whisk on a medium heat, continuing until the sauce becomes thick, smooth and glossy. Then turn the heat to its lowest setting and give it 5 minutes to cook. After that, whisk in the cheese until it has melted, then season with the nutmeg, salt and freshly milled black pepper.

Next, pre-heat the grill to its highest setting, then place a saucepan on the heat, add some boiling water from the kettle, fit a steamer in it and add the cauliflower. Put a lid on and time it for 4 minutes. After that, add the broccoli to join the cauliflower, lid on again, and time it for another 4 minutes.

Now arrange the cooked rice in the baking dish, then top with the cauliflower and broccoli florets. Next pour the sauce over, then, finally, mix the parmesan with the breadcrumbs and parsley. Sprinkle this all over the top, then place the whole thing under the grill and cook for 2-3 minutes, until the sauce is bubbling and golden brown ■

Roasted and Mi-cuit Tomato Risotto
Serves 2, or 6 as a starter

Oven-roasted tomatoes, which have been slightly blackened and become really concentrated in flavour, are the mainstay of this superb dish. Add to them some mi-cuit or sun-blush tomatoes, parmesan, a hint of saffron and some creamy rice and you have one of the nicest risottos imaginable.

For the roasted tomatoes:

1 lb 8 oz (700 g) tomatoes

1 dessertspoon extra virgin olive oil (or oil reserved from sun-blush tomatoes, if using, see below)

1 fat clove garlic, peeled and chopped

½ oz (10 g) fresh basil leaves

salt and freshly milled black pepper

For the risotto:

9 fl oz (250 ml) Italian carnaroli rice

2 teaspoons sun-dried tomato paste

4 oz (110 g) mi-cuit tomatoes, roughly chopped, or 2 oz (50 g) sun-blush tomatoes (drained and oil reserved, see above)

1 oz (25 g) butter

1 red onion, finely chopped

¼ teaspoon saffron stamens

10 fl oz (275 ml) dry white wine

2 oz (50 g) parmesan, freshly grated, plus 1 oz (25 g) extra, shaved into flakes with a potato peeler, to garnish

1 tablespoon double cream

salt and freshly milled black pepper

You will also need a solid baking tray 14 x 10 inches (35 x 25.5 cm), lightly oiled and a 9 inch (23 cm) shallow, ovenproof dish of about 3 pint (1.75 litre) capacity.

Pre-heat the oven to gas mark 6, 400°F (200°C).

First of all, skin the fresh tomatoes by pouring boiling water over them, then leave them for 1 minute exactly before draining them and slipping the skins off (if they're too hot protect your hands with a cloth). Now slice each tomato in half and arrange the halves on the baking tray, cut side uppermost, then season with salt and freshly milled black pepper. Then sprinkle a few droplets of olive oil (or oil reserved from the sun-blush tomatoes) on each one, followed by the garlic, then finally, top each one with half a basil leaf dipped in oil first.

Now pop the whole lot into the oven and roast for 50-60 minutes or until the edges of the tomatoes are slightly blackened. After that, remove them from the oven and then put the dish in the oven to pre-heat it, reducing the temperature to gas mark 4, 350°F (180°C) first. Now put the tomatoes and all their juices into a processor and blend.

Next, melt the butter in a large saucepan and fry the onion for about 7 minutes until it is just tinged brown at the edges. After that, add the rice and stir to coat all the grains with the buttery juices. Now crush the saffron to a powder with a pestle and mortar, then add this, together with the wine. Bring it up to boiling point, let it bubble for a minute, then add the tomato paste and 12 fl oz (340 ml) boiling water. Give it all a good stir, season with salt and pepper and then add all the processed tomato mixture, plus the mi-cuit or sun-blush tomatoes. Stir again and bring up to simmering point, then transfer the whole lot to the warm dish, return the dish to the oven and give it 35 minutes (use a timer).

After that, stir in the grated parmesan, then give it another 5 minutes in the oven – what you'll have to do here is to bite a grain of rice to check when it's ready. It should be tender but still retain some bite. Before serving, stir in the cream and top with shavings of parmesan and the remaining basil leaves ■

Perfect Rice
Serves 4

If you want to cook perfect rice – the kind that always stays light and fluffy, with absolutely every grain remaining separate – then I can teach you. But first you will have to make a promise, and that is to memorise three simple little words: leave it alone! If you can do this you will always be able to cook long-grain rice perfectly, and never have to worry about it.

10 fl oz (275 ml) white basmati rice

1½ teaspoons groundnut or other flavourless oil

1 small onion, peeled and finely chopped

1 rounded teaspoon salt

You will also need a frying pan with a 10 inch (25.5 cm) base and a tight-fitting lid.

Begin by warming the frying pan over a medium heat, then add the oil and the onions and let them cook for 3-4 minutes, until lightly tinged brown. Next, stir in the rice – there's no need to wash it – and turn the grains over in the pan so they become lightly coated and glistening with oil. Then add 1 pint (570 ml) of boiling water, along with the salt, stir once only, then cover with the lid. Turn the heat to its very lowest setting and let the rice cook gently for exactly 15 minutes. Don't remove the lid and don't stir the rice during cooking, because this is what will break the grains and release their starch, which makes the rice sticky.

After 15 minutes, tilt the pan to check that no liquid is left; if there is, pop it back on the heat for another minute. When there is no water left, take the pan off the heat, remove the lid and cover with a clean tea cloth for 5-10 minutes before serving, then transfer the rice to a warm serving dish and fluff it lightly with a fork before it goes to the table ■

Non-meat Loaf
Serves 4

This is delicious warm with a home-made tomato sauce, or cold with pickles and salad.

3 oz (75 g) yellow or green dried split peas

2 oz (50 g) Puy lentils

2 oz (50 g) green-brown lentils

3 oz (75g) finely chopped fennel

1 carrot, peeled and chopped

1 small stick celery, finely chopped

1 small leek, rinsed and finely chopped

½ red pepper, deseeded and chopped

15 fl oz (425 ml) vegetable stock made with Marigold Swiss vegetable bouillon powder

1½ oz (40 g) butter

1 clove garlic, peeled and crushed

¼ teaspoon cayenne pepper

¼ teaspoon ground mace

1 large egg, beaten

2 tablespoons chopped fresh parsley

salt and freshly milled black pepper

You will also need a 1 lb (450 g) loaf tin, the base lined with baking parchment and well greased.

Start by bringing the stock to boiling point, stir in the split peas and Puy lentils and simmer, covered, for 5 minutes. Then add the other lentils and simmer for 25-30 minutes or until the peas and lentils are soft.

Now pre-heat the oven to gas mark 5, 375°F (190°C). Heat the butter in a frying pan, add all the vegetables and the garlic and fry for 10 minutes or until softened and golden. Now stir the peas and lentils into the vegetables, together with the cayenne, mace, beaten egg and parsley, mix well, then season. Spoon the mixture into the tin, pressing it down firmly. Then cover with foil and bake for 40 minutes. Leave to rest for 15 minutes, then slip a knife around the inside of the tin and turn on to a warmed serving dish. Serve, cut in slices ■

Roasted Vegetable Couscous Salad with Harissa-style Dressing
Serves 4, or 8 as a starter

In this salad, the combination of goats' cheese and roasted vegetables on a cool bed of couscous mixed with salad leaves and a spicy dressing is positively five star.

For the roasted vegetables:

1 small aubergine

2 medium courgettes

1 lb (450 g) cherry tomatoes, skinned

1 small red or yellow pepper, deseeded and cut into 1 inch (2.5 cm) squares

1 small bulb fennel, chopped

1 large onion, peeled, sliced and cut into 1 inch (2.5 cm) squares

2 fat cloves garlic, peeled and crushed

2 tablespoons fresh basil leaves, torn so that they stay quite visible

3 tablespoons extra virgin olive oil

2 oz (50 g) pitted black olives, chopped

1 heaped tablespoon capers, drained

sea salt and freshly milled black pepper

For the couscous:

10 oz (275 g) couscous

18 fl oz (510 ml) hot vegetable stock made with Marigold Swiss vegetable bouillon powder

4 oz (110 g) firm goats' cheese

salt and freshly milled black pepper

For the salad:

3 oz (75 g) mixed salad leaves (such as lettuce, coriander, flat-leaf parsley, rocket)

1 tablespoon black onion seeds, to garnish

For the dressing:

4 fl oz (120 ml) extra virgin olive oil

1 rounded teaspoon cayenne pepper

2 tablespoons ground cumin

2 heaped tablespoons tomato purée

4 tablespoons lime juice (about 2 limes)

You will also need a large, shallow roasting tin or baking tray.

First, prepare the roasted vegetables: prepare the aubergine and courgettes ahead of time by cutting them into 1 inch (2.5 cm) dice, leaving the skins on. Then toss them in a dessertspoon of salt and pack them into a colander with a plate on top and a heavy weight on top of the plate. Leave them on one side for an hour so that some of the bitter juices drain out. After that, squeeze out any juices left, and dry them thoroughly in a clean cloth. Pre-heat the oven to gas mark 9, 475°F (240°C).

Now arrange the aubergine, courgettes, tomatoes, pepper, fennel and onion in the roasting tin, sprinkle with the crushed garlic, basil and olive oil, toss everything around in the oil to get a good coating and season with salt and pepper. Place the tin on the highest shelf of the oven for 30-40 minutes or until the vegetables are toasted brown at the edges. When the vegetables are done, remove them from the oven and stir in the chopped olives and the capers, then remove them to a plate to cool.

When you're ready to assemble the salad, first place the couscous in a large, heatproof bowl, then pour the hot stock over it, add some salt and pepper, stir it with a fork, then leave on one side for 5 minutes, by which time it will have absorbed all the stock and softened. Meanwhile, cut the cheese into sugar-cube-sized pieces. Make up the dressing by whisking all the ingredients together in a bowl, then pour into a serving jug.

To serve the salad, place the couscous in a large, wide salad bowl and gently fork in the cubes of cheese, along with the roasted vegetables. Next, arrange the salad leaves on top and, just before serving, drizzle a little of the dressing over the top, followed by a sprinkling of onion seeds and hand the rest of the dressing around separately ■

Oven-baked Wild Mushroom Risotto

Oven-baked
Wild Mushroom Risotto
Serves 2, or 6 as a starter

I've always loved real Italian risotto, a creamy mass with the rice grains *al dente* – but oh, the bother of all that stirring to make it. This is another oven-baked risotto – it works like a dream and leaves you in peace to enjoy the company of your friends while it's cooking.

½ oz (10 g) dried porcini mushrooms

8 oz (225 g) fresh, dark-gilled mushrooms

2½ oz (60 g) butter

1 medium onion, peeled
and finely chopped

7 fl oz (200 ml) Italian carnaroli rice

5 fl oz (150 ml) dry Madeira

2 tablespoons freshly grated parmesan,
plus 2 oz (50 g) extra, shaved into flakes
with a potato peeler

salt and freshly milled black pepper

You will also need a 9 inch (23 cm) square shallow, ovenproof dish, approximately 2 inches (5 cm) deep.

Pre-heat the oven to gas mark 2, 300°F (150°C).

First of all, you need to soak the dried mushrooms and, to do this, you place them in a bowl and pour 1 pint (570 ml) of boiling water over them. Then just leave them to soak and soften for half an hour. Meanwhile, chop the fresh mushrooms into ½ inch (1 cm) chunks – not too small, as they shrink down quite a bit in the cooking.

Now melt the butter in a medium saucepan, add the onion and let it cook over a gentle heat for about 5 minutes, then add the fresh mushrooms, stir well and leave on one side while you deal with the porcini.

When they have had their half-hour soak, place a sieve over a bowl, line the sieve with a double sheet of kitchen paper and strain the porcini mushrooms, reserving the liquid. Squeeze any excess liquid out of them, then chop them finely and transfer to the pan to join the other mushrooms and the onion. Keep the heat low and let the onions and mushrooms sweat gently and release their juices – which will take about 20 minutes.

Meanwhile, put the dish in the oven to warm. Now add the rice and stir it around to get a good coating of butter, then add the Madeira, followed by the strained mushroom soaking liquid. Add a teaspoon of salt and some freshly milled black pepper, bring up to simmering point, then transfer the whole lot from the pan to the warmed dish. Stir once, then place it on the centre shelf of the oven without covering. Set a timer and give it 20 minutes exactly.

After that, gently stir in the grated parmesan, turning the rice grains over. Now put the timer on again and give it a further 15 minutes, then remove from the oven and put a clean tea cloth over it while you invite everyone to be seated. Like soufflés, risottos won't wait, so serve *presto pronto* on warmed plates and sprinkle with the shavings of parmesan ■

Chilladas
Serves 8 (makes 24)

These spiced lentil cakes really are delicious. Serve with a home-made tomato sauce.

1 lb (450 g) whole green-brown lentils

2 medium carrots

2 medium onions

4 oz (110 g) butter

2 cloves garlic, peeled and crushed

1 large green pepper, deseeded and finely chopped

1 teaspoon cayenne pepper

½ teaspoon ground mace

1 teaspoon chopped fresh thyme

1 dessertspoon chopped fresh parsley

4 teaspoons tomato purée

salt and freshly milled black pepper

For the coating:

2 large eggs, lightly beaten

4 oz (110 g) fresh, fine breadcrumbs

groundnut or other flavourless oil
for shallow-frying

Place the lentils in a large saucepan with 2 pints (1.2 litres) water. Bring them to the boil, then cover and simmer gently for 35-40 minutes or until they are mushy. Meanwhile, peel and finely chop the carrots and onions. Then, heat the butter in a large frying pan and soften the onions, garlic and carrots in it for 5 minutes; now add the chopped pepper and cook for a further 5-10 minutes.

Next, season the lentils and tip them into a bowl to mash them to a pulp with a fork – but not too smooth. Now mix in the vegetables, cayenne, mace, herbs and tomato purée and leave the mixture to cool. Then divide and shape the mixture into 24 small rounds. Dip the chilladas first into the beaten egg, then into the breadcrumbs, and shallow-fry in batches in about ¼ inch (5 mm) of oil for about a minute on each side or till golden. Drain on kitchen paper before serving ■

Dolmades (stuffed vine leaves)
Serves 4, or 6 as a starter

You will find the vine leaves for this favourite easy recipe in packets in supermarkets.

12 large vine leaves in brine, 4 oz/110 g

2 fl oz (75 ml) basmati rice, cooked in
4 fl oz (120 ml) water (see page 122)

1½ tablespoons olive oil

1 oz (25 g) pine nuts

1 lb 8 oz (700 g), peeled and chopped fresh or same quantity tinned tomatoes

2 teaspoons tomato purée

1½ teaspoons fresh or 1 teaspoon dried oregano

1 tablespoon each chopped fresh mint and parsley

¼ teaspoon ground cinnamon

3 small cloves garlic, peeled and crushed

juice ½ lemon

salt and freshly milled black pepper

You will also need a 2 pint (1.2 litre) lidded, flameproof casserole.

First, soak the vine leaves in boiling water for 20 minutes, then drain and spread out each leaf flat – vein side uppermost. Heat the oil in a frying pan and fry the pine nuts till golden. Then add the cooked rice, one-third of the tomatoes, the purée, half the oregano, the mint, parsley, cinnamon and garlic. Stir well, then cook for 2 minutes. Now add the lemon juice and season. Spoon a dessertspoonful of the mixture on to the stalk end of a leaf and fold once, pressing the filling to a sausage shape. Then tuck in the sides of the leaf and roll it up to make a tight, cylindrical parcel. When all the leaves are filled, spoon half of the leftover tomatoes into the casserole. Now pack the dolmades in and spoon the remaining tomatoes and oregano on top. Add a seasoning of salt and pepper, pour over 2½ fl oz (65 ml) of water, put a lid on and simmer very gently for 1 hour. Serve hot or cold with the juices spooned over ■

Left: Stir-fried Rice with Egg and Spring Onions
Top right: Risotto Verde

Risotto Verde
Serves 4, or 6 as a starter

A wonderful creamy luscious taste of summer – be sure to make it before the English asparagus season ends.

6 fl oz (175 ml) Italian carnaroli rice

2½ oz (60 g) butter

1 small onion, peeled and finely chopped

3 fl oz (75 ml) dry white wine

18 fl oz (510 ml) hot vegetable stock made with Marigold Swiss vegetable bouillon powder

1 dessertspoon fresh chopped sage

4 oz (110 g) skinned young broad beans (you'll need about 6 oz (175 g) unskinned weight)

4 oz (110 g) asparagus, cut into 1 inch (2.5 cm) pieces

1 bunch spring onions, trimmed and chopped

2 tablespoons Pecorino Romano or parmesan cheese, freshly grated

1 bunch snipped fresh chives

salt and freshly milled black pepper

To serve:

4 tablespoons groundnut or other flavourless oil

12 sage leaves

2 oz (50 g) Pecorino Romano or parmesan cheese, freshly grated

You will also need a 2 inch (5 cm) deep, ovenproof baking dish measuring 9 inches (23 cm) square.

Preheat the oven to gas mark 2, 300°F (150°C).

Begin by melting the butter in a medium saucepan, then add the onion and let it cook over a gentle heat for 5-7 minutes or until the onion is soft and golden. Meanwhile, place the baking dish in the oven to warm through. Now add the rice to the saucepan, stirring it around to get a good coating of butter (it will look like there's not nearly enough rice at this stage, but it swells up during the cooking), then add the white wine and vegetable stock.

Next, add the chopped sage, half a teaspoon of salt and some freshly milled black pepper and bring it up to simmering point, then transfer the whole lot from the pan to the warmed dish. Stir once, then place it on the centre shelf of the oven (without covering) to cook for exactly 20 minutes – a timer is useful here.

Meanwhile, heat the oil in a small frying pan. Add the whole sage leaves, a few at a time, and cook for 30 seconds to 1 minute until crispy, then remove with a slotted spoon to a plate lined with kitchen paper.

After the 20 minutes are up, remove the risotto from the oven and gently stir in the broad beans, asparagus and spring onions, along with the 2 tablespoons of Pecorino (or parmesan) cheese, turning the rice grains over. Now put the timer on again and cook the risotto for a further 15 minutes, then remove the dish from the oven, stir in the chives and put a clean tea cloth over it while you invite everyone to sit down. Risottos won't wait, so serve *presto pronto* on warmed plates and finished with a couple of crispy fried sage leaves and the extra grated Pecorino or parmesan ▪

Stir-fried Rice
with Egg and Spring Onions
Serves 2

The golden rule of stir-frying rice successfully is to always make sure the cooked rice is absolutely cold. In other words, you can't boil it and stir-fry straightaway because it goes all sticky.

4 fl oz (120 ml) white basmati rice

1 large egg, beaten

1 spring onion, split lengthways and finely chopped (including green part)

½ teaspoon salt

1 dessertspoon groundnut or other flavourless oil

½ onion, peeled and finely chopped

1 dessertspoon Japanese soy sauce

You will also need a frying pan with a 10 inch (25.5 cm) base and a tight-fitting lid, or a wok with a lid.

First, warm the frying pan or wok over a medium heat. Next, add the rice, then add 8 fl oz (225 ml) boiling water, along with the salt, stir once only, then cover with a lid. Turn the heat to its lowest setting and let the rice cook gently for exactly 15 minutes. Don't remove the lid and don't stir the rice during cooking, because this is what will break the grains and release their starch, which makes the rice sticky.

After 15 minutes, tilt the pan to check that no liquid is left; if there is, pop it back on the heat for another minute. When there is no water left in the pan, take it off the heat, remove the lid and cover with a clean tea cloth for 5-10 minutes, then transfer the rice to a dish and fluff it lightly with a fork and allow it to become completely cold.

When you are ready to stir-fry, heat half the oil in the frying pan or wok and when it's really hot, quickly fry the chopped onions for 3 minutes, moving them around in the pan until they are tinged brown. Next, add the remaining oil to the pan and, when it's smoking hot, add the rice and stir-fry – this time for about 30 seconds.

Now spread the ingredients out in the pan and pour in the beaten egg. It won't look very good at this stage, but keep on stir-frying, turning the mixture over, and the egg will soon cook into little shreds that mingle with the other ingredients. Finally, add the spring onion and soy sauce, give it one more good stir and serve ▪

Thai Bean Salad
with Pink Grapefruit and Grapes
Serves 4, or 6 as a starter

In Thailand they use pomelo in salads, which is very similar to grapefruit. I have used pink grapefruit here, but when they're not available, you could ring the changes and use a thinly sliced, medium-sized mango.

For the salad:

4 oz (110 g) cannellini beans, soaked overnight in cold water, cooked for 1¼-1½ hours, or until tender, drained and cooled

1 medium pink grapefruit, peeled and the segments separated and halved

2 oz (50 g) red seedless grapes, halved

grated zest 1 lime (reserve the juice for the dressing)

1 teaspoon sesame seeds

3 tablespoons chopped fresh coriander

3 tablespoons chopped fresh mint leaves

4 oz (110 g) rocket leaves, stalks removed

2 oz (50 g) beansprouts

1 stem lemon grass, trimmed, tough outer layer discarded, then very finely sliced

3 kaffir lime leaves (if available), rolled into a cigar shape and very finely shredded

For the dressing:

2-3 medium-sized red chillies, halved and deseeded

2 cloves garlic, peeled

1 inch (2.5 cm) piece fresh root ginger, peeled

6 sprigs fresh coriander

1 sprig fresh mint

juice 3 large limes (about 4 tablespoons including the reserved juice from the salad ingredients, see above)

2 tablespoons groundnut or other flavourless oil

1 teaspoon light (or dark) soft brown sugar

a generous pinch of salt

First, pre-heat a small frying pan over a medium heat, then add the sesame seeds. Keep them on the move until they're golden and begin to splutter – about a minute. Then remove the pan from the heat and allow them to cool.

Meanwhile, make the dressing. Blend the chillies, garlic, ginger, and the sprigs of coriander and mint in a food processor or blender until finely chopped, and add the lime juice, oil, sugar and salt and whiz again.

Next, put the cooked beans into a bowl and pour over three-quarters of the dressing, then add the lime zest and most of the chopped coriander and mint (saving some to sprinkle over later), then toss so it's well coated.

Just before serving, put the rocket leaves and beansprouts into a large mixing bowl, toss them in the remaining dressing with the beans, then arrange the salad on an oblong serving dish, along with the chunks of grapefruit and the grapes here and there. Then sprinkle over the lemon grass, lime leaves (if using), the remaining coriander and mint, and the sesame seeds. Serve immediately ▪

Frijolemole
Serves 4-6

This rather exotic title simply means 'bean purée' – but a rather special one, made with chickpeas, chillies, fresh lime juice and coriander. It has a crunchy texture and is lovely for a first course or light lunch with some toasted bread and a salad.

6 oz (175 g) dried chickpeas, soaked overnight in 1 pint (570 ml) cold water

1 fresh chilli

2 tablespoons fresh lime juice

1 heaped tablespoon chopped fresh coriander

1 tablespoon groundnut or other flavourless oil

1 medium Spanish onion, peeled and chopped

2 cloves garlic, peeled and chopped

3 spring onions

1 large tomato, skinned and chopped

½ teaspoon Tabasco sauce

2 tablespoons soured cream or fromage frais

salt and freshly milled black pepper

To garnish:

black olives

flat-leaf parsley

Begin by draining the soaked chickpeas and place them in a saucepan with enough cold water to cover. Bring them up to simmering point, put a lid on and simmer gently for about 45 minutes or until the chickpeas are tender when tested with a skewer.

Meanwhile, heat the oil in a small frying pan and gently sauté the onion for 5 minutes, then add the garlic and cook for another 5 minutes.

The spring onions should now be trimmed and chopped small and the chilli should be split, deseeded under a cold running tap,

and also chopped small. Don't forget to wash your hands straight away!

When the chickpeas are ready, drain them in a sieve set over a bowl, then transfer them to a food processor, along with some salt, the sautéed onion and garlic and any oil left in the pan. Now add the lime juice and blend until you have a smoothish purée – if it's too stiff add a couple of tablespoons of the cooking liquid from the chickpeas. What you need is a soft purée, like hummus in texture.

Now empty the contents of the processor into a bowl and add the tomato, chilli, spring onions, Tabasco, coriander and 2 tablespoons of soured cream (or fromage frais). Taste to check the seasoning and add a few more drops of Tabasco if it needs a little more kick. Cover the bowl and chill till needed. Serve, garnished with black olives and some flat-leaf parsley ▪

Stuffed Cabbage Leaves with Toasted Pistachios and Pine Nuts
Serves 2

You can make all sorts of stuffings if you follow the basic recipe – you could use cooked lentils or other chopped nuts or whatever ingredients happen to be handy.

1 smallish head of spring cabbage
12 oz (350 g) red, ripe tomatoes, peeled and roughly chopped

For the stuffing:
5 fl oz (150 ml) brown basmati rice
6 fresh mint leaves, chopped
1 oz (25 g) unsalted, shelled pistachio nuts
1 oz (25 g) pine nuts
2 tablespoons olive oil
1 medium onion, peeled and chopped
2 oz (50 g) currants
2 small cinnamon sticks
salt and freshly milled black pepper

You will also need a small frying pan with a lid, and a casserole with a capacity of 4 pints (2.25 litres).

First of all, cook the rice. Begin by warming the frying pan over a medium heat, then add the oil and add the onions and let them cook for 3-4 minutes, or until lightly tinged brown. Next, stir in the rice, give it a stir so it is glistening with oil. Then pour in 10 fl oz (275 ml) of boiling water and season with salt. Stir, once only, and then cover with the lid. Turn the heat to its lowest setting and let the rice cook for 45 minutes, or until all the liquid has been absorbed and the grains are tender.

Take the pan off the heat, remove the lid and cover with a clean tea cloth for 5 minutes, then turn the cooked rice into a mixing bowl and leave it to cool a little. Meanwhile, pre-heat the oven to gas mark 4, 350°F (180°C).

Now place the pistachios and the pine nuts on a baking tray and toast in the oven for 7-8 minutes (make sure you set a timer).

Then remove the tray from the oven and leave the nuts to cool. Now you can prepare the cabbage. To do this, discard the tough outer leaves and then carefully peel off about 6 or 7 whole leaves. In each one of these make a V-shaped cut with a sharp knife to snip out the hard stalky bits. Next, chop up the heart of the cabbage and bring a large saucepan of water to the boil. Blanch the whole leaves and chopped cabbage, separately, by cooking them in the boiling water; the whole leaves will take 5 minutes and the chopped will take 2-3 minutes. Then drain the cabbage in a colander, rinse in cold water and drain again. Shake off as much moisture from the leaves as you can and wrap them in a clean tea cloth or piece of kitchen paper to dry.

Then add the chopped cabbage to the cooled rice, with the currants, pistachios, pine nuts and mint and a generous seasoning of salt and pepper. Now take a heaped tablespoon of the rice and chopped cabbage mixture and wrap it in one of the prepared leaves – squeezing gently till you have a neat package and tucking the ends underneath to prevent the parcels bursting open while they are in the oven.

Fill and roll the remaining cabbage leaves with the rest of the stuffing, then pack the parcels closely together in a casserole, tucking the cinnamon sticks in amongst them. Season with salt and pepper and pour the chopped tomatoes over the parcels. Cover and bake for 1 hour in the oven ■

Mixed Vegetable Salad à la Grècque
Serves 6

This salad has lots of gutsy flavours, can be made well in advance and doesn't need any last-minute attention. I love to serve it at buffet parties. I think this is best left covered in the fridge overnight to allow the flavours to develop

1 large onion, peeled
1 lb 8 oz (700 g) ripe, red tomatoes (or 1 lb 5 oz/600 g tinned Italian chopped tomatoes)
8 shallots, peeled
6 oz (175 g) cauliflower
6 oz (175 g) small to medium open-cap mushrooms, wiped
1 tablespoon coriander seeds
12 black peppercorns
2½ fl oz (65 ml) olive oil
1 fat clove garlic, peeled and crushed
3½ fl oz (100 ml) red wine vinegar
1 dessertspoon chopped fresh oregano (or 1 teaspoon dried oregano)
juice 2 lemons, about 2 fl oz (55 ml)
3 fl oz (75 ml) water, mixed with
1 tablespoon tomato purée
3 oz (75 g) dried butter beans (or judion beans), soaked overnight in cold water, cooked for 30-40 minutes, or until tender, and drained
salt and freshly milled black pepper

To serve:
2½ fl oz (65 ml) olive oil
1 oz (25 g) chopped fresh flat-leaf parsley
3 spring onions, finely chopped (including the green parts)

You will also need a large, shallow serving dish.

First of all, you need to dry-roast the coriander seeds. To do this, place them in a small frying pan over a medium heat and stir and toss them around for 1-2 minutes, or until they begin to look toasted and start to jump in the pan. Now crush them quite coarsely with a pestle and mortar, along with the peppercorns.

Next, finely chop the onion, heat the oil in a medium-sized saucepan and soften the onion in it for 10 minutes. Meanwhile, skin the fresh tomatoes, if using. Place them in a heatproof bowl and pour boiling water on to them. Leave them for exactly a minute (or 15-30 seconds, if they are small), then remove them and slip off their skins (protecting your hands with a cloth if they are hot). Now quarter them and add them (or the tinned tomatoes) to the pan. Then add the crushed coriander seeds and peppercorns, garlic, vinegar, oregano, lemon juice, water and tomato purée, and a teaspoon of salt. Bring everything up to the boil, stir in the shallots, cover the pan and simmer for 20 minutes.

Next, break the cauliflower into 1 inch (2.5 cm) florets, halve the mushrooms and add them both, along with the beans, to the pan. Cover it again and simmer for a further 20 minutes, stirring the vegetables around once or twice during the cooking time. After 20 minutes, test them with a skewer – they should be tender but still firm. Now taste to check the seasoning. Then pour the contents of the pan into the serving dish and leave to cool.

To serve, remove the dish from the fridge an hour in advance, drizzle the vegetables with the oil, then scatter over the chopped parsley and spring onions ■

Spiced Pilau Rice with Nuts
Serves 4

I've always loved the fragrant flavour of spiced pilau rice, and could easily eat it just on its own, adding nuts to give it some crunch.

10 fl oz (275 ml) white basmati rice
1 oz (25 g) unsalted cashew nuts
1 oz (25 g) unsalted, shelled pistachio nuts
1 oz (25 g) pine nuts
2 cardamom pods
¾ teaspoon cumin seeds
½ teaspoon coriander seeds
1½ tablespoons groundnut or other flavourless oil
1 small onion, peeled and finely chopped
1 inch (2.5 cm) piece cinnamon stick
1 bay leaf
1 rounded teaspoon salt

You will also need a lidded frying pan with a 10 inch (25.5 cm) base.

First of all, in the pestle and mortar, crush the cardamom pods and the cumin and coriander seeds. Then warm the frying pan over a medium heat, add the crushed spices (the cardamom pods as well as the seeds), turn the heat up high and toss them around in the heat to dry-roast them and draw out the flavour – this will take about 1 minute. After that, turn the heat back to medium and add the oil, onion and nuts and fry until everything is lightly tinged brown.

Next, stir in the rice and turn the grains over until they are nicely coated and glistening with oil, then pour in 1 pint (570 ml) of boiling water. Add the cinnamon, bay leaf and salt, stir once only, then put the lid on, turn the heat down to its lowest setting and let the rice cook for exactly 15 minutes. Now take the pan off the heat, remove the lid and cover with a clean tea cloth for 5 minutes. Then empty the rice into a warm serving dish and fluff up lightly with a fork before it goes to the table ■

Roasted Vegetable and Brown Rice Gratin
Serves 4

There is a lovely combination of vegetables in this supper dish but you can vary the vegetables you use, depending on whatever is seasonally available.

For the rice:
10 fl oz (275 ml) brown basmati rice
1 tablespoon olive oil
2 medium onions, peeled and finely chopped
1 pint (570 ml) hot stock made with Marigold Swiss vegetable bouillon powder
1 rounded teaspoon salt

For the vegetables:
10 oz (275 g) butternut squash (peeled weight)
5 oz (150 g) each celeriac, swede, carrots, parsnips (peeled weight)
2 medium red onions, peeled
1 heaped tablespoon chopped mixed fresh herbs (such as parsley, thyme and tarragon)
1 fat clove garlic, peeled and crushed
2 tablespoons olive oil
salt and freshly milled black pepper

For the cheese sauce:
1 pint (570 ml) milk
1½ oz (40 g) plain flour
1½ oz (40 g) butter
a little cayenne pepper
2 oz (50 g) mature Cheddar, grated
1 oz (25 g) parmesan, finely grated
a little freshly grated nutmeg
salt and freshly milled black pepper

You will also need a baking sheet measuring 16 x 12 inches (40 x 30 cm), and an 8 x 6 inch (20 x 15 cm) ovenproof dish, and a 10 inch (25.5 cm) lidded frying pan.

Pre-heat the oven to gas mark 8, 450°F (230°C).

For the vegetables, begin by cutting the squash, celeriac, swede, carrots and parsnips into 1 inch (2.5 cm) cubes. Place them and the red onions, each cut into 6 through the root, in a large bowl, along with the herbs, garlic, a good seasoning of salt and pepper and the olive oil, then toss them around so they get a good coating of oil and herbs. Now arrange them evenly all over the baking sheet, then place this on the highest shelf of the oven to roast for about 30 minutes, or until they are nicely brown at the edges. As soon as they are ready, take them out and reduce the oven temperature to gas mark 6, 400°F (200°C).

For the rice, begin by warming the frying pan over a medium heat, then add the oil and the onions and let them cook for 3-4 minutes, until lightly tinged brown. Next stir in the rice – there's no need to wash it – and turn the grains over in the pan so they become lightly coated and glistening with oil.

Then add the boiling stock, along with the salt, stir once only, then cover with the lid, turn the heat to the very lowest setting and cook for 40-45 minutes. Don't remove the lid and don't stir the rice during cooking, because this is what will break the grains and release their starch, which makes the rice sticky.

Meanwhile, make the cheese sauce by placing the milk, flour, butter and a pinch of the cayenne pepper into a medium-sized saucepan, then whisk it all together over a gentle heat until you have a smooth, glossy sauce. Let it cook on the lowest heat for 5 minutes, and after that, add half the cheeses. Whisk again and allow them to melt into it, then season the sauce with salt, freshly milled black pepper and freshly grated nutmeg. When the vegetables and rice are cooked, arrange the rice in

the ovenproof dish, then the vegetables on top of that, followed by the sauce, pouring it over and around the vegetables as evenly as possible.

Finally, scatter over the remaining cheeses with a sprinkling of cayenne pepper, then return the dish to the oven and give it about 20 minutes or until the sauce is browned and bubbling ■

Above: Cauliflower and Broccoli Gratin with Blue Cheese. Top: Roasted Vegetable and Brown Rice Gratin

Camargue Red Rice Salad with Feta Cheese

Camargue Red Rice Salad with Feta Cheese
Serves 4

This is a lovely salad for outdoor eating on a warm, sunny summer's day.

10 fl oz (275 ml) Camargue red rice

7 oz (200 g) feta cheese

2 shallots, peeled and finely chopped

2 oz (50 g) fresh rocket leaves, finely shredded

3 spring onions, trimmed and finely chopped (including the green ends)

salt and freshly milled black pepper

For the dressing:

1 small clove garlic, peeled and crushed

½ teaspoon salt

1 teaspoon grain mustard

1 tablespoon balsamic vinegar

2 tablespoons extra virgin olive oil

freshly milled black pepper

You will also need a 10 inch (25.5 cm) frying pan with a lid.

First put the rice in the frying pan with a teaspoon of salt, then pour in 1 pint (570 ml) boiling water, bring it back up to simmering point, then put a lid on and let it cook very gently for 40 minutes. After that, don't remove the lid, just turn the heat off and leave it for another 15 minutes to finish off.

Meanwhile, make the dressing by crushing the garlic and ½ teaspoon salt in a pestle and mortar, then, when it becomes a purée, add the mustard and work that in, followed by the vinegar and some freshly milled black pepper. Now add the oil and, using a small whisk, whisk everything thoroughly to combine it. Then transfer the warm rice to a serving dish, pour the dressing over and mix thoroughly. Taste to check the seasoning and leave aside until cold. Next, add the shallots, the rocket and the spring onions. Finally, just before serving, crumble the feta cheese all over ■

Turkish Stuffed Tomatoes
Serves 4

These are good for a light lunch with salad for four, or this will serve eight as a starter.

8 really large ripe tomatoes

5 fl oz (150 ml) carnaroli rice

1 small onion, peeled and finely chopped

1 dessertspoon olive oil, plus extra for drizzling

1 clove garlic, peeled and crushed

1 teaspoon ground cinnamon

1 tablespoon each pine nuts and currants

10 fl oz (275 ml) hot stock made with Marigold Swiss vegetable bouillon powder

1 teaspoon chopped fresh thyme

2 teaspoons golden caster sugar

salt and freshly milled black pepper

You will also need a small frying pan with a tight-fitting lid, and a roasting tin measuring 11 x 8 x 2 inches (28 x 20 x 5 cm).

Begin by cooking the rice. Fry the onion in the olive oil in the frying pan until softened, then add the crushed garlic and pour in the rice. Add the cinnamon, pine nuts and the currants and give everything a good stir to get it well coated. Then season with salt and pepper and pour in the hot stock. Stir just once, cover and simmer gently for 15-20 minutes or until all the liquid is absorbed and the grains are tender. Then remove the rice from the heat, add the thyme and fluff with a skewer. Pre-heat the oven to gas mark 4, 350°F (180°C).

Prepare the tomatoes by slicing off a little of the stalk end and scooping out all the core and seeds – trying to leave as much of the actual flesh as possible. Put a pinch of sugar into each hollowed-out tomato, then pack with the rice mixture and replace the lids. Place the tomatoes in the roasting tin with a little water at the bottom, drizzle a few drops of olive oil over each and bake for 25-30 minutes. They are lovely eaten hot or cold ■

Vegetable Tagine with Apricots and Coriander Couscous
Serves 4

This recipe has been given to me by Sarah Randell, our Editor. It's a warming, spicy stew that will do wonders to cheer up long winter nights. It is served with couscous, flavoured with cinnamon and fresh coriander. Preserved lemons are now sold in jars in larger supermarkets.

1 medium aubergine, trimmed and cut into 1½ inch (4 cm) chunks

4 oz (110 g) peeled butternut squash, cut into 1½ inch (4 cm) chunks

4 oz (110 g) peeled parsnip, cut into 1½ inch (4 cm) chunks

3 oz (75 g) ready-to-eat dried apricots, chopped

2 tablespoons olive oil

1 large onion, peeled and sliced

2 fat cloves garlic, peeled and finely chopped

1 teaspoon ground cumin

1 teaspoon ground cinnamon

1 teaspoon ground ginger

1 teaspoon saffron stamens

2 x 14 oz (400 g) tins chopped tomatoes

1½ tablespoons clear honey

2-3 teaspoons harissa paste (mild-medium spiciness)

a cinnamon stick

a strip of lemon peel

1½ oz (40 g) butter

2 oz (50 g) whole blanched almonds

1 tablespoon chopped preserved lemon

salt

For the couscous:

8 oz (225 g) couscous

generous pinch of ground cinnamon

2 tablespoons chopped coriander leaves

First of all, heat the oil in a large saucepan, add the onion and cook over a medium heat for 7-10 minutes or until golden. Then add the garlic, ground cumin, cinnamon and the ginger and cook for another 2 minutes, stirring, before adding the aubergine and cook for a further 5 minutes or until the aubergine is beginning to soften. Next, stir in the saffron, tomatoes, honey, harissa paste, apricots, cinnamon stick, lemon peel and a half teaspoon of salt.

Now stir the butternut and parsnip chunks into the sauce, bring the liquid back to the boil, then reduce the heat and gently simmer the vegetables, covered, for 15-20 minutes, or until they are just tender.

Towards the end of the cooking time, put the couscous into a mixing bowl and pour on 14 fl oz (400 ml) of boiling water, cover with a clean cloth and then leave aside for 10 minutes. Meanwhile, melt ½ oz (10 g) of the butter in a small frying pan and add the almonds and cook, stirring, until they are golden brown. Stir the remaining butter (in small pieces), the pinch of ground cinnamon and the coriander leaves into the hot couscous and fluff it up with a fork.

Transfer the vegetable stew to a warm serving dish and, using a draining spoon, scatter the almonds over the top, followed by the preserved lemon. Serve with the coriander couscous ■

Three Bean Salad with Cider Dressing
Serves 4

'Not Pork' Pies
Makes 6

A delicious salad to serve at any time of the year with crusty bread to mop up the juices.

3 oz (75 g) each of flageolet, kidney and cannellini beans, and chickpeas, pre-soaked overnight and drained (see below)

1 onion, peeled and studded with 6 cloves

a few parsley stalks and a sprig of fresh thyme

1 bay leaf

1 clove garlic, peeled

1 oz (25 g) rocket, stalks removed

½ medium red onion, peeled and thinly sliced

2 tablespoons chopped fresh parsley

For the dressing:

1 tablespoon dry cider

2 cloves garlic, peeled

1 heaped teaspoon mustard powder

2 tablespoons red or white wine vinegar

3½ fl oz (100 ml) extra virgin olive oil

sea salt and freshly milled black pepper

Begin by placing the beans in a saucepan with the onion, parsley, thyme, bay leaf and garlic. Cover with water and fast-boil for 10 minutes to purify the kidney beans. Now simmer gently for 1¼-1½ hours. Cook the chickpeas separately, in the same way, for 1½-2 hours or until tender.

For the dressing, crush the garlic with a teaspoon of sea salt in a pestle and mortar, then work in the mustard. Add some pepper, the vinegar and cider, and the oil, giving everything a good whisking. Then season to taste – this needs to be well seasoned. Drain the beans and chickpeas, discarding the flavourings, and whilst warm, mix with the dressing, then leave for an hour. Arrange three-quarters of the rocket in a serving dish, spoon on the beans and add the rest of the leaves, pushing some in amongst the beans. Finally, top with the onion slices and parsley ■

I've always wanted to do a non-meat equivalent of a pork pie and at last I've achieved it – serve with home-made pickles or chutney. This is perfect food for outdoor eating and picnics.

For the filling:

2 oz (50 g) Puy lentils

1 dessertspoon olive oil

1 shallot, peeled and finely chopped

2 oz (50 g) carrot, peeled and finely chopped

1 fat clove garlic, peeled and crushed

4 oz (110 g) red pepper, finely chopped

1 medium, ripe plum tomato, peeled and finely chopped

2 teaspoons tomato purée

1½ oz (40 g) sun-blush or mi-cuit tomatoes, finely chopped

2 large eggs, lightly beaten

¾ teaspoon ground mace

¼ teaspoon cayenne pepper

1 tablespoon each chopped fresh thyme and parsley

1 dessertspoon chopped fresh sage

salt and freshly milled black pepper

For the pastry:

1 fl oz (25 ml) milk

3 oz (75 g) pure vegetable fat

8 oz (225 g) strong plain white flour, plus a little extra for dusting

½ teaspoon each dry English mustard, mixed spice and sea salt

good grating nutmeg

2 large egg yolks (1 yolk to be used for glazing the pies)

You will also need a muffin tin with 6 cups, each one 3 inches (7.5 cm) across the top, and about 1¼ inches (3 cm) deep, lightly greased, a plain 3¼ inch (8 cm) pastry cutter, and a small baking sheet.

First of all prepare the filling. To do this, first wash the lentils, then place them in a small saucepan with a generous pinch of salt and cover with water. Let them come to the boil, then simmer very gently, covered, for 40-45 minutes, or until they are tender.

Meanwhile, heat the oil in a medium-sized frying pan and add the shallot and carrot and cook for 5 minutes, then add the garlic and red pepper, mixing everything together thoroughly and cook for a further 5 minutes or until all the vegetables are softened. Remove from the heat and stir in the peeled tomato, tomato purée and the sun-blush (or mi-cuit) tomatoes.

Next, drain the lentils and tip them into a mixing bowl, then add the vegetable mixture and stir to combine everything thoroughly, then leave the filling to cool a little.

Now mix the eggs, mace, cayenne, thyme, parsley and sage into the mixture and season generously with salt and freshly milled black pepper.

Now pre-heat the oven to gas mark 4, 350°F, (180°C). For the pastry, put the milk and 2 fl oz (55 ml) water into a small saucepan and add the vegetable fat, cut up into small pieces. Place the pan over a gentle heat and simmer until the fat has dissolved. Sift the flour, mustard, mixed spice, sea salt and nutmeg into a large mixing bowl, and mix in 1 of the egg yolks so that it is evenly distributed. When the fat has completely melted in the liquid, turn up the heat to bring it just up to the boil, and pour it on to the dry ingredients and, using a wooden spoon, mix everything together.

Then turn the dough out on to a lightly floured work surface and bring it together with your hands to make a ball. You have to work quickly now, as it's important that the

pies go into the tin whilst this dough is still warm. Take two-thirds of the dough and cut this up into 6 equal parts. Roll each of these into a ball and put 1 into each of the holes in the tin. Using your thumb, quickly press each ball flat on to the base and then up to the top edge. Press the pastry over the rim of the top edge, it should overlap by at least ¼ inch (5 mm).

Using a teaspoon, divide the filling between the 6 pies. It will be quite sloppy at this stage, but don't worry, that is normal. Then roll out the remaining pastry and cut out six 3¼ inch (8 cm) rounds; the pastry will be quite thin, so you may need to sprinkle the work surface with a little extra flour. Next, using a pastry brush, paint some of the second egg yolk round the upper edge of the pies and gently press on the lids. Using a small fork, press the rim of each lid against the top of the pie case, make a hole in the top of each pie and glaze with the rest of the yolk.

Now place the muffin tin on the baking sheet and bake the pies for 30 minutes on the middle shelf. After this time, carefully and using oven gloves or a thick cloth, remove the hot pies from the tin and place them directly on to the hot baking sheet; this will make the sides and base crispy.

Bake for a further 20-25 minutes or until the sides and base of the pies are crispy, then leave them to cool on a wire rack ■

Above: 'Not Pork' Pies

Hummus bi Tahina

Hummus bi Tahina
Serves 4

Mashed Black-eyed Beancakes with Ginger Onion Marmalade
Serves 4

Yes, I do know hummus is sold absolutely everywhere but let me tell you, this home-made version is way above anything you will have bought.

4 oz (110 g) dried chickpeas, pre-soaked, then drained and the water discarded

5 fl oz (150 ml) tahina paste

juice 2 lemons

2 fat cloves garlic, peeled

4 tablespoons olive oil, plus a little extra for drizzling

cayenne pepper

black olives, Greek-style pickled chillies, and pitta breads, to serve

salt

To begin with, put the drained chickpeas in a medium-sized saucepan, cover them with fresh water and bring them to the boil, along with a pinch of salt. Then reduce the heat to low, cover and simmer gently for 1½-2 hours, or until they are tender.

Then, drain them, reserving the cooking liquid, and put them into a blender, together with the lemon juice, garlic, olive oil and 5 fl oz (150 ml) of the cooking liquid. Switch on and blend, adding the tahina paste to the mixture as the blades revolve, stopping the blender every now and then to push the mixture down into the goblet. The consistency should be something like mayonnaise so, if you think it's too thick, add a little more of the cooking liquid. Then season to taste with cayenne pepper and salt.

Now place the hummus in a serving bowl and drizzle with olive oil. Serve with olives, pickled chillies and warm pitta breads ▪

Black-eyed beans are the lovely nutty beans popular in recipes from the deep south of America and, with the addition of other vegetables, they make very good beancakes. Fried crisp and crunchy on the outside and served with delectable ginger onion marmalade, this makes a splendid main course. The marmalade is not only a wonderful accompaniment but is great as a relish for all kinds of other dishes. It can be served warm – or I think it's quite nice cold with the hot beancakes.

4 oz (110 g) black-eyed beans

4 oz (110 g) green-brown lentils

1 bay leaf

5-6 tablespoons olive oil

1 red onion, peeled and finely chopped

1 medium carrot, finely chopped

1 small red pepper, deseeded and finely chopped

1 green chilli, deseeded and finely chopped

1 clove garlic, peeled and chopped

¼ teaspoon ground mace

1 teaspoon chopped fresh thyme, plus 2 sprigs

1 tablespoon sun-dried tomato paste

2 tablespoons wholemeal flour

watercress sprigs, to garnish

salt and freshly milled black pepper

For the ginger onion marmalade:

1 rounded dessertspoon freshly grated ginger

12 oz (350 g) onions

2 tablespoons olive oil

3 rosemary sprigs

8 fl oz (225 ml) dry white wine

3 tablespoons white wine vinegar

2 tablespoons dark soft brown sugar

salt and freshly milled black pepper

First of all, the black-eyed beans need soaking – this can be done by covering them with twice their volume of cold water and leaving them overnight or, alternatively, bringing them up to the boil, boiling for 10 minutes and then leaving to soak for 2 hours. The green lentils won't need soaking.

To make the marmalade, peel and slice the onions into ¼ inch (5 mm) rings (slice any really large outer rings in half). Then take a solid, medium-sized saucepan and heat the olive oil. When it's hot, add the onions and the rosemary, stir well, and toss the onions around till they're golden and tinged brown at the edges (about 10 minutes).

After that, pour in the white wine and white wine vinegar, followed by the brown sugar and the grated ginger, stir and bring everything up to simmering point. Add salt and pepper, then turn the heat down to low again and let everything simmer very gently for 1¼ hours or until all the liquid has almost disappeared. Then remove the rosemary and pour everything into a serving bowl.

To make the beancakes, once the soaking is done, take a medium-sized saucepan, add the drained beans, and the lentils, then pour in 1 pint (570 ml) water, add the bay leaf and sprigs of thyme, then bring everything up to a gentle simmer and let them cook for about 40-45 minutes, by which time all the water should have been absorbed and the beans and lentils will be completely soft. If there's any liquid still left, drain them in a colander. Remove the bay leaf and thyme sprigs.

Now you need to mash them to a pulp and you can do this using a fork, potato masher or electric hand whisk. After that, give them a really good seasoning with salt and freshly milled black pepper and put a clean tea cloth over them to stop them becoming dry. Now

take a really large frying pan, add 1 tablespoon of olive oil, then heat it over a medium heat and add the onion, carrot, pepper, chilli and garlic. Sauté them all together for about 6 minutes, moving them around the pan to soften and turn golden brown at the edges.

After that, mix all the vegetables into the mashed bean and lentil mixture, add the mace and chopped thyme and tomato paste, then dampen your hands and form the mixture into 12 round cakes, measuring approximately 2½-3 inches (6-7.5 cm) in diameter. Then place them on a plate or a lightly oiled tray, cover with clingfilm and keep them in the fridge until needed, but for 1 hour minimum.

When you're ready to serve the beancakes, coat them lightly with wholemeal flour seasoned with salt and freshly milled black pepper, then heat 2 tablespoons of olive oil. When it is really hot, reduce the heat to medium and fry the beancakes in 2 batches for 3 minutes on each side until they're crisp and golden, adding more oil, if needed.

Drain them on kitchen paper and serve, garnished with sprigs of watercress and the ginger onion marmalade ▪

Roasted Vegetable Biryani with Toasted Cashews
Serves 4-6

This is a fragrant, spicy dish of rice, layered with roasted vegetables in a rich tomato sauce, and is based on a recipe which was kindly given to me by my friend Pami Dhanani.

For the vegetables:

10 fl oz (275 ml) white basmati rice, to be cooked following the Perfect Rice recipe on page 122

4 oz (110 g) aubergine

4 oz (110 g) peeled potato

4 oz (110 g) peeled carrots

4 oz (110 g) small cauliflower florets

4 oz (110 g) fine green beans, halved

4-5 oz (110-150 g) fresh sweetcorn, off the cob (about 1 cob)

2 oz (50 g) unsalted cashew nuts

2 tablespoons groundnut or olive oil

1 green pepper, deseeded and thinly sliced

1 medium ripe tomato, thinly sliced

For the sauce:

1 oz (25 g) butter

1 teaspoon groundnut or olive oil

8 black peppercorns

4 cloves

2 cardamom pods, seeds removed

1 tablespoon each of poppy, fennel coriander and cumin seeds

2 tablespoons desiccated (or fresh grated) coconut (see page 225)

2 medium onions, peeled and chopped

1 x 14 oz (400 g) tin chopped tomatoes

3 cloves garlic, peeled and finely chopped

2 inch (5 cm) piece of fresh root ginger, peeled and finely chopped

1 green chilli, deseeded and finely chopped

10 curry (or mint) leaves, chopped

2 inch (5 cm) cinnamon stick

1 teaspoon sugar

1 teaspoon salt

You will also need a baking tray measuring 14 x 10 inches (35 x 25.5 cm) and a serving dish measuring 8 x 8 inches (20 x 20 cm), 2 inches (5 cm) deep.

Begin by making the sauce. Heat half the butter and all the oil in a medium-sized frying pan. Add the peppercorns, cloves, cardamom, poppy, fennel, coriander and cumin seeds and the coconut. Fry over a low heat for 2-3 minutes, stirring, then tip them into a pestle and mortar. When they have cooled a little, grind to a rough paste. Next, heat the remaining butter in the pan and cook the onions for 8-10 minutes. Now stir in the tomatoes, garlic, ginger, chilli, curry (or mint) leaves, cinnamon stick and sugar and gently cook for 4-5 minutes, stirring now and then. Then take the pan off the heat, remove the cinnamon stick and purée the ingredients in a blender. Next, add the curry paste and the teaspoon of salt and whiz the sauce again until the ingredients are combined, then transfer them to a large mixing bowl. Pre-heat the oven to gas mark 4, 350°F (180°C). Now put the cashews on the baking tray and toast in the oven for 10 minutes or until golden.

Meanwhile, chop the aubergine, potato and carrots into 1 inch (2.5 cm) chunks. Put the cashews to one side, and scatter the aubergine, potatoes, carrots, cauliflower and beans on the tray. Lightly brush vegetables with the oil, then roast them in the oven for 25 minutes. Now cook the rice. After the 25 minutes, scatter the sweetcorn over the vegetables and return them all to the oven for 5 minutes. (Pop the serving dish in to pre-heat, too.) Now toss the vegetables in the sauce till they are coated. Then spread half the rice in the serving dish, spoon the vegetables and sauce on top, and finally, cover with the remaining rice. Garnish with the cashews, pepper and tomato ■

Stuffed Yellow Peppers with Pilau Rice, Currants and Toasted Pine Nuts
Serves 6

The beauty of these peppers is that they can be made well in advance, then warmed through and filled with the pilau rice just before serving.

For the roasted peppers:

3 large yellow peppers

1 clove garlic, peeled and chopped

4-5 tablespoons olive oil

salt and freshly milled black pepper

For the pilau rice:

10 fl oz (275 ml) basmati rice (use a measuring jug)

2 oz (50 g) currants

2 oz (50 g) pine nuts

1½ tablespoons olive oil

1 medium onion, peeled and finely chopped

1 cinnamon stick, halved

1 clove garlic, peeled and crushed

1 pint (570 ml) of hot stock made with Marigold Swiss vegetable bouillon powder

6 sprigs fresh mint, to garnish

salt

You will also need a baking tray measuring 14 x 10 inches (35 x 25.5 cm), greased, and a medium-sized, lidded frying pan.

Pre-heat the oven to gas mark 4, 350°F (180°C).

All you do is cut the peppers in half lengthways through the stalk, then scrape out the seeds and place the halves on the baking tray. Now sprinkle a little of the garlic into each one and follow that with a teaspoon of oil. Brush a little more oil around the edges of the peppers, add a seasoning of salt and freshly milled black pepper, then bake them on a high shelf in the oven for 50-60 minutes, or until they are well browned at the edges.

Meanwhile, prepare the rice. Heat the 1½ tablespoons of oil in the frying pan over a medium heat. Add the onions and pine nuts and fry for 10 minutes, or until everything is golden. Then add the currants, cinnamon and garlic. Stir the rice into the pan and turn the grains over until they are thoroughly coated in the oil. Then pour in the hot stock and season with salt. Stir once only, then put the lid on, turn the heat down to its lowest setting and let the rice cook for exactly 15 minutes. After that, take the pan off the heat, remove the lid and cover the pan with a clean tea cloth until the rice is needed.

When the peppers are cooked, transfer them to a warmed dish and fill each one with the rice, adding the mint at the last moment. Serve the remaining rice in a warmed bowl to accompany the peppers ■

Right: Stuffed Yellow Peppers with Pilau Rice, Currants
and Toasted Pine Nuts. Top left: Perfect Rice.

Chapter Seven
Food for
Friends

Vegetarian Moussaka with Ricotta Topping
Serves 4-6

This Greek-style moussaka tastes every bit as good as the meat version. Serve it with a crunchy salad and some warm pitta bread.

2 aubergines, each 8 oz (225 g)
10 fl oz (275 ml) hot stock
made with Marigold Swiss vegetable
bouillon powder
2 oz (50 g) Puy lentils
2 oz (50 g) green-brown lentils
4 tablespoons olive oil
2 medium onions, peeled and finely
chopped
1 large red pepper, deseeded and
chopped into ¼ inch (5 mm) dice
2 cloves garlic, peeled and crushed
1 x 14 oz (400 g) tin chopped tomatoes,
drained
7 fl oz (200 ml) red wine
2 tablespoons tomato purée
or sun-dried tomato paste
1 teaspoon ground cinnamon
2 tablespoons chopped fresh parsley
sea salt and freshly milled black pepper

For the topping:
9 oz (250 g) ricotta
10 fl oz (275 ml) whole milk
1 oz (25 g) plain flour
1 oz (25 g) butter
¼ whole nutmeg, grated
1 large egg, beaten
1 oz (25 g) parmesan, freshly grated
salt and freshly milled black pepper

You will also need a shallow dish, about
9 x 9 x 2½ inches (23 x 23 x 6 cm) deep.

Pre-heat the oven to gas mark 4, 350°F (180°C).

Begin by preparing the aubergines: to do this cut them into ½ inch (1 cm) dice, leaving the skins on. Place them in a colander, sprinkling with salt between each layer, then put a small plate with a heavy weight on top – this will draw out any excess juices. Now pour the stock into a saucepan, together with the Puy lentils, cover and simmer for 15 minutes before adding the green lentils. Cover again and cook for a further 15 minutes or until all the lentils are soft.

Meanwhile, heat 2 tablespoons of oil in a large solid frying pan and fry the onions until they're soft and tinged brown at the edges (about 5 minutes), then add the chopped pepper and soften and brown that, too, for about another 4 minutes. Next, add the garlic, cook for 1 minute more, then transfer the whole lot to a plate. Now transfer the aubergines to a clean tea cloth to squeeze them dry, then add a further 2 tablespoons of oil to the frying pan, turn the heat up to high and toss the aubergines in it so they get evenly cooked. When they're starting to brown a little, add the drained tomatoes and the onion and pepper mixture to the pan.

Then in a bowl mix the wine, tomato purée and cinnamon together and pour it over the vegetables. Add the lentils and the chopped parsley, season well and let everything simmer gently while you make the topping. All you do is place the milk, flour, butter and nutmeg in a saucepan and, using a balloon whisk, whisk until it comes to simmering point and becomes a smooth sauce. Season with salt and pepper, remove it from the heat and let it cool a little before whisking in the ricotta, followed by the egg. Finally, transfer the vegetable and lentil mixture to the dish and spoon the cheese sauce over the top, taking it right up to the edges. Sprinkle with the parmesan and transfer the dish to the pre-heated oven to bake on the middle shelf for 1 hour. Then allow the moussaka to rest for 15 minutes before serving ■

Thick Onion Tart
Serves 4-6

The secret of this tart, with its wholemeal cheese pastry, is to cook the onions until they almost caramelise, so they form a lovely thick, brown layer over the base.

For the pastry:
2 oz (50 g) self-raising flour
2 oz (50 g) wholemeal flour
pinch salt
½ teaspoon mustard powder
2 oz (50 g) butter
1½ oz (40 g) Cheddar, grated

For the filling:
1½ lb (700 g) onions, peeled
and chopped fairly small
2 oz (50 g) butter
2 large eggs, beaten
4 fl oz (110 ml) double cream,
natural yoghurt or milk
1 tablespoon grated Cheddar
salt and freshly milled black pepper

You will also need a 7½ inch (19 cm)
diameter fluted quiche tin with
a removable base, 1¼ inches (3 cm)
deep, lightly buttered, and a small,
solid baking sheet.

Pre-heat the oven, and the baking sheet, to gas mark 4, 350°F (180°C).

First, make the pastry by sifting the flours, salt and mustard powder into a mixing bowl, then rubbing in the fat until the mixture becomes crumbly. Then stir in the grated cheese and add enough cold water to make a dough that leaves the bowl clean (about 1-2 tablespoons). Wrap the dough in a polythene bag and leave to rest in the fridge for half an hour.

Meanwhile, you can be preparing the filling. Melt the butter in a large, heavy-based saucepan, then add the chopped onions, stir to get them well coated in the butter, and cook them, uncovered, over a medium heat for about half an hour until they have reduced and turned a deep brown. Give them a stir from time to time to prevent them catching on the bottom of the pan and, if at the end of the time, they haven't turned almost mahogany brown, turn the heat up and cook for a further 10 minutes.

Then roll out the pastry to line the tart tin, prick the base with a fork, place it on the pre-heated baking sheet, and bake in the centre of the oven for 15 minutes. After that, remove from the oven and brush the inside of the pastry case with a little beaten egg (from the filling ingredients), and return to the oven for another 5 minutes.

Next, spread the onions all over the base of the tart, whisk the beaten eggs together with the cream and some seasoning, and slowly pour half the egg and cream mixture in, allowing the liquid to settle between each addition. Then place the baking sheet in the oven, gradually add the remainder of the filling (depending on how much the onions have reduced – there may be a tiny spot left over).

Finally, sprinkle the cheese over the top, and bake for 30 minutes or till the filling is puffy and golden brown ■

Thick Onion Tart

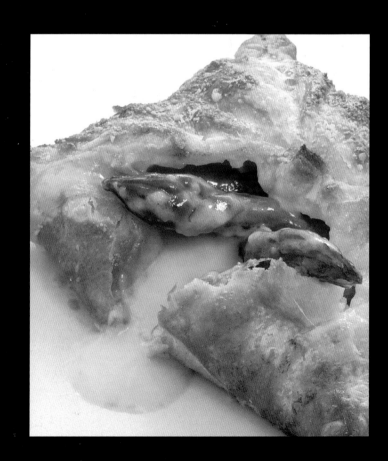

Above: Asparagus and Gruyère Feuilletés

Asparagus and Gruyère Feuilletés
Serves 6

In this recipe, asparagus is encased in very thin, crisp parcels of puff pastry with melted cheese. A lovely main course for a summer's lunch or supper party or you could make 8 smaller ones for a first course.

For the filling:

12 oz (350 g) fresh asparagus

6 oz (175 g) Gruyère or Emmental, in one piece

3 tablespoons freshly grated parmesan, plus a little extra, to sprinkle

7 fl oz (200 ml) crème fraîche

a few sprigs of watercress, to garnish

salt and freshly milled black pepper

For the pastry:

1 x 375 g pack fresh, ready-rolled puff pastry

flour for dusting

2 large egg yolks, beaten with a tablespoon of milk

You will also need a large baking tray measuring 16 x 12 inches (40 x 30 cm), lightly oiled.

First, remove the pastry from the fridge and let it come to room temperature (about 10 minutes). Meanwhile, wash the asparagus in cold water, then take each stalk in both hands and bend and snap off the woody end. Then arrange the stalks in an opened fan steamer. Place the steamer in a frying pan or saucepan, pour in about 1 inch (2.5 cm) of boiling water from the kettle, then add some salt, put a lid on and steam for 2-3 minutes or until the stalks feel just tender when tested with a skewer.

After that, remove them from the steamer and allow them to cool. Then dry the stalks with kitchen paper and cut each one into 3, on the diagonal. Next, using a small sharp knife, remove the rind from the Gruyère

(or Emmental) and cut it into ½ inch (1 cm) cubes. Then, in a small bowl, mix the parmesan, crème fraîche and add some salt and freshly milled black pepper.

Now, carefully unroll the sheet of pastry on to a lightly floured work surface and cut it into 3 widthways. Roll out one-third until it measures 7 x 14 inches (18 x 35 cm) and then cut that into two 7 x 7 inch (18 x 18 cm) squares. Then repeat the rolling and cutting with the other 2 pieces of pastry so you end up with 6 squares in all.

Next, you need to carefully brush the edges of 3 of the pastry squares with some of the beaten egg yolk and milk. Then divide half of the crème fraîche filling between the 3 pieces of pastry, about a tablespoon into the centre of each square. Next, lay about half the quantity of asparagus on top of the crème fraîche and several cubes of cheese tucked in between. Now pull up the opposite corners of each square to meet in the centre like an envelope.

Carefully pinch the seams together to seal them and make a small hole in the centre of each one to allow the steam to escape. Then, using a fish slice, transfer the parcels to the baking tray and now make the other 3.

Cover the parcels on the baking sheet with clingfilm and chill until you are ready to cook them. To do that, pre-heat the oven to gas mark 6, 400°F (200°C). Then, brush each one with some of the remaining beaten egg mix and lightly sprinkle each one with some parmesan. Bake on a high shelf for 20-25 minutes or until they are golden brown and serve them straight from the oven, garnished with a few sprigs of watercress ■

Frying-pan Pizza with Mozzarella and Sun-dried Tomatoes
Serves 2 or 4 as a starter

This is the easiest home-made pizza in the world. It's made with a scone dough which, happily, does not require proving. The topping can, of course, be varied to include whatever you like best, but the combination below is, I think, one of the nicest. If you don't have time to make up the tomato sauce, you can substitute 4 tablespoons of tomato purée.

For the tomato sauce:

1 tablespoon olive oil

1 small onion, peeled and chopped

1 medium clove garlic, peeled and crushed

1 lb (450 g) ripe tomatoes, skinned and chopped

1 dessertspoon chopped fresh basil

salt and freshly milled black pepper

For the base:

8 oz (225 g) self-raising flour, plus a little extra for dusting

½ teaspoon salt

1 tablespoon chopped fresh herbs

4 tablespoons olive oil

freshly milled black pepper

For the topping:

5 oz (150 g) plain or smoked mozzarella, cut into 1 inch (2.5 cm) pieces

4 oz (110 g) sun-dried tomatoes preserved in oil, drained (reserving 2 tablespoons of the oil), and chopped

12 black olives, pitted and sliced

2 oz (50 g) mushrooms, sliced

2 tablespoons capers, drained

2 tablespoons torn fresh basil leaves

salt and freshly milled black pepper

You will also need a frying pan with a 9-10 inch (23-25 cm) base.

First, make up the tomato sauce by heating the olive oil in a small saucepan, adding the onion and garlic and cooking for 2-3 minutes to soften. Then add the chopped tomatoes and basil, season with salt and pepper, and continue to cook over a medium heat for 20-25 minutes until the tomatoes have reduced and concentrated their flavour. (While you're at it, why not make a larger quantity of this – it freezes very well!) Now for the pizza base: sift the flour into a bowl, along with the salt and some pepper and add the herbs. Make a well in the centre and pour in 2 tablespoons of the olive oil, followed by 4 tablespoons of water. Now mix to a soft (though not sticky) dough – you may find that you have to add a further tablespoon or so of water to get the right consistency.

Next, prepare a floured surface, turn the dough out on to it and knead lightly before rolling out to a round to fit the base of the frying pan. Heat 1 tablespoon of the remaining olive oil in the pan, place the circle of dough in it and cook over a low heat for about 5 minutes, or until the base is lightly browned. Have ready an oiled plate and turn the pizza base out on to it. Then, after heating the remaining olive oil in the pan, slide the pizza back in and cook the reverse side for 5 minutes.

During this time, spread the reduced tomato sauce over the surface of the pizza, then scatter over the pieces of mozzarella, the sun-dried tomatoes, olives, mushrooms, capers and torn basil leaves. Season, then drizzle the oil from the preserved tomatoes over the top. To see if the underside of the pizza is cooked, you can lift up an edge with a palette knife and have a look. When it's ready, transfer the pan to a pre-heated grill for 2-3 minutes to melt the cheese and heat the topping. Serve straightaway ■

Cheese and Parsnip Roulade with Sage and Onion Stuffing
Serves 4

This recipe was originally written in response to a letter I received from a vegetarian who asked if I could devise something that had stuffing, sauce and all the trimmings – so that he could feel as festive as everyone else on Christmas Day.

For the roulade:

4 oz (110 g) Sage Derby
or Lancashire cheese, grated

1½ oz (40 g) butter

1 oz (25 g) plain flour

10 fl oz (275 ml) cold milk

3 large eggs, separated

1½ oz (40 g) hazelnuts, toasted and chopped

1 tablespoon grated parmesan for dusting

salt and freshly milled pepper

For the stuffing:

1 teaspoon chopped fresh sage

8 oz (225 g) onions, peeled and chopped

1½ oz (40 g) butter

1 tablespoon chopped fresh parsley

3 oz (75 g) white breadcrumbs

salt and freshly milled black pepper

For the filling:

12 oz (350 g) parsnips (prepared weight)

1 oz (25 g) butter

2 tablespoons double cream

freshly grated nutmeg

salt and freshly milled black pepper

You will also need a Swiss-roll tin 13 x 9 inches (32 x 23 cm), lined with baking parchment.

Pre-heat the oven to gas mark 6, 400°F (200°C).

First, make up the stuffing by melting the butter in a small, heavy-based saucepan, then add the onions and cook them for about 6 minutes or until they are transparent. Next,

add the herbs, breadcrumbs and seasoning, stirring well to combine everything, then sprinkle the mixture evenly over the lined tin.

Now for the roulade: place the butter, flour and milk in a saucepan and whisk them together over a medium heat until thickened, then season with salt and pepper and leave the sauce to cook over a gentle heat for 3 minutes. Then draw the pan off the heat to cool slightly. Next, add the egg yolks, whisking them in. Now add the grated cheese and taste to check the seasoning. In a large bowl (and with a spanking clean whisk), beat the egg whites until they form soft peaks. Gently fold one spoonful of the egg whites into the cheese mixture, to loosen it. Then spoon this mixture, a little at a time, into the rest of the egg white. Now spread the whole lot evenly into the tin over the stuffing mixture, and bake on the top shelf of the oven for 20-25 minutes or until it feels springy and firm in the centre.

Meanwhile, cook the parsnips in a steamer for 10-15 minutes until they're soft, then cream them, together with the butter, double cream and a seasoning of nutmeg, salt and pepper (this can be done by hand or in a food processor). When they're ready, keep them warm while you lay a sheet of baking parchment, slightly longer than the roulade, on a work surface and sprinkle the hazelnuts all over it.

When the roulade is cooked, turn it out on to the hazelnuts and carefully peel off the base paper. Spread the creamed parsnip evenly all over the sage and onion stuffing. Then roll up the roulade along the longest side, using the paper underneath to help you pull it into a round (it's not difficult, it behaves very well). Transfer the roulade to a serving plate and dust with the grated parmesan ■

Toasted Hazelnut and Vegetable Burgers with Sweet Pepper and Coriander Relish
Serves 4

These burgers, made with hazelnuts and vegetables, are simple, honest and quite delicious. The relish is made in moments and you won't believe how good it tastes.

3 oz (75 g) hazelnuts

2 medium carrots, peeled and grated

2 celery stalks, finely chopped

1 medium onion, peeled and finely chopped

2 tablespoons finely chopped cabbage

½ oz/10 g (2 tablespoons) fresh breadcrumbs

1 teaspoon chopped fresh parsley

a couple of pinches of cayenne pepper

pinch ground mace

1 large egg

1 tablespoon tomato purée

1 tablespoon natural yoghurt

salt and freshly milled black pepper

For the coating:

1 large egg, lightly beaten

3 oz (75 g) fresh breadcrumbs

For the sweet pepper and coriander relish:

1 small fresh green chilli

1 small red pepper, deseeded

½ small red onion, peeled

2 tablespoons chopped fresh coriander

2 tablespoons fresh lime juice (1 lime)

1 large tomato, skinned, deseeded and chopped

You will also need a baking sheet measuring 14 x 10 inches (35 x 25.5 cm), greased.

Pre-heat the oven to gas mark 6, 400°F (200°C).

You need to start by making the burgers which are quite simple to make, once you've done the chopping and grating. First of all,

spread the hazelnuts out on a small baking tray and toast them in the oven for 5-6 minutes, using a timer. After that, turn the oven off and allow the nuts to cool, then whiz them in a food processor until they are ground to a powder.

Next, put the ground hazelnuts in a mixing bowl with the grated and chopped vegetables, the breadcrumbs, parsley, cayenne and mace and mix well. In another small bowl, place the egg, tomato purée and yoghurt and whisk together, then add this mixture to the vegetable mixture. Season to taste with salt and freshly milled black pepper and give everything another mix.

Next, form the mixture into 8 small patties. Place them on some kitchen paper on a plate and chill, uncovered, for a few hours in the fridge. This will help to firm up the burgers and prevent them breaking during cooking.

Meanwhile, place all the ingredients for the sweet pepper and coriander relish in a food processor and switch on to blend evenly to the stage where it looks as though everything has been chopped minutely small but hasn't lost its identity. Leave on one side (covered) in a cool place.

Shortly before you are ready to cook the burgers, pre-heat the oven to gas mark 4, 350°F (180°C). Now dip each one into the beaten egg first, then into the breadcrumbs, and place on the baking sheet. Bake for 15 minutes, then turn the burgers over with care and bake for a further 15 minutes. Stir the relish well before serving and serve it with the burgers ■

Top left: Quattro Formaggio (four cheese) Pizza
Left and top right: Pizza dough

Quattro Formaggio (four cheese) Pizza

Serves 2 (makes one
10 inch/25.5 cm pizza)

This is the classic version of one of the most wonderful combinations of bread and cheese imaginable.

For the pizza base:

6 oz (175 g) plain flour

1 teaspoon salt

1 teaspoon easy-blend dried yeast

½ teaspoon golden caster sugar

1 tablespoon olive oil

2-3 tablespoons polenta (cornmeal) to roll out, plus a little extra for dusting

For the topping:

2½ oz (60 g) ricotta

2 oz (50 g) mozzarella, cut into 1 inch (2.5 cm) slices

2 oz (50 g) Gorgonzola Piccante, Shropshire Blue or Cashel Blue, cut into 1 inch (2.5 cm) slices

1 oz (25 g) parmesan, grated

You will also need a pizza stone or solid baking sheet measuring 14 x 10 inches (35 x 25.5 cm).

Pre-heat the oven to its lowest setting.

Begin by warming the flour slightly in the oven for about 10 minutes, then turn the oven off. Sift the flour, salt, yeast and sugar into a bowl and make a well in the centre of the mixture, then add the olive oil and pour in 4 fl oz (120 ml) hand-hot water.

Now mix to a dough, starting off with a wooden spoon and using your hands in the final stages of mixing. Wipe the bowl clean with the dough, adding a spot more water if there are any dry bits left, and transfer it to a flat work surface (there shouldn't be any need to flour this). Knead the dough for 3 minutes or until it develops a sheen and blisters under the surface (it should also be springy and elastic). You can now either

leave the dough on the surface covered by the upturned bowl or transfer the dough to a clean bowl and cover it with clingfilm that has been lightly oiled on the side that is facing the dough. Leave it until it looks as though it has doubled in bulk, which will be about an hour at room temperature.

Having made the dough and left it to rise, pre-heat the oven to gas mark 8, 450°F (230°C), along with the pizza stone or baking sheet. The next stage is to tip the dough back on to a work surface that has been sprinkled generously with polenta to prevent it from sticking. Knock all the air out of the dough and knead it for a couple of seconds to begin shaping it into a ball. Then dust your rolling pin with polenta and roll the dough out to a circle that is approximately 10 inches (25.5 cm) in diameter. Finish by stretching it out with your hands, working from the centre and using the flat of your fingers to push the dough out; it doesn't need to be a perfect round, but you want it to be a fairly thin-based pizza, with slightly raised edges.

Then, using a thick oven glove, very carefully lift the baking sheet or pizza stone out of the oven and sprinkle it with a little polenta (cornmeal). Now carefully lift the pizza dough on to the stone or baking sheet and quickly arrange teaspoonfuls of ricotta here and there all over. After that, scatter the mozzarella and Gorgonzola pieces (or other cheese) in between and, finally, scatter the parmesan over. Bake the whole thing on a high shelf for 10-12 minutes, until the crust is golden brown and the cheese is bubbling. You can lift the edge up slightly to check that the underneath is crisp and brown. Finally, carefully remove the baking sheet or pizza stone from the oven, again using a thick oven glove, and serve the pizza on hot plates straightaway ■

Wild Mushroom Stroganoff

Serves 4

Serve this wild mushroom stroganoff with some plain rice and a crisp green salad or some lightly buttered spinach.

2 lb (900 g) mixed fresh wild mushrooms or other mushrooms (such as flat, chestnut or shiitake), thickly sliced

½ oz (10 g) dried porcini mushrooms

10 fl oz (275 ml) dry white wine or Madeira

2 large onions, peeled

2-3 oz (50-75 g) butter

7 fl oz (200 ml) crème fraîche

freshly grated nutmeg

salt and freshly milled black pepper

You will also need a lidded, heavy-based frying pan, approximately 10 inches (25.5 cm) in diameter.

First of all, heat the wine (or Madeira) in a small saucepan until it just begins to bubble around the edges. Then remove it from the heat, add the porcini and leave it aside to soak. What you now need to do is to cut each onion in half, then each half needs to be sliced and the layers separated out into half-moon shapes.

Now melt 2 oz (50 g) of the butter in the frying pan and gently soften the onions for about 10 minutes or until they have turned golden brown. Then, with a draining spoon, remove them to a plate. Next, turn the heat up high, and add a third of the fresh mushrooms (you need to cook them in batches). Brown them and then transfer them to join the onions, adding a little extra butter if it is needed.

When all the mushrooms are browned, return the whole lot to the pan, along with the onions. Meanwhile, drain the porcini, reserving the liquid and chop them. Next, add the porcini to the pan with the wine

(or Madeira) and season with salt and freshly milled black pepper. Now bring it up to a gentle simmer, turn the heat to low, put a lid on and leave to cook gently for 30 minutes.

Next, taste to check the seasoning, remove the pan from the heat and stir in the crème fraîche with a few good gratings of fresh nutmeg. Re-heat, without allowing it to come back to the boil ■

Wild Mushrooms in Madeira En Croûte with Foaming Hollandaise
Serves 6

This recipe is ideal for entertaining; you can make the filling and pastry parcels the day before. Serve with Foaming Hollandaise, which can also be made ahead.

For the pastry:

1 lb 2 oz (500 g) ready-made puff pastry

1 large egg yolk, lightly beaten, to glaze

¾ oz (20 g) finely grated parmesan

a little flour, for dusting

For the filling:

¾ oz (20 g) dried porcini mushrooms

9 oz (250 g) of both chestnut mushrooms and oyster mushrooms, roughly chopped

5 fl oz (150 ml) dry (Secco) Madeira

1½ oz (40 g) butter

1 large onion, peeled and finely chopped

3 cloves garlic, peeled and crushed

1 rounded tablespoon plain flour

¾ teaspoon chopped fresh thyme

freshly grated nutmeg

3 fl oz (75 ml) double cream

a few sprigs watercress, to garnish

salt and freshly milled black pepper

To serve:

Foaming Hollandaise (see page 46)

You will also need 2 medium-sized, solid baking sheets, lightly oiled.

Begin by making the filling: put the dried mushrooms in a jug and cover them with 10 fl oz (275 ml) boiling water, then leave them to soak for 30 minutes.

To make the sauce, melt the butter in a large saucepan and soften the chopped onions and garlic in it till pale gold (about 5 minutes). Then stir in the flour, followed by all the fresh mushrooms, the soaked mushrooms (snipped a bit with a pair of scissors, if they're large) and their soaking water. Season with salt and pepper and add the thyme and a few good gratings of nutmeg. Now pour in the Madeira, cover the pan with a tight-fitting lid and let the mushrooms cook as slowly as possible for 1½ hours: the liquid should barely simmer, and you should check and stir it from time to time to make sure the liquid hasn't evaporated. Now divide the pastry in half and on a lightly floured surface, roll one half into a 5 x 15 inch (13 x 39 cm) square, about ¾ inch (2 cm) thick, then cut this into three 5 x 5 inch (13 x 13 cm) squares. Repeat with the remaining pastry, so you end up with 6 squares. Then transfer 3 to each baking sheet and brush each one with egg yolk. Next, using a sharp knife, carefully score a line all the way around the inside of each square, about ¾ inches (2 cm) in from the edge, being careful not to cut all the way through. Now sprinkle each one with parmesan and transfer the sheets to the fridge to allow the pastry to rest for 30 minutes. Pre-heat the oven to gas mark 7, 425°F (220°C).

Bake the pastry on a high shelf of the oven for 12-14 minutes or until golden brown and crisp. Then remove from the oven and transfer the squares to a wire cooling rack. Using a small sharp knife, cut around the scored line on each square and remove the lids. If there is any uncooked pastry in the centre, scrape it out. Then leave the pastry cases and lids to cool. To serve, warm the pastry in a low oven and re-heat the hollandaise over a saucepan of barely simmering water. Stir the cream into the mushrooms and re-heat them. Put each parcel on to a warm plate and fill with mushrooms. Replace the lids and spoon a little hollandaise over each one; serve the rest separately in a warm jug. Garnish with watercress and serve straightaway ■

Caramelised Balsamic and Red Onion Tarts with Goats' Cheese
Makes 8

The long, slow cooking of red onions and balsamic vinegar gives a lovely sweet, concentrated, caramel consistency. These are then spooned into crispy cheese-pastry cases and topped with goats' cheese and sage. Serve with some balsamic-dressed salad leaves.

For the pastry:

3 oz (75 g) butter, at room temperature

6 oz (175 g) plain flour, plus a little extra for rolling

2 oz (50 g) mature Cheddar, finely grated

½ teaspoon mustard powder

pinch cayenne pepper

1 large egg, beaten, for brushing

For the filling:

6 tablespoons balsamic vinegar

2 lb (900 g) red onions, peeled and very finely sliced

2 x 4 oz (110 g) soft-rind goats' cheeses, top and bottom rinds removed and discarded, each sliced into 4 rounds

1 oz (25 g) butter

1 dessertspoon chopped fresh sage, plus 8 sage leaves for topping

a little olive oil

cayenne pepper for sprinkling

salt and freshly milled black pepper

You will also need eight ¾ inch (2 cm) deep, mini quiche tins with a base diameter of 4¼ inches (11 cm), greased, and a 6 inch (15 cm) cutter or plate to cut around.

Pre-heat the oven to gas mark 4, 350°F (180°C).

First, make the pastry by rubbing the butter lightly into the flour, then add the cheese, mustard and cayenne, plus just enough cold water to make a smooth dough – 1-2 tablespoons. Then place the dough in a polythene bag to rest in the fridge for 20 minutes. After that, roll it out as thinly as possible and use the cutter or plate as a guide to cut out 8 rounds. Line the greased quiche tins with the pastry and lightly prick the bases with a fork, then place on a baking sheet and cook on the centre shelf of the oven for 15-20 minutes, or until the pastry is cooked through but not coloured. Then allow the pastry cases to cool on a wire rack. (They can be made ahead and stored in an airtight container until needed.)

To make the filling, melt the butter in a heavy-based, medium-sized saucepan, stir in the onions, balsamic vinegar and chopped sage, season and let everything cook very gently, without a lid, stirring often, for about 30 minutes, until the mixture has reduced down, taken on a lovely glazed appearance and all the excess liquid has evaporated. Then let the mixture cool until you are ready to fill the tarts.

To finish the tarts, brush a little beaten egg over each pastry case and pop them back into the oven – same temperature as before – for 5 minutes: this helps to provide a seal for the pastry and stops it from becoming soggy. Now spoon the onion mixture into the cases and top each one with a slice of goats' cheese and a sage leaf that has first been dipped in the olive oil. Finally, sprinkle with a little cayenne pepper and bake for 20 minutes ■

Caramelised Balsamic and Red Onion Tarts with Goats' Cheese

Vegetarian Shepherd's Pie with Goats' Cheese Mash

Vegetarian Shepherd's Pie with Goats' Cheese Mash
Serves 4

I really love this alternative version of shepherd's pie, with its diverse combination of dried pulses and fresh vegetables. It's extremely popular with vegetarian customers in our Norwich restaurant.

4 oz (110 g) dried black-eyed beans, pre-soaked overnight in cold water and drained

3 oz (75 g) green split peas (no need to soak), rinsed

3 oz (75 g) green lentils (no need to soak), rinsed

2 oz (50 g) peeled carrots

2 oz (50 g) peeled swede

2 oz (50 g) peeled celeriac

1 large onion, peeled

1 small green pepper, deseeded

2 oz (50 g) butter

1 heaped tablespoon chopped mixed fresh herbs (such as sage, rosemary, thyme and parsley)

¼ teaspoon ground mace

¼ teaspoon cayenne pepper

salt and freshly milled black pepper

For the topping:

4 oz (110 g) soft goats' cheese

1 lb 8 oz (700 g) potatoes, peeled

8 oz (225 g) tomatoes

2 oz (50 g) butter

2 tablespoons milk

1 oz (25 g) pecorino or parmesan, grated

salt and freshly milled black pepper

You will also need a steamer, and a round baking dish with a diameter of 9 inches (23 cm), 2 inches (5 cm) deep, buttered.

First, put the drained beans into a saucepan with the split peas and lentils. Add 1¼ pints (725 ml) boiling water and some salt, cover and simmer gently for 50-60 minutes, or until the pulses have absorbed the water

and are soft. Then remove them from the heat and mash them just a little with a large fork.

Now pre-heat the oven to gas mark 5, 375°F (190°C), and put the potatoes for the topping on to steam. Next, roughly chop all the vegetables for the filling, pile the whole lot into a food processor and process until chopped small. Next, melt the butter for the filling in a large frying pan over a medium heat, add the vegetables and cook gently for 10-15 minutes, stirring now and then until they're softened and tinged gold at the edges.

Meanwhile, skin the tomatoes for the topping. Place them in a heatproof bowl and pour boiling water on to them. After exactly a minute (or 15-30 seconds, if they are small), remove them (protecting your hands with a cloth if the tomatoes are hot), slip off their skins and slice them.

After that, add the vegetables to the pulses mixture, along with the herbs, spices, and salt and freshly milled black pepper to taste. Then spoon the mixture into the baking dish and arrange the tomatoes in overlapping slices on the top.

As soon as the potatoes are cooked, place them in a bowl, add the butter, milk and goats' cheese, and using an electric hand whisk, whisk to a smooth purée. Then season with salt and freshly milled black pepper and spread the potato over the rest of the ingredients in the dish.

Finally, sprinkle over the pecorino or parmesan and bake the pie on the top shelf of the oven for 20-25 minutes, or until the top is lightly browned. If you want to prepare this in advance, it will need about 40 minutes in the oven ■

Spinach Pasties
Makes 6

These are very easy to make and you can use either bought puff or home-made quick flaky pastry.

8 oz (225 g) bought puff pastry or quick flaky pastry, made with 6 oz (175 g) flour and 4 oz (110 g) butter (see page 37)

flour for dusting

1 egg, beaten, to glaze

For the filling:

1 lb (450 g) young leaf spinach

1 oz (25 g) soft butter

2 oz (50 g) cottage cheese, fromage frais or quark

1½ oz (40 g) parmesan, freshly grated

1 small clove garlic, peeled and finely crushed

¼ teaspoon dried dillweed

freshly grated nutmeg

lemon juice, to taste

salt and freshly milled black pepper

Pre-heat the oven to gas mark 7, 425°F (220°C).

You will also need a solid baking sheet measuring 11 x 16 inches (28 x 40 cm), lightly greased, and a 6 inch (15 cm) round pastry cutter or saucer of a similar size.

Begin by placing the spinach in a saucepan with a little salt. Put a lid on and place it over a medium heat. Just let it collapse down into its own juices, timing it for 2-3 minutes and turning if over halfway through. Drain the spinach in a colander, pressing it with a saucer to extract every last bit of juice – you should end up with about 8 oz (225 g) of cooked spinach.

After that transfer the spinach to a mixing bowl and beat in the butter, cheeses, garlic and the dillweed. Season with nutmeg, salt and freshly milled black pepper and add

a little lemon juice, then leave the mixture to cool. On a lightly floured surface, roll out the pastry fairly thinly, then using the cutter or a saucer to cut around, cut out 6 rounds that are 6 inches (15 cm) in diameter. It will be necessary to re-roll the pastry scraps to get 6 rounds. Then put about a tablespoon of the cooled spinach mixture on one half of each pastry circle.

Brush the pastry edges with beaten egg, then bring one half of a pastry circle over to cover the spinach filling on the other half, pressing the edges together to seal well and form the pasty. Repeat this with the other 5 circles. Glaze with beaten egg, then place the 6 pasties on the greased baking sheet.

Make a small ventilation hole in the centre of each one and bake on the second shelf from the top of the oven for about 15 minutes or until the pasties have risen and are golden brown ■

Twice-baked Goats' Cheese Soufflés with Chives
Serves 4

These can be made two or three days in advance (or even weeks if you want to freeze them). All you then do is turn them out and bake them 25 minutes before you need them. Serve with a rocket leaf salad.

4 oz (110 g) peppered (or other) goats' cheese, cut into ¼ inch (5 mm) cubes
1 dessertspoon chopped fresh chives
8 fl oz (225 ml) milk
1 small onion, peeled and cut in half
1 bay leaf
a grating of fresh nutmeg
a few whole black peppercorns
1 oz (25 g) unsalted butter
1 oz (25 g) self-raising flour
2 large eggs, separated
freshly grated parmesan, to serve
salt

You will also need four ramekins, 3 inches (7.5 cm) across and 1½ inches (4 cm) deep, well buttered, a small roasting tin and a solid baking sheet.

Pre-heat the oven to gas mark 4, 350°F (180°C).

Begin by placing the milk, onion, bay leaf, a good grating of nutmeg, a few whole peppercorns and a pinch of salt in a small saucepan. Slowly bring it up to simmering point, then strain it into a jug and discard the onion, bay leaf and peppercorns.

Now rinse and dry the saucepan, place it back on the heat and melt the butter in it. Stir in the flour and cook gently for 1 minute, stirring all the time, to make a smooth, glossy paste. Next, add the hot milk, little by little, stirring well after each addition. When all the milk is incorporated, let the sauce barely bubble and thicken, then leave it on the lowest possible heat for 2 minutes. Now take the sauce off the heat and transfer it to a large mixing bowl. Beat

in first the egg yolks, followed by the chives. Mix everything thoroughly together and taste to check the seasoning. Finally, fold in three-quarters of the cubed goats' cheese.

Next, the egg whites should go into another clean bowl and be whisked up to the soft-peak stage. Then take a heaped tablespoon at a time and fold the egg whites into the cheese-and-egg mixture, using cutting and folding movements so as not to lose the air. Now divide the mixture between the buttered ramekins, place them in the roasting tin and pour about ½ inch (1 cm) of boiling water straight from the kettle into the tin.

Place the roasting tin on a high shelf in the oven and bake the soufflés for 15 minutes or until they are set and feel springy in the centre (it is important not to under-cook them at this stage, because on the second cooking they are going to be turned out). Don't worry if they rise up a lot – as they cool they will sink back into the dish. Remove them from the roasting tin straightaway, cool and then chill in the fridge until needed (they can also be frozen at this stage).

To serve the soufflés, pre-heat the oven to gas mark 6, 400°F (200°C). Butter the solid baking sheet, then slide the point of a small knife round each soufflé, turn it out on to the palm of your hand and place it, the right way up, on the baking sheet, keeping it well apart from its neighbours.

Sprinkle the remaining goats' cheese on top of each one, then pop them into the oven on the middle shelf and bake for 20-25 minutes or until they're puffy, well risen and golden brown. Using a fish slice, slide each soufflé on to a hot serving plate and serve straightaway with some freshly grated parmesan ■

Savoury Feta Cheesecake
Serves 6-8

The savoury cheesecake is a real winner. Feta cheese lightened with fromage frais makes a lovely cool summer cheesecake, just right for a light lunch served with a salad or Spiced Pickled Pears (see page 158).

For the base:
3 oz (75 g) white breadcrumbs
1½ oz (40 g) Pecorino Romano or parmesan, finely grated
1 oz (25 g) butter, melted
freshly milled black pepper

For the filling:
8 oz (225 g) feta
8 oz (225 g) medium-fat curd cheese
6 oz (175 g) 8 per cent fat fromage frais
4 heaped tablespoons chopped fresh chives
3 spring onions, finely sliced
2 tablespoons fresh lemon juice
2 teaspoons vegetarian gelatine powder
2 large egg whites
freshly milled black pepper

You will also need an 8 inch (20 cm) round cake tin with a loose base, lightly oiled. If it is less than 2 inches (5 cm) deep, line the sides with baking parchment to give a depth of 2 inches (5 cm).

Pre-heat the oven to gas mark 6, 400°F (200°C).

Begin by putting the breadcrumbs in a bowl and adding the cheese, the melted butter and a seasoning of pepper (no salt because the cheese is quite salty).

Now press the crumb mixture into the base of the prepared tin, pressing it firmly flat with the back of a spatula. Then pop it into the oven on a high shelf and bake for 15 minutes or until it is crisp and toasted

golden brown. Then remove from the oven. Now make the filling by first breaking up the feta cheese with a fork and then adding this to a food processor, along with the curd cheese and fromage frais, and blend until completely smooth. Then transfer to a bowl and stir in the chives, spring onions and some freshly milled pepper.

Next, measure the lemon juice and 2 fl oz (55 ml) water into a small saucepan, sprinkle in the gelatine, stir to dissolve the granules and then leave to one side. Then in a separate clean bowl, whisk the egg whites to the soft-peak stage.

Now heat the gelatine mixture to boiling point and add it to the cheese; use an electric hand whisk or stir quickly with a wooden spoon to combine it thoroughly. Then follow this with the whisked egg whites, first folding 1 tablespoon of the whites into the cheese mixture to loosen it, then stirring in the remaining whites. Now immediately pour the whole lot on to the cooled base, cover with clingfilm and transfer the cheesecake to the fridge to chill and set until needed, preferably overnight ■

Note: This recipe contains raw eggs.

Right: Savoury Feta Cheesecake
Top left: Twice-baked Goats' Cheese Soufflés with Chives

Gorgonzola Cheese and Apple Strudel with Spiced Pickled Pears
Serves 6

A brilliant combination of crisp pastry, melting cheese and the sharpness of the pears.

For the strudel:

6 oz (175 g) Gorgonzola Piccante, Shropshire Blue or Cashel Blue cut in ½ inch (1 cm) cubes

1 small Bramley apple

1 small Cox's apple

10 sheets of frozen filo pastry, each 18 x 11 inches (45 x 28 cm), thawed

1 lb 8 oz (700 g) young leeks (this will be about 12 oz (350 g) weighed after trimming)

8 oz (225 g) prepared weight of celery (reserve the leaves)

8 oz (225 g) mozzarella, cut in ½ inch (1 cm) cubes

12 spring onions (white parts only), chopped

4 oz (110 g) ready-chopped walnuts

3 tablespoons chopped parsley

1 oz (25 g) white bread, crust removed

2 medium cloves garlic, peeled

4 oz (110 g) butter

salt and freshly milled black pepper

For the spiced pickled pears:

6 hard pears (Conference or similar variety)

4 oz (110 g) soft brown sugar

12 fl oz (340 ml) cider vinegar

1 tablespoon balsamic vinegar

1 tablespoon whole mixed peppercorns

4 whole cloves

6 juniper berries, crushed

You will also need a large flat baking sheet, approximately 16 x 12 inches (40 x 30 cm), buttered, and a flameproof casserole, approximately 10 inches (25.5 cm) in diameter, large enough to hold the pears.

Pre-heat oven to gas mark 5, 375°F (190°C).

First, you need to pickle the pears; peel the pears using a potato peeler, but be very careful to leave the stalks intact as they look much prettier. Place all the rest of the ingredients in the flameproof casserole, bring everything up to simmering point, stirring all the time to dissolve the sugar. Now carefully lower the pears into the hot liquid, laying them on their sides, then cover with a lid and transfer the pears to the oven for 30 minutes.

After that, remove the lid and carefully turn the pears over. Test with a skewer to see how they are cooking – they'll probably need about another 30 minutes altogether, so cover with the lid and leave them in the oven till they feel tender when pierced with a skewer. Then remove them and allow them to cool in their liquid until needed. When serving, there's no need to re-heat the pears as they taste much better cold.

Now prepare the leeks by trimming and discarding the outer layers, then slice each one vertically almost in half and wash them under a cold running tap, fanning them out to get rid of any grit and dust. Then dry them in a cloth and cut them into ½ inch (1 cm) pieces.

Now chop the celery into slightly smaller pieces. Then melt 1½ oz (40 g) of the butter in a frying pan 9 inches (23 cm) in diameter. Keeping the heat at medium, sauté the leeks and celery for about 7-8 minutes until just tinged brown, stir them and keep them on the move to stop them catching at the edges. Then tip them into a large bowl and while they are cooling you can deal with the other ingredients.

The apples need to be cored and chopped into ½ inch (1 cm) pieces, leaving the skins on, then as soon as the leeks and celery have cooled, add the apples, diced mozzarella, spring onions, walnuts and 1 tablespoon of chopped parsley. Season everything well and stir to mix it all together.

Now you need to make a breadcrumb mixture and to do this, place the bread, garlic, the rest of the parsley and reserved celery leaves in a food processor. Switch it on and blend until everything is smooth. If you don't have a food processor, grate the bread, and chop everything else finely and mix together.

Next, take a large clean tea cloth and dampen it under cold water, lay it out on a work surface, then carefully unwrap the filo pastry sheets and lay them on the damp cloth, folding it over. It is important to keep the pastry sheets in the cloth to prevent them from drying out.

It is quite complicated to explain how to assemble the strudel, but to actually *do* it is very easy and only takes a few minutes. Place the buttered baking sheet on a work surface. Because the filo sheets are too small to make this strudel, we're going to have to 'weld' them together. To do this, first of all melt the remaining butter in a small saucepan, then take 1 sheet of filo pastry (remembering to keep the rest covered), lay it on one end of the baking sheet and brush it with melted butter. Then place another sheet beside it, overlapping it by about 2 inches/5 cm, then brush that with melted butter. Place a third sheet next to the second, overlapping it again by 2 inches (5 cm).

Now sprinkle a quarter of the breadcrumb mixture all over the sheets and then place 2 more sheets of filo, this time in the opposite direction, buttering the first one with melted butter and welding the other one with a 2 inch (5 cm) join. Brush that layer as before with melted butter and repeat the sprinkling of breadcrumbs. Then place the next 3 sheets as you did the first 3, again brushing with butter and sprinkling with crumbs. Then place the final 2 sheets as the second ones and brush with butter.

After that, place half the cheese and vegetable mixture all the way along the filo, sprinkle the cubes of Gorgonzola (or other cheese) on top of that, then finish off with the rest of the mixture on top.

Now just pat it together firmly with your hands. Take the edge of the pastry that is nearest to you, bring it up over the filling, then flip the whole lot over as if you were making a giant sausage roll. Neatly push in the vegetables, before tucking the pastry ends underneath. Now brush the entire surface with the remaining butter, scatter the rest of the crumb mixture over the top and bake in the oven for 25-30 minutes or until it has turned a nice golden brown colour.

To serve the strudel, cut off the ends (they are great for the bird table but not for your guests) and cut the strudel into slices, giving each person one pickled pear ■

Stir-fried Tofu with Oyster Mushrooms
Serves 2

Winter Vegetable Pie with a Parmesan Crust
Serves 4-6

My thanks to cookery writer Lulu Grimes for this delightful recipe. Tofu has a bland flavour, which Lulu thinks goes very well with strong sauces, such as soy and hoisin sauce. Serve the stir-fry with rice or noodles.

7 oz (200 g) firm tofu, drained

12 oyster mushrooms, halved

2 tablespoons groundnut or other flavourless oil

1 teaspoon sesame oil

1 clove garlic, peeled and crushed

2 teaspoons freshly grated root ginger

2 tablespoons hoisin sauce

2 tablespoons Japanese soy sauce

2 teaspoons sugar

2 spring onions, cut into pieces on the diagonal

2 baby pak choi, cut into 6 wedges through the root

a handful of coriander leaves

First of all, cut the tofu into bite-size pieces with a sharp knife. Now, heat a wok or large frying pan over a high heat, add the groundnut oil and heat it until it is very hot and almost smoking, then add the sesame oil. Next, you need to add the tofu and cook it until it is golden brown on all sides, move it around gently with a spatula, or it will stick and break.

Now, reduce the heat to medium and add the garlic, ginger, hoisin sauce, soy sauce and sugar and spring onions to the tofu and toss together until everything is thoroughly mixed and the sauce has coated all of the tofu. Then add the oyster mushrooms and pak choi and simmer for a minute or two until the sauce has reduced a little and the pak choi has softened slightly.

Garnish the stir-fry with coriander and serve immediately ■

I like to serve this homely pot pie with creamy mashed potato. You can vary the vegetables used with other roots, such as swede or parsnips.

8 oz (225 g) each butternut squash, celeriac and sweet potato, peeled and cut into 1 inch (2.5 cm) chunks

4 oz (110 g) carrots, peeled and cut into 1 inch (2.5 cm) chunks

8 oz (225 g) leeks, trimmed, halved lengthways and cut into 2 inch (5 cm) thick chunks

a little freshly grated nutmeg

4 oz (110 g) Gruyère or Emmental, grated

1 egg, beaten, to glaze

salt

For the parmesan pastry:

1 oz (25 g) finely grated parmesan

4 oz (110 g) plain flour, plus a little extra for dusting

pinch salt

1 oz (25 g) pure vegetable fat

1 oz (25 g) softened butter

For the sauce:

1½ oz (40 g) butter

1 medium onion, peeled and finely chopped

1½ oz (40 g) plain flour

1 pint (570 ml) milk

a little freshly grated nutmeg

1 tablespoon wholegrain mustard

2 oz (50 g) Gruyère or Emmental, grated

1 oz (25 g) parmesan, finely grated

1 dessertspoon each finely chopped fresh rosemary and thyme

salt and freshly milled black pepper

You will also need a round baking dish with a diameter of 9 inches (23 cm), 2 inches (5 cm) deep.

First of all, place the butternut squash, celeriac, carrots and leeks in a steamer (the sweet potato is added later on). Pour in some boiling water from the kettle, add the freshly grated nutmeg and salt, then cover and steam the vegetables for 10 minutes. Now add the chunks of sweet potato and steam for another 10 minutes or until the thickest parts of the root vegetables feel tender when tested with a skewer. Then tip all the vegetables into a large bowl and allow them to cool.

Meanwhile, make the sauce and the pastry. For the sauce, in a smallish saucepan, melt the butter and add the onion, and when you've stirred it so it's nice and buttery, let it cook on the lowest possible heat for about 20 minutes. It's important not to let it colour, so give it a stir from time to time. Now using a wooden spoon, stir in the flour until smooth, then add the milk a little at a time, switching to a balloon whisk, and whisking well after each addition. Now season the sauce with nutmeg and salt and freshly milled black pepper to taste, and let it barely simmer for 5 minutes. After that, stir in the grain mustard, the cheeses and the herbs. Then leave to cool.

To make the pastry, first sift the flour with the pinch of salt into a large bowl, holding the sieve up high to give it a good airing. Then add the vegetable fat and butter and, using only your fingertips, lightly and gently rub the fat into the flour. When everything is crumbly, add the parmesan and then sprinkle in some cold water – about 1 tablespoon. Start to mix the pastry with a knife and then finish off with your hands, adding more drops of water till you have a smooth dough that will leave the bowl clean. Then pop the pastry into a polythene bag and let it rest in the fridge for 30 minutes.

When you are ready to bake the pie, pre-heat the oven to gas mark 7, 425°F (220°C). Carefully mix the steamed vegetables with the sauce and pile half the mixture into the dish. Now sprinkle half the Gruyère (or other cheese) from the filling ingredients over the top and then repeat with the remaining mixture and cheese. Next, roll the pastry out on a surface lightly dusted with flour, and as you roll, give it quarter turns to make a round shape. Then cut out a 12 inch (30 cm) circle and after you have cut the round, roll out the trimmings and cut a ½ inch (1 cm) strip to go around the edge of the dish.

Now dampen the edge of the dish with water and place the strip of pastry around the rim, pressing down well. Dampen the strip and then transfer the circle of pastry, rolling it over the pin, to the dish and press it lightly and firmly over the edges to seal. Next, using the blunt side of a knife, knock up the edges, then flute them using your thumb to push out and your forefinger to pull in again. Now make a hole in the centre of the pastry lid to let the steam out, and brush the surface with beaten egg.

Now place the dish on the baking sheet and bake it for 25 to 30 minutes on the centre shelf or until the pie is bubbling hot and the pastry is golden brown and crusty ■

Roasted Tomato and Goats' Cheese Tart with Thyme
Serves 6

I guarantee, once you've made this tart, you will go on making it because it's just about the easiest and most sublime tomato recipe on record. It's great as a starter or as a main course with a salad. Serve it at barbecues or any outdoor eating event (it's even good cold on a picnic). You'll just have to make it to believe it.

1 lb 10 oz (740 g) ripe plum tomatoes

5 oz (150 g) soft goats' cheese

4 teaspoons fresh chopped thyme, plus a few small sprigs

1 x 375 g pack fresh, ready-rolled puff pastry

2 cloves garlic, peeled and crushed

2 tablespoons extra virgin olive oil

salt and freshly milled black pepper

You will also need a large baking tray measuring 12 x 16 inches (30 x 40 cm), lightly oiled.

Pre-heat the oven to gas mark 5, 375°F, (190°C).

To begin the recipe, first of all unwrap the pastry and then place it on the baking sheet. Then, using a sharp knife, carefully score a line on the pastry, about ½ inch (1 cm) in from the edge, all the way around but be careful not to cut it all the way through.

Now tip the goats' cheese into a small bowl, add the crushed garlic, chopped thyme and a good seasoning of salt and freshly milled black pepper. Then give it all a good mixing, and using a small palette or other round-bladed knife, carefully spread the cheese mixture evenly all over the surface of the pastry, right up to the line.

Next, thinly slice all the tomatoes (there is no need to peel them) and arrange them on top of the goats' cheese in overlapping lines lengthways; overlap one line one way and the other next to it the other way. After that, season the tomatoes and then drizzle the olive oil and scatter the sprigs of thyme all over them.

Bake in the pre-heated oven on a middle shelf for 55 minutes or until the pastry is golden brown and the tomatoes are roasted and slightly charred at the edges. If you are going to serve the tart warm, leave it to settle for about 10 minutes before cutting into squares ■

Italian Stuffed Aubergines
Serves 2, or 4 as a starter

Apart from tasting superb, this is particularly pretty to look at. I like to serve it as a first course, but with a salad and some good bread, it would make a lovely supper dish for two people.

1 medium to large aubergine, about 12-14 oz (350-400 g)

2-3 tablespoons olive oil

3 large, ripe tomatoes

1 medium onion, peeled and finely chopped

1 large clove garlic, peeled and crushed

1 tablespoon torn fresh basil leaves

2 teaspoons sun-dried tomato paste

1 heaped tablespoon drained small capers

5 oz (150 g) mozzarella, drained

1½ tablespoons fine fresh breadcrumbs

2 tablespoons freshly grated parmesan

8 basil leaves, lightly oiled

salt and freshly milled black pepper

You will also need a large, solid baking sheet 16 x 12 inches (40 x 30 cm), lightly oiled, and a baking dish 16 x 12 inches (40 x 30 cm), also oiled.

Pre-heat the oven to gas mark 4, 350°F (180°C).

First of all, wipe the aubergine and trim off the stalk end, then use the very sharpest knife you have to cut it lengthways into 8 thin slices about ¼ inch (5 mm) thick. When you get to the bulbous sides, these slices should be chopped into small pieces and kept aside for the filling. Now arrange the slices of aubergine in rows on the baking sheet, then brush each slice lightly with olive oil and season with salt and freshly milled black pepper. Pop them into the oven on a high shelf and let them pre-cook for 15 minutes, by which time they will have softened enough for you to roll them up easily.

Next, pour boiling water on the tomatoes and after 1 minute, drain and slip the skins off (protecting your hands with a cloth if they are hot). Then cut each tomato in half and, holding them in the palm of your hand, gently squeeze them until the seeds come out (you don't need these) – it's best to do this over a plate or a bowl! Now, using a sharp knife, chop the tomatoes into approximately ¼ inch (5 mm) dice.

Next, heat 1 tablespoon of oil in a large, solid frying pan and fry the onion, the chopped pieces of aubergine and crushed garlic for about 5 minutes. Then add the chopped tomatoes, torn basil leaves and tomato paste and continue to cook for about another 5 minutes. Give everything a good seasoning and add the capers. Then remove the pan from the heat and let the mixture cool slightly.

Now chop the mozzarella into very small dice. As soon as the aubergines are cool enough to handle, sprinkle each one with chopped mozzarella, placing it all along the centre of each slice. On top of that, put an equal amount of stuffing ingredients, leaving a border all round to allow for expansion. Roll up the slices and put them in the baking dish, making sure the overlapping ends are tucked underneath.

Finally, brush each one with oil, combine the fresh breadcrumbs and grated parmesan, sprinkle the mixture over them, pop a basil leaf on top, then bake in the oven (same temperature) for about 20 minutes and serve immediately ■

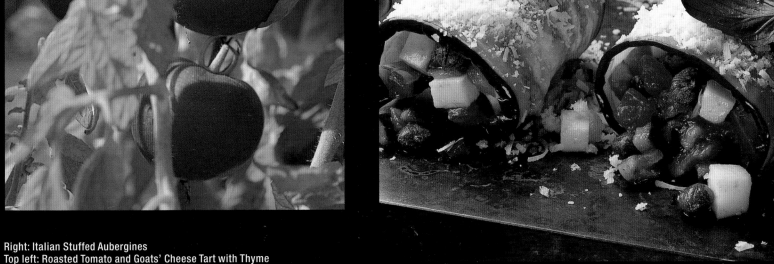

Right: Italian Stuffed Aubergines
Top left: Roasted Tomato and Goats' Cheese Tart with Thyme

Oven-roasted Ratatouille

Oven-roasted Ratatouille and Mozzarella Strudel with Parmesan and Pecans
Serves 6

Filo pastry is made ready to use, so no tedious rolling out and all that buttery, wafer-thin crunchiness is guaranteed. This filling makes a very special strudel, perfect for entertaining.

For the strudel:

four 18 x 11 inch (45 x 28 cm) sheets of frozen filo pastry, defrosted

4 oz (110 g) mozzarella, cubed

3 tablespoons finely grated parmesan

4 oz (110 g) pecan nuts

3 oz (75 g) butter

For the oven-roasted ratatouille:

2 medium courgettes

1 small aubergine

1 lb (450 g) ripe plum tomatoes or any other ripe, red tomatoes

1 small red pepper, deseeded and cut into 1 inch (2.5 cm) squares

1 small yellow pepper, deseeded and cut into 1 inch (2.5 cm) squares

1 medium onion, peeled and chopped into 1 inch (2.5 cm) squares

2 large garlic cloves, peeled and finely chopped

a handful of torn fresh basil leaves, about ½ oz (10 g)

1 heaped teaspoon coriander seeds, crushed

3 tablespoons olive oil

sea salt and freshly milled black pepper

You will also need a 16 x 12 inch (40 x 30 cm) shallow roasting tray and a large baking sheet measuring 16 x 12 inches (40 x 30 cm), greased, and some baking parchment.

First, you need to roast the vegetables. Prepare the courgettes and aubergine ahead of time by cutting them into 1 inch (2.5 cm) dice, leaving the skins on. Now place them in a colander and mix them with a rounded dessertspoon of salt. Then place a plate on top of them and weigh it down with a heavy weight, making sure you have a plate underneath the colander to catch the drips. Leave them like this for an hour so that any bitter juices can drain out.

Meanwhile, pour boiling water over the tomatoes, leave them for 1 minute exactly, then drain, slip the skins off and quarter the flesh. When the aubergines and courgettes have drained, squeeze out any excess juice, then dry them thoroughly in a clean cloth. Pre-heat the oven to gas mark 9, 475°F (240°C). Now arrange the tomatoes, aubergines, courgettes, peppers and onion on the roasting tray, sprinkle with the garlic, torn basil leaves, crushed coriander seeds and season with freshly milled pepper. Drizzle the oil over, then mix thoroughly to get a good coating of oil. Roast on the highest shelf of the oven for 30-40 minutes, or until the vegetables are tender and tinged brown at the edges. Remove from the oven and leave until cold.

When you are ready to make the strudel, pre-heat the oven to gas mark 4, 350°F (180°C) and pop the nuts on to a baking sheet to toast for 6 minutes. While they toast, melt the butter. When the nuts are ready, remove them from the oven and allow to cool a little. Now pulse them in a processor to chop them small, transfer them to a small bowl and mix them with 2 tablespoons of the parmesan.

Now spread a sheet of baking parchment out on the baking sheet. Follow this with a sheet of filo, covering the remaining sheets of filo with a clean, slightly damp, tea cloth. Brush all over the filo sheet with some of the melted butter. Sprinkle on a quarter of the nuts and parmesan. Then do this another 3 times with the other filo sheets. Now scatter half the cubes of mozzarella in the middle of the pastry and then, using a draining spoon, transfer the roasted ratatouille on top of that, leaving a gap of 2 inches (5 cm) at either end, followed by the other half of the mozzarella.

Then use the parchment paper to help you roll the filo over the filling and then over again. What you need to end up with is the seam and the ends tucked in underneath. You can discard the paper now.

Now brush the rest of the butter all over and bake on the centre shelf of the oven for 40 minutes. If you want to, you can make the strudel in advance and bake it when you want to serve it. Or I sometimes cook it in advance and whack it back in the oven to warm at the same temperature for 10 minutes. Sprinkle with the remaining tablespoon of parmesan before serving ◼

Vegetarian Goulash with Smoked Pimentón
Serves 4

The pimentón (smoked paprika) in this goulash, is from southern Spain and adds a spicy, deep flavour. I like to serve the goulash with whole-grain brown rice cooked with onion or some buttered noodles.

14 oz (400 g) tin chopped Italian tomatoes

10 fl oz (275 ml) hot water, enriched with 1 teaspoon tomato purée

8 oz (225 g) cauliflower florets

8 oz (225 g) each carrots and courgettes, cut into 1 inch (2.5 cm) chunks

8 oz (225 g) new potatoes, halved

½ green pepper, deseeded and chopped

1 heaped tablespoon sweet, smoked pimentón (mild, smoked paprika), plus a little extra, to sprinkle

2 medium onions, peeled and sliced

2 tablespoons olive oil

1 rounded dessertspoon plain flour

5 fl oz (150 ml) soured cream

salt and freshly milled black pepper

Pre-heat the oven to gas mark 4, 350°F (180°C).

You will also need a lidded, flameproof casserole with a capacity of 4 pints (2.25 litres).

Begin by heating the oil in the casserole, then fry the onions until softened. Next, stir in the flour and the tablespoon of pimentón. Cook for a minute, then stir in the tomatoes and the water. Bring the sauce up to boiling point, stirring all the time, and add all the other vegetables. Stir everything together, season with salt and freshly milled black pepper, then cover and transfer to the oven for 30-40 minutes.

Finally, stir in the soured cream and sprinkle a little more pimentón on top and serve ◼

Left: Pancake Cannelloni with Spinach and Four Cheeses
Top right: Courgette and Potato Cakes with Mint and Feta Cheese

Pancake Cannelloni
with Spinach and Four Cheeses
Serves 4-6

Pancakes make brilliant cannelloni – lighter, I think, than pasta. The cannelloni can also be served as a starter in individual heatproof gratin dishes, with two pancakes per person, in which case bake them for 20 minutes only.

For the pancakes:

4 oz (110 g) plain flour

pinch salt

2 large eggs

7 fl oz (200 ml) milk mixed with

3 fl oz (75 ml) water

2 oz (50 g) butter, melted

For the sauce.

1 pint (570 ml) milk

2 oz (50 g) butter

1¼ oz (30 g) plain flour

1 bay leaf

good grating of fresh nutmeg

2½ fl oz (65 ml) double cream

salt and freshly milled black pepper

For the filling:

1 lb (450 g) young leaf spinach

½ oz (10 g) butter

5 oz (150 g) ricotta

5 oz (150 g) Gorgonzola or Cashel Blue, crumbled

2½ oz (60 g) parmesan, grated

whole nutmeg

1 bunch spring onions, finely sliced (including the green parts)

freshly milled black pepper

For the topping:

4 oz (110 g) mozzarella, grated

1½ oz (40 g) parmesan, grated

You will also need a solid 7 inch (18 cm) frying pan, some greaseproof paper, and a well-buttered dish measuring 9 x 9 x 2 inches (23 x 23 x 5 cm).

First of all, make the pancakes as described for the crepes (on page 252) omitting the orange zest and sugar from the batter. These pancakes should be thicker than the crepes so use 2 tablespoons of batter for each pancake. You should end up with 12-14 pancakes. Now make the sauce by placing the milk, butter, flour and bay leaf in a saucepan and bring everything up to simmering point, whisking all the time until the sauce has thickened. Season it with salt, pepper and a good grating of fresh nutmeg. Then turn the heat down to its lowest setting and let the sauce simmer gently for 2 minutes, and remove it from the heat before stirring in the cream.

Meanwhile, cook the spinach by placing it in a large saucepan with the butter and cooking it briefly for 1-2 minutes, tossing it around until it wilts and collapses down, then drain it in a colander and squeeze it hard to get rid of all the excess juice. Pre-heat the oven to gas mark 6, 400°F (200°C).

Now place the spinach in a bowl, chop it roughly with a knife and then add the ricotta, Gorgonzola, parmesan and a grating of the nutmeg. Mix everything together, seasoning with pepper, but no salt, as the cheeses can be quite salty. Next, add the chopped spring onions and 4 or 5 tablespoons of the sauce.

Then lay a pancake out and place a tablespoonful of the filling on to it, then roll it up, tucking in the edges and repeat this with the remaining pancakes. Lay the filled pancakes side by side in the baking dish and scatter the mozzarella all over them. Next, pour over the sauce. Finally, sprinkle the parmesan all over the surface. Then bake the cannelloni on the highest shelf of the oven for 25-30 minutes until the top is brown and sauce is bubbling ■

Courgette and Potato Cakes
with Mint and Feta Cheese
Serves 6

These quite brilliant little courgette cakes used to be fried. However, we then tried baking them in the oven, which worked a treat, making them particularly ideal to serve as part of a buffet party. To serve 12, just double the quantities.

3 medium courgettes, weighing about 12 oz (350 g) in total

2 medium Desirée potatoes, weighing about 12 oz (350 g) in total

2 tablespoons chopped fresh mint

8 oz (225 g) feta, crumbled

2 spring onions, finely chopped

1 large egg, lightly beaten

1 tablespoon plain flour

1 oz (25 g) butter

1 tablespoon olive oil

sea salt and freshly milled black pepper

You will also need a baking tray, measuring 14 x 10 inches (35 x 25.5 cm).

First, you need to coarsely grate the courgettes – a food processor is good for this – and put them into a colander. Then sprinkle them with a teaspoon of salt to draw out some of their excess moisture and leave them to drain for about an hour, with a plate or bowl underneath to catch the juices.

Meanwhile, scrub the potatoes and place them in a saucepan, with a little salt. Pour just enough boiling water over them to cover them, then simmer gently with a lid on for 8 minutes to parboil them. After that, drain them and leave them aside until they're cool enough to handle. Then peel them and, using the coarse side of a grater, grate them into a large bowl and season with more salt and some freshly milled black pepper.

When the hour is up, rinse the courgettes under cold, running water, squeeze out as much moisture as possible with your hands, then spread them out on a clean tea cloth and roll it up to wring out every last drop – this is very important, so the cakes are not wet.

Now add the courgettes to the grated potatoes, along with the spring onions, mint, feta and beaten egg, and using two forks, lightly toss it all together. Next, divide the mixture into 8 and shape into rounds about ½ inch (1 cm) thick, pressing them firmly together to form little cakes. They don't have to be very neat – it's nice to have a few jagged edges. Then lightly dust the cakes with the flour.

To cook them, first pre-heat the oven to gas mark 7, 425°F (220°C) and also pre-heat the baking tray. Meanwhile, melt the butter and oil in a small saucepan, then brush the cakes on both sides with it. When the oven is up to heat, place the cakes on the tray and then put it on to the top shelf for 15 minutes. After that, carefully turn the cakes over using a palette knife and a fork and return them to the middle shelf of the oven for a further 10-15 minutes. Serve hot ■

Silken Tofu with Chilli, Spring Onion and Frizzled Leek
Serves 2

Red Onion Tarte Tatin
Serves 4, or 6 as a starter

This is another Lulu Grimes recipe and she explains that as silken tofu is very soft, it is often served scrambled up with stronger flavours, or used as a textural element in soups. Here, it has hot oil poured over it at the end, to heat the outside and cook the garnishes. Eat with steaming hot rice.

8 oz (225 g) silken tofu

3 spring onions, finely sliced

1 or 2 red chillies, finely chopped

¼ oz (5 g) fresh coriander leaves, roughly chopped

1 tablespoon sweet chilli sauce

2 tablespoons soy sauce

3 tablespoons groundnut oil

1 teaspoon sesame oil

2 inches (5 cm) trimmed leek, finely shredded

First of all, open the tofu and drain off any excess liquid, then gently tip it on to a heatproof plate. Next, carefully cut the tofu into cubes using a sharp knife. It is easier to leave it in its block shape but you can arrange it more attractively if you like.

Then, scatter the spring onions, chilli, and coriander over the tofu and drizzle on the sweet chilli sauce and soy sauce. Now you need to put the oils into a small saucepan and heat them until they are smoking hot, then add the leek and cook it for barely a minute until it frizzles and starts to brown. Be careful not to let the oil burn.

Now, pour the hot oil and leek evenly over the tofu, it should be hot enough to splutter. Serve the tofu immediately with rice ▪

This is simply the old favourite apple tarte tatin turned into a savoury version. The red onions are mellowed and caramelised with balsamic vinegar, and look spectacularly good. And the cheese and thyme pastry provides the perfect background. Everyone in my family thinks this is ace.

2 lb 8 oz (1.15 kg) red onions

1 oz (25 g) butter

1 teaspoon golden caster sugar

6 small thyme sprigs, plus 1 tablespoon chopped fresh thyme

1 tablespoon balsamic vinegar

a few shavings of parmesan, to serve

salt and freshly milled black pepper

For the pastry:

3 oz (75 g) plain flour

2 oz (50 g) plain wholemeal flour

2 oz (50 g) soft butter

1 oz (25 g) Cheddar cheese, grated

1 teaspoon chopped fresh thyme leaves

You will also need a cast-iron, ovenproof pan with a base diameter of 9 inches (23 cm), or a good solid baking tin of the same size.

Pre-heat the oven to gas mark 4, 350°F (180°C), and pre-heat a solid baking sheet as well.

Begin by preparing the onions, which should have their outer papery skins removed and then be cut in half lengthways from stem to root. After that, place the pan over a medium heat and, as soon as it's hot, add the butter and the sugar, then as soon as the butter begins to sizzle, quickly scatter the sprigs of thyme in, then arrange the onions on the base of the pan, cut side down. As you do this you need to think 'jigsaw puzzle', so that after the onion halves have been placed in the pan to cover the surface, all of those left over need to be cut into wedges and fitted in between to fit all of the gaps. Bear in mind that when you turn the tart out, it is the cut side of the onions you see. When the onions have all been fitted in, give them a good seasoning of salt and freshly milled black pepper, then scatter over the chopped thyme and sprinkle in the vinegar.

Now turn the heat down under the pan and let the onions cook very gently for about 10 minutes. After that, cover the pan with foil and place it on the baking sheet on the shelf just above the centre of the oven and leave it there for the onions to cook for 50-60 minutes.

While the onions are cooking, make the pastry and this can be done by hand, or, if you like, by mixing all the ingredients in a processor. When the mixture resembles fine crumbs, gradually add enough cold water to make a soft dough (you'll need 2-3 tablespoons). Then pop the dough into the fridge in a polythene bag for 30 minutes to rest.

As soon as the onions have had their cooking time, test them with a skewer: they should be cooked through, but still retain some texture. Then, protecting your hands well, remove the pan from the oven and place it back on to the hob, increasing the oven temperature to gas mark 6, 400°F (200°C). Then turn on the heat under the pan containing the onions to medium, as what you now need to do is reduce all the lovely, buttery, oniony juices – this will probably take about 10 minutes, but do watch them carefully so that they do not burn. By this time you'll be left with very little syrupy liquid at the base of the pan.

While that's all happening, roll out the pastry to a circle about 10 inches (25.5 cm) in diameter, then – again being careful to protect your hands – turn the heat off under the pan, fit the pastry over the onions, pushing down and tucking in the edges all round the inside of the pan. Then return the tart to the oven on the same baking sheet, but this time on the higher shelf and give it another 25-30 minutes until the pastry is crisp and golden.

When the tart is cooked, remove it from the oven and allow it to cool for 20 minutes before turning it out. When turning it out it's important to have a completely flat plate or board. Then, protecting your hands with a tea cloth, place the plate on top of the pan, then turn it upside down, give it a good shake and hey presto – Red Onion Tarte Tatin! If for any reason some of the onions are still in the pan, fear not: all you need to do is lift them off with a palette knife and replace them into their own space in the tart. We think it's nice to serve this tart just warm with a few shavings of parmesan sprinkled over ▪

Red Onion Tarte Tatin

Leek and Soured Cream Flan
Serves 6

This flan has a very crisp, cheese, wholemeal pastry and makes a very good lunch dish with a salad.

For the pastry:
3 oz (75 g) self-raising flour
3 oz (75 g) plain wholemeal flour, plus extra for dusting
pinch salt
¾ teaspoon mustard powder
1½ oz (40 g) pure vegetable fat
1½ oz (40 g) softened butter
2 oz (50 g) Cheddar, finely grated

For the filling:
3 lb (1.35 kg) leeks
5 fl oz (150 ml) soured cream
2 oz (50 g) butter
1 clove garlic, peeled and crushed
2 tablespoons double cream
1 large egg, beaten
2 oz (50 g) Cheddar, grated
salt and freshly milled black pepper

You will also need a 9 inch (23 cm), loose-bottomed, fluted tart tin, 1½ inches (4 cm) deep, lightly greased, and a small, solid baking sheet.

To make the pastry, sift the flours, salt and mustard into a large bowl, then rub in the fats until the mixture resembles fine breadcrumbs, lifting everything up and letting it fall back into the bowl to give it a good airing.

Now stir in the cheese, and add enough cold water, about a tablespoon, to make a dough that leaves the bowl clean. Pop the pastry into a polythene bag and leave to rest in the fridge for 30 minutes. Meanwhile, pre-heat the oven to gas mark 4, 350°F (180°C), and put the baking sheet in to pre-heat as well. Now for the filling. First, prepare the leeks. Begin by making a vertical split about

halfway down the centre of each one and clean them by running them under cold water while you fan out the layers. Then slice them in half lengthways and leaving 1½ inches (4 cm) of green on the ends, slice them thinly.

Now melt the butter in a large pan, add the leeks and garlic, and some seasoning. Cover and cook gently, without browning, for 10-15 minutes or until the juice runs out of them. Then you need to transfer them to a large sieve set over a bowl to drain, placing a saucer with a weight on top of them to press out every last drop.

Next, roll out the pastry on a lightly floured surface and line the tin with it, using any surplus pastry to reinforce the sides and base and carefully smoothing it into place. Now prick the base all over with a fork (to prevent it rising), then bake the flan case in the centre of the oven on the baking sheet for 15 minutes.

After that, remove from the oven and brush all over with a little beaten egg (from the filling ingredients). Return to the oven for 5 minutes more, then remove and turn the heat up to gas mark 5, 375°F (190°C).

Now return the leeks to the pan and combine the soured cream and double cream with the remaining beaten egg, and then stir this into the leek mixture, seasoning to taste. Spread the mixture over the pastry case, sprinkle with the cheese and bake in the centre of the oven for 40 minutes or until brown and crispy ■

Thai Green Vegetable Curry
Serves 4

This recipe is so simple and easy. If you prefer a milder curry, use fewer chillies in the paste. You can vary the vegetables – try open-cap mushrooms, pak choi or spinach to ring the changes. Serve with Thai fragrant rice.

6 oz (175 g) shiitake mushrooms, sliced
5 oz (150 g) small broccoli florets
5 oz (150 g) fine green beans, halved
4 oz (110 g) asparagus tips
2 x 14 fl oz (400 ml) tins coconut milk
1 teaspoon palm or soft brown sugar
3 dessertspoons fresh green peppercorns or green peppercorns in brine, drained
4 kaffir lime leaves (optional)
½ oz (10 g) each Thai basil (or other basil leaves) and coriander leaves
½ mild red chilli, deseeded and cut into hair-like shreds
salt

For the green curry paste:
6-8 whole green bird eye chillies, de-stalked
1 lemon grass stalk, trimmed, sliced thinly and soaked for 30 minutes in 2 tablespoons lime juice
1 rounded teaspoon thinly shredded kaffir lime peel (or other lime peel)
1 inch (2.5 cm) piece peeled fresh galangal or other fresh ginger, sliced
1 heaped teaspoon chopped fresh coriander stalks
½ teaspoon each cumin and coriander seeds, dry-roasted in a small frying pan until toasted, then ground in a pestle and mortar
3 garlic cloves, peeled
5 Thai shallots, peeled (or other shallots)

You will also need a wok or a large flameproof casserole.

All you do is pop all the paste ingredients in a processor or blender and whiz it to a paste (stopping once or twice to push the mixture back down from the sides on to the blades). To make the curry, first place the tins of coconut milk on a work surface, upside down. Then open them and inside, you will see the whole thing has separated into thick cream below and thin watery milk on top. Divide these by pouring the milk into one bowl and the cream into another.

Next, place the wok, or casserole, without any oil in it, over a very high heat and then, as soon as it becomes really hot, add three-quarters of the coconut cream. What you do now is literally fry it until it separates, stirring all the time so it doesn't catch. As it starts to separate, the oil will begin to seep out and it will reduce. Ignore the curdled look – this is normal.

Next, add the curry paste and three-quarters of the coconut milk, which should be added a little at a time, keeping the heat high and letting it reduce down slightly. Stay with it and keep stirring to prevent it sticking. Then add the palm sugar and the peppercorns. Stir again and gently simmer everything, uncovered, for 5 minutes. Now add the remaining coconut cream and milk and a generous pinch of salt, along with all the vegetables. Gently stir them in, then bring the liquid back to the boil before simmering for 5 minutes or until the vegetables are just tender.

Just before serving, place the lime leaves (if using) one on top of the other, roll them up tightly and slice them into very fine shreds. Stir the basil and coriander into the curry and scatter the lime leaves and red chilli over the top ■

Souffléed Butternut Creams with Foaming Herb Butter Sauce
Serves 6

This is blissfully easy and I find it works well if you make the sauce the day before (just stir in the chopped herbs before warming it). It is so named as butternut is the best squash for this recipe.

12 oz (350 g) peeled butternut squash, cut into 2 inch (5 cm) cubes
1 large egg and 1 large yolk, lightly beaten
whole nutmeg
10 fl oz (275 ml) double cream
6 small sprigs chervil, to garnish
salt and freshly milled black pepper

For the sauce:
1½ oz (40 g) young leaf spinach
¾ oz (20 g) watercress
¾ oz (20 g) flat-leaf parsley
1 tablespoon chopped fresh tarragon
1 dessertspoon snipped fresh chives
4 oz (110 g) butter
2 large eggs, separated
1-2 dessertspoons lemon juice
1 dessertspoon white wine vinegar
salt and freshly milled black pepper

You will also need six 1½ inch (4 cm) deep ramekins with a base diameter of 3 inches (7.5 cm), buttered, and a shallow roasting tin.

Start by making the sauce. First, rinse the spinach, watercress and parsley and put these into a saucepan over a medium heat. Stir them around until they have just wilted, tip them into a colander and rinse under cold water. Now carefully squeeze out the excess moisture, pressing with a wooden spoon, then put the leaves in the processor with the tarragon and chives and finely chop. Transfer the mixture to a bowl and rinse the processor. Next, place the egg yolks in the processor with some salt and pepper, switch on and

blend well. In a small saucepan heat 1 dessertspoon of the lemon juice and the vinegar till simmering, then with the processor on, pour the hot liquid on to the yolks in a steady stream. Switch off, and in the same saucepan melt the butter. When it's foaming, switch on and pour in the butter in a steady, thin stream, until it's all incorporated and the sauce has thickened. Next, whisk the egg whites to soft peaks and then fold the sauce, a tablespoon at a time, into them. Now do a bit of tasting, adding lemon juice, salt and pepper. Cover and chill the chopped herbs and sauce separately till needed.

For the creams, begin by steaming the butternut for 10 minutes or until tender when tested with a skewer. Now cover with a clean tea cloth and leave it to get cold. To cook the creams, pre-heat the oven to gas mark 5, 375°F (190°C). Then, place the butternut in a fine sieve over a bowl and press it through, to remove any fibres. Now mix the beaten egg and yolk into the butternut and lightly whip the cream. Then fold the butternut mixture into the cream, followed by a generous grating of nutmeg and some salt and pepper. Now place the ramekins in the tin and fill each one. Pour an inch (2.5 cm) of boiling water into the tin and place in the centre of the oven to cook for 30 minutes.

Meanwhile, fold the chopped herbs into the sauce and place the bowl over a pan of barely simmering water to warm. Leave the cooked creams for 10 minutes, then holding each one with a cloth, slide a small palette knife round the edge and tip the creams briefly, upside down, on to your palm, then straight on to a warm plate, the right way up. Spoon over a little sauce (serve the rest at table) and garnish with chervil ■

Note: This recipe contains raw eggs.

Spinach and Ricotta Soufflés with Fonduta Sauce
Serves 8

Everything in this recipe can be made well in advance and then all that needs to happen is the egg whites get whisked and incorporated just before cooking. The soufflés are served with an Italian fonduta, a creamy melted cheese sauce, and make a lovely starter.

For the soufflés:
2 lb (900 g) young leaf spinach
2 oz (50 g) ricotta cheese
4 large eggs, separated
2 oz (50 g) butter, plus a little extra for greasing the ramekins
freshly grated parmesan
for dusting the insides of the ramekins and sprinkling on top of the soufflés
10 fl oz (275 ml) milk
2 oz (50 g) plain flour
freshly grated nutmeg
pinch cayenne pepper
salt and freshly milled black pepper

For the fonduta sauce:
7 fl oz (200 ml) crème fraîche
6 oz (175 g) Fontina, Gruyère or Emmental, cut into very small cubes
a good pinch cayenne pepper
a squeeze of lemon juice

You will also need eight 1½ inch (4 cm) deep ramekins, with a base diameter of 3 inches (7.5 cm), and a large baking sheet.

Pre-heat the oven to gas mark 5, 375°F (190°C), and pop the baking sheet in to pre-heat, too.

First of all, butter the ramekins and lightly dust the insides with parmesan. Then thoroughly wash the spinach in several changes of cold water and pick it over, removing any thick, tough stalks or damaged leaves. Next, press the leaves into a large, saucepan, sprinkle in some salt (but don't add

water), cover and cook over a medium heat for 4-5 minutes. Just let it collapse down into its own juices and then give it a stir halfway through. Now drain the spinach thoroughly in a colander, pressing it very firmly with a saucer to extract every last bit of juice, it needs to be quite dry. Then chop it fairly finely.

For the soufflés, put the milk in a saucepan, then simply add the flour and butter and bring everything gradually up to simmering point, whisking continuously with a balloon whisk, until the sauce has thickened and becomes smooth and glossy. Then turn the heat down to its lowest possible setting and let the sauce cook very gently for 5 minutes, stirring from time to time. Now remove the pan from the heat and transfer the sauce to a large bowl. Next, beat the chopped spinach and the ricotta into the sauce with the egg yolks. Now season with salt, pepper, a generous amount of nutmeg and the cayenne. Beat the egg whites in a large clean bowl till stiff, then using a large metal spoon, fold one spoonful into the spinach sauce to 'loosen' it. Now carefully fold the remaining egg whites into the spinach mixture before dividing it equally between the 8 ramekins. Sprinkle the tops of the soufflés with a little parmesan and bake on the baking sheet for 25-30 minutes, or until well risen and slightly browned on top.

Whilst the soufflés are cooking you can make the fonduta sauce. Put the crème fraîche into a small saucepan with the cheese and slowly bring it up to simmering point, with the cayenne and a good squeeze of lemon juice, whisking as the cheese melts. The soufflés need to be served hot and puffy from the oven. Make an incision into each soufflé with a knife and pour in a little sauce, then hand the rest around separately in a jug ■

Above: Spinach and Ricotta Soufflés with Fonduta Sauce

Chapter Eight
Simply
Vegetables

Welsh Rabbit Jacket Potatoes
Serves 2

This makes a lovely lunch dish served with a salad. You can make your own relish for this (see below) or you could buy it ready-made.

2 large baked potatoes, 8-10 oz
(225-275 g) each
3 oz (75 g) mature Cheddar, grated
a little olive oil
1 tablespoon bought or home-made
relish (see below)
1 heaped teaspoon finely grated onion
1 large egg, lightly beaten
1 tablespoon finely snipped fresh chives
sea salt

For the red onion, tomato and chilli relish:
1 small red onion, peeled
and finely chopped
8 oz (225 g) ripe red tomatoes
½ small red chilli, deseeded
and finely chopped
1 clove garlic, peeled and crushed
1 tablespoon dark soft brown sugar
4 fl oz (120 ml) balsamic vinegar
salt and freshly milled black pepper

Pre-heat the oven to gas mark 5, 375°F
(190°C).

First, you need to make the relish. Begin by skinning the tomatoes: pour boiling water over them and leave for exactly 1 minute before draining them (or 15-30 seconds if they are small) and slipping off the skins (protect your hands with a cloth if they are too hot). Put the onion, chilli, garlic and tomatoes in a food processor and blend until finely chopped, then place the mixture in a saucepan and add the sugar and vinegar.

Place the pan over a gentle heat and simmer very gently, without a lid, for 2 hours, by which time the mixture will have reduced to a thick sauce. Towards the end of the cooking time, stir frequently so the sauce doesn't stick to the bottom of the pan. Then taste to check the seasoning.

Meanwhile, wash the potatoes and dry them thoroughly in a cloth, then all you need to do is to prick them a few times with a fork and rub a few drops of olive oil into the skin of each one, followed by some crushed salt. Put the potatoes straight on to the centre shelf of the oven and let them bake for 1¼-1½ hours or until the skins are really crisp.

Pre-heat the grill to its highest setting for 10 minutes before the potatoes are ready. Now all you do here is combine the onion, egg and chives for the filling, together with the cheese and 1 tablespoon of relish, in a bowl. Then, when the potatoes are ready, cut them in half lengthways and make some criss-cross slits in them, being careful not to cut through the skins and using a cloth to protect your hands.

Then divide the topping mixture between the potatoes, place them on the grill pan and grill 2 inches (5 cm) from the heat for 3-4 minutes, until the cheese has puffed up and turned golden brown on top.

The leftover relish will keep, covered, in the fridge, for several days. It can be served hot or cold or used in other recipes (see pages 79 and 91) ■

Oven-Roasted Cauliflower and Broccoli with Garlic
Serves 4

These two particular vegetables can become a bit repetitive as winter wears on, so here's a deliciously different way to cook them – no water, just in the heat of the oven, which concentrates their flavour wonderfully.

8 oz (225 g) cauliflower
8 oz (225 g) broccoli
2 garlic cloves, peeled
1 heaped teaspoon whole coriander seeds,
coarsely crushed
2 tablespoons olive oil
salt and freshly milled black pepper

You will also need a large, solid
roasting tray.

Pre-heat the oven to gas mark 6, 400°F
(200°C).

All you do is trim the cauliflower and broccoli into florets, 1 inch (2.5cm) in diameter, and place them in a mixing bowl, then sprinkle in the crushed coriander seeds. Crush the cloves of garlic, together with ¾ teaspoon salt, in a pestle and mortar until you have a paste. Whisk the oil into this, then pour the whole mixture over the broccoli and cauliflower.

Now use your hands to toss and mix everything together to get a nice coating of oil and coriander, then arrange the florets on the roasting tray and season with salt and pepper. Bake for 25-35 minutes or until tender when tested with a skewer, and serve straightaway ■

Gruyère Jacket Potato Halves with Chives
Makes 12 halves

Desirée is my all-round reliable favourite potato – it's full-flavoured, firm and waxy. You need to top these potato halves while they are still hot so that the cheese melts well – on a cold potato, it has a tendency to go hard and crispy. I like to serve these as part of a hot buffet.

6 medium-sized Desirée potatoes,
about 4 oz (110 g) each
3 oz (75 g) Gruyère or Emmental,
finely grated
2 tablespoons snipped fresh chives
a little olive oil
sea salt

Pre-heat the oven to gas mark 5, 375°F
(190°C).

First, wash the potatoes, then dry them very thoroughly with a cloth. Leave them aside to dry as much as possible. If they are already washed, all you need to do is wipe them with damp kitchen paper. Next, prick the skins a few times with a fork, then put a few drops of olive oil on to each potato and rub it all over the skin. After that, rub on some crushed salt. Place the potatoes straight on to the centre shelf of the oven and let them bake for 1-1¼ hours, until the skins are really very crisp.

Now cut each potato in half lengthways and score the flesh in a diamond pattern to break it up a bit. Then place the potatoes on a baking sheet and divide the grated Gruyère (or Emmental) between them. Then return them to the oven for 15 minutes, until the cheese is melted and golden. Sprinkle with the chives just before serving ■

Clockwise from left: Purple Sprouting Broccoli with Chilli, Lime and Sesame Dressing; Cauliflower with Two Cheeses and Crème Fraîche; Oven-roasted Winter Vegetables

Cauliflower with Two Cheeses and Crème Fraîche
Serves 4

No need to make a white sauce for this one – the beauty of half-fat crème fraîche is that you can simmer it into a creamy sauce in moments. This could be an accompanying vegetable for four, it could make a main course for two served with rice, or I like it with penne pasta – England meets Italy, sort of thing!

1 medium cauliflower, separated into florets (reserve a few inner leaves)
1½ oz (40 g) parmesan, finely grated, plus 1 heaped tablespoon extra, to finish
1½ oz (40 g) Gruyère or Emmental, finely grated
2 heaped tablespoons half-fat crème fraîche
2 bay leaves, torn in half
a little freshly grated nutmeg
2 spring onions, very finely chopped (including the green parts)
pinch cayenne pepper
salt and freshly milled black pepper

You will also need an ovenproof baking dish measuring 7½ inches (19 cm) square and 2 inches (5 cm) deep.

Pre-heat the grill to its highest setting.

First of all, place the cauliflower florets and a few of the inner leaves in a steamer with the pieces of bay leaf tucked amongst it. Pour in some boiling water from the kettle, add some freshly grated nutmeg and salt, then cover and steam the cauliflower till tender – about 12 minutes. After this time, test the thickest parts with a skewer to see if they are tender, then remove it to the baking dish and cover with a cloth to keep warm.

Now pour 3 fl oz (75 ml) of the steaming water into a saucepan, add the crème fraîche and simmer, whisking well, until it has thickened very slightly, then add the

cheeses. Heat this gently for about 1 minute, whisking, until the cheeses have melted, then season the sauce to taste.

Now pour the sauce over the cauliflower and scatter the spring onions and remaining parmesan over, then sprinkle with the cayenne. Finally, place the dish under the hot grill until the cauliflower has browned and the sauce is bubbling ■

Oven-roasted Winter Vegetables
Serves 6

This is always going to be an easy option if you're entertaining, as all the vegetables get cooked without any attention. One thing I have found invaluable, too, is being able to prepare them well ahead, which gives you that organised feeling. This is a particularly lovely combination of vegetables, but you can vary it with whatever is available.

Vegetable quantities (below) are prepared weights
12 shallots, peeled
12 oz (350 g) peeled and deseeded butternut squash
12 oz (350 g) peeled sweet potato
12 oz (350 g) peeled swede
12 oz (350 g) peeled celeriac
1 tablespoon freshly chopped mixed herbs (such as rosemary and thyme)
2 large cloves garlic, peeled and crushed
3 tablespoons olive oil
salt and freshly milled black pepper

You will also need a baking tray measuring 11 x 16 inches (28 x 40 cm).

Pre-heat the oven to gas mark 7, 425°F (220°C).

All you do is cut the vegetables into large, chunky pieces (no smaller than 1½ inches/ 4 cm) – leaving the celeriac until last, as it may discolour if left for too long – place in a large bowl, then add the herbs, garlic, olive oil and lots of seasoning and just use your hands to mix them. (The prepared vegetables can now be kept in a sealed plastic bag in the fridge for 2-3 days.)

To cook the vegetables, spread them out on the baking tray and cook in the pre-heated oven on a high shelf for 30-40 minutes, until they're tender and turning brown at the edges ■

Purple Sprouting Broccoli with Chilli, Lime and Sesame Dressing
Serves 3-4

This is something a little different to ring the changes when sprouting broccoli is in season. I think it goes very well with most oriental dishes or just by itself with some steamed rice.

12 oz (350 g) purple sprouting broccoli
salt

For the dressing:
1 small red chilli, deseeded and finely chopped
1 dessertspoon lime juice
1 teaspoon sesame seeds
1 dessertspoon sesame oil
1 dessertspoon Japanese soy sauce

You will also need a saucepan fitted with a fan steamer.

First, prepare the broccoli by cutting it into even-sized pieces – stalks and all. Then place the saucepan fitted with a fan steamer on the heat, add the broccoli, pour in about an inch (2.5 cm) of boiling water from the kettle and sprinkle with salt. Put a lid on and time it for about 4 minutes.

Meanwhile, to make the dressing, you need first to toast the sesame seeds. To do this, use a small, solid frying pan, pre-heat it over a medium heat without oil, then add the sesame seeds and toast them, moving them around in the pan to brown them evenly. As soon as they begin to splutter, pop and turn golden, they're ready, which will take about 1-2 minutes. Now remove them to a serving bowl and simply stir in all the rest of the ingredients. When it's cooked, remove the broccoli from the steamer and transfer to the bowl. Toss it around in the dressing and serve straightaway ■

Traditional Braised Red Cabbage with Apples
Serves 8

This recipe is great because it can be made the day before and gently re-heated with no last-minute bother.

2 lb (900 g) red cabbage

1 lb (450 g) cooking apples, peeled, cored and chopped small

1 lb (450 g) onions, peeled and chopped small

1 clove garlic, peeled and chopped very small

¼ whole nutmeg, freshly grated

¼ teaspoon ground cinnamon

¼ teaspoon ground cloves

3 tablespoons brown sugar

3 tablespoons wine vinegar

½ oz (10 g) butter

salt and freshly milled black pepper

Pre-heat the oven to gas mark 2, 300°F (150°C).

First, discard the tough outer leaves of the cabbage, cut it into quarters and remove the hard stalk. Then shred the rest of the cabbage finely, using your sharpest knife (although you can shred it in a food processor, I prefer to do it by hand: it doesn't come out so uniform).

Next, in a fairly large casserole, arrange a layer of shredded cabbage seasoned with salt and pepper, then a layer of chopped onions and apples with a sprinkling of garlic, spices and sugar. Continue with these alternate layers until everything is in. Now pour in the wine vinegar, and lastly, add dots of butter on the top. Put a tight-fitting lid on the casserole and let it cook very slowly in the oven for 2-2½ hours, stirring everything around once or twice during the cooking. Red cabbage, once cooked, will keep warm without coming to any harm, and it will also re-heat very successfully. And, yes, it does freeze well so, all in all, it's a real winner of a recipe ■

Baked Aubergines with Tomatoes
Serves 4

This is a good accompaniment, or can even be eaten as a lunch dish on its own.

1 lb 12 oz (800 g) aubergines

6 largish tomatoes, skinned and chopped

4 tablespoons oil

1 large onion, peeled and finely chopped

2 cloves garlic, peeled and crushed

2 tablespoons finely chopped parsley

a good pinch each of ground allspice, cinnamon and caster sugar

1 tablespoon grated Cheddar

2-3 tablespoons dry white breadcrumbs

1 oz (25 g) butter

sea salt and freshly milled black pepper

You will also need an ovenproof, baking dish with a diameter of 9 inches (23 cm) and 2 inches (5 cm) deep, generously buttered.

First, cut each aubergine into smallish pieces, pile them all in a colander, sprinkle with salt (2 heaped teaspoons), then place a plate on top of them. Weight it down with a scale weight and leave to drain for 1 hour.

When you're ready to cook, pre-heat the oven to gas mark 5, 375°F (190°C). Drain the aubergines and dry them thoroughly on kitchen paper, then heat the oil in a frying pan. Add the aubergines to the pan and fry to a pale golden colour, then add the chopped onion and carry on cooking until that has softened a bit. Next, add the tomatoes, garlic and parsley, the spices and sugar, and season with salt and pepper. Let everything simmer gently for about 5 minutes, stirring occasionally. Then transfer the mixture to the baking dish, sprinkle the top with a mixture of the cheese and breadcrumbs, and dot the surface with flecks of butter. Bake near the top of the oven for about 30 minutes, or until browned ■

Sliced Potatoes Baked with Tomatoes and Basil
Serves 4-6

Just when the new potatoes are getting too big to be really new, the red ripe tomatoes of summer are at their best and the basil leaves are large and opulent. This dish is a wonderful way to combine all three.

2 lb (900 g) potatoes, skins on

1 lb (450 g) red ripe tomatoes

3 tablespoons torn fresh basil leaves

1 fat clove garlic, peeled and finely chopped

1 onion, peeled and finely chopped

1 tablespoon extra virgin olive oil

salt and freshly milled black pepper

You will also need a round or oval gratin dish, about 9 inches (23 cm) wide, lightly oiled.

Pre-heat the oven to gas mark 5, 375°F (190°C).

First of all, pour boiling water over the tomatoes, leave them for 1 minute exactly (or 15-30 seconds if they are small), then drain them and slip the skins off (protecting your hands with a cloth, as necessary). Chop the flesh quite small. Then slice the potatoes thinly.

Now, in the gratin dish, arrange first a layer of sliced potato, a little chopped garlic and onion and some seasoning, followed by some chopped tomato, some more seasoning and a few torn basil leaves. Repeat all this until you have incorporated all the ingredients, then drizzle a little oil over the surface and bake in the oven for about 1 hour or until the potatoes are tender ■

Mashed Potato with Garlic-infused Olive Oil
Serves 4

If you enjoy the taste of really fine olive oil, you'll know how dipping bread directly into it brings out the full flavour. The same happens with potatoes – a sublime combination.

2 lb (900 g) potatoes (Desirée or King Edward), peeled and cut into even-sized chunks

3 fat garlic cloves, peeled and halved lengthways

8 tablespoons best-quality extra virgin olive oil

salt and freshly milled black pepper

First, place the garlic cloves and olive oil in a small saucepan over the gentlest heat possible – a heat diffuser is good for this – and leave for 1 hour for the garlic to infuse and become really soft.

Now put the potato chunks in a steamer fitted over a large pan of boiling water, sprinkle 1 dessertspoon of salt all over them, put a lid on and steam the potatoes until they are absolutely tender – they should take 20-25 minutes. To tell if they are ready, pierce them with a skewer in the thickest part: they should not be hard in the centre, and you need to be careful here, because if they are slightly underdone, you do get lumps.

When the potatoes are cooked, remove from the steamer, drain off the water, return to the pan and cover with a clean tea cloth for about 4 minutes to absorb some steam, then, using an electric hand whisk on a low speed, begin to break them up using half the garlic and oil. As soon as all that is incorporated, add the rest of the garlic and oil and whisk until smooth, seasoning well with salt and freshly milled black pepper ■

Mashed Potato with Garlic-infused Olive Oil

Left: Oven-roasted Red Potatoes with Red Onion and Red Wine Vinegar
Top right: Bubble and Squeak Rösti

Oven-roasted Red Potatoes with Red Onion and Red Wine Vinegar
Serves 6

This is a nice, easy way to cook potatoes, there's no need to peel them either, which does make life easier.

2 lb 8 oz (1.15 kg) red potatoes (Romano or Desirée)
3 tablespoons olive oil
2 medium red onions
1½ tablespoons red wine vinegar
salt and freshly milled black pepper

You will also need a large, shallow roasting tray measuring 16 x 12 inches (40 x 30 cm).

Pre-heat the oven to gas mark 7, 425°F (220°F).

First of all, place the tray with the oil into the pre-heated oven to get really hot (which will take about 10 minutes). Meanwhile, wipe the potatoes with a piece of kitchen paper and then cut them into chunks measuring approximately ¾ inch (2 cm), leaving the skin on. Peel and chop the onions fairly roughly into slivers.

Now remove the roasting tray from the oven and place it over a direct heat. Then carefully spread the potatoes and onions into the hot oil, turning them over to get a good covering. Then sprinkle the wine vinegar over, season well with salt and freshly milled black pepper, then return the tray to the highest shelf of the oven for 40-45 minutes, or until the potatoes are crisp and the onion is slightly charred at the edges. As soon as they are ready, serve immediately ■

Bubble and Squeak Rösti
Serves 4 (makes 8 rösti)

Bubble and squeak is a classic leftover recipe for greens, but making it rösti-style and adding some mature Cheddar adds a new dimension. These little individual rösti are brilliant served with a selection of pickles.

1 lb (450 g) potatoes (Romano or Desirée), this should be 3 evenly sized potatoes, about 5 oz/150 g each)
3 oz (75 g) spring greens or green cabbage (trimmed weight)
2 oz (50 g) mature Cheddar, coarsely grated
1 tablespoon plain flour
1 oz (25 g) butter
1 dessertspoon olive oil
salt and freshly milled black pepper

You will also need a baking tray measuring 10 x 14 inches (25.5 x 35 cm).

First, scrub the potatoes, then place them in a medium saucepan with a little salt. Pour boiling water over to just cover them, then simmer gently with a lid on for 8 minutes.

Drain the potatoes, then, while they are cooling, finely shred the spring greens or cabbage leaves into ¼ inch (5 mm) slices. This is easy if you form them into a roll and then slice them. Drop the spring greens or cabbage into boiling water for 2 minutes only, then drain and dry well.

When the potatoes have cooled, peel them, then, using the coarse side of a grater, grate them into a bowl. Season with salt and freshly milled black pepper, then add the grated cheese and greens or cabbage, and using 2 forks, lightly toss together.

To assemble the rösti, shape the mixture into rounds 3 inches (7.5 cm) wide and ½ inch (1 cm) thick. Press them firmly together to form little cakes and dust lightly with the flour. If you want to make them ahead, place them on a plate and cover with clingfilm – they will happily sit in the fridge for up to 6 hours.

To cook the rösti, pre-heat the oven to gas mark 7, 425°F (220°C), placing the baking tray on the top shelf of the oven. Melt the butter and add the oil, then brush the rösti on both sides with the mixture.

When the oven is up to heat, place the rösti on the baking tray and return it to the top shelf of the oven for 15 minutes, then turn the rösti over and cook them for a further 10 minutes. Once cooked, it's all right to keep them warm for up to 30 minutes ■

Compote of Glazed Shallots
Serves 8

This recipe is dead simple, yet it draws out all the sweet, fragrant flavour of the shallots and at the same time gives them a glazed pink, jewel-like appearance. Cider and cider vinegar can be used instead of wine to make it more economical.

1 lb 8 oz (700 g), about 24 small, even-sized shallots, peeled and left whole (ones that split into twins count as 2)
2 fl oz (55 ml) red wine vinegar
14 fl oz (400 ml) dry red wine
pinch salt
1 teaspoon sugar

Use a wide, shallow saucepan that will take the shallots in one layer, then simply place all the above ingredients except the sugar in it and bring everything up to simmering point. Then turn the heat down to its lowest setting and let the shallots simmer, uncovered (just a few bubbles breaking the surface), for 1-1¼ hours.

Turn the shallots over at half-time, and 10 minutes before the end of the cooking time, sprinkle in the sugar. You should end up with tender shallots glistening with a lovely glaze. If your heat source is not low enough, you may need to use a diffuser. If it's more convenient, you can cook the shallots in advance, and gently re-heat them before serving ■

Compote of Garlic and Sweet Peppers
Serves 6-8

This is a really robust, deliciously full-bodied combination and is ideal as part of a buffet, just see how many people go back for seconds!

10 cloves garlic, peeled
and finely chopped
2 lb (900 g) peppers (red, yellow and
orange – but not green)
2 rounded teaspoons cumin seeds,
lightly crushed
3 tablespoons olive oil
2 teaspoons mild chilli powder
5 tablespoons tomato purée,
plus a little extra, if needed
salt

Begin by washing, halving and deseeding the peppers, and cut the halves into quarters and the quarters into ¼ inch (5 mm) thick strips. Then place a large saucepan over a medium heat, add the crushed cumin seeds and toss them around in the heat to draw out their flavour. Then add the oil and let it gently heat for a minute. Now stir in the sliced peppers, garlic and chilli powder, cook for 1 minute, stirring so that the ingredients are thoroughly mixed, cover the pan and continue to cook over a low heat for a further 30-40 minutes or until the pepper strips are quite soft.

Now uncover the pan, increase the heat to medium and stir in the tomato purée. Continue to cook, uncovered, until no free liquid remains – this takes about 15 minutes. Finally, taste and add salt and a little more tomato purée if the mixture seems to need a little more body and sweetness. Serve the compote warm or at room temperature ■

Parsnips with a Mustard and Maple Glaze
Serves 4-6

This is a very good combination of flavours, and if you get bored with plain roast parsnips at the end of winter, this is just what's needed.

3 lb (1.35 kg) medium-sized parsnips
3 tablespoons groundnut or other
flavourless oil
2 tablespoons each wholegrain mustard
and maple syrup, mixed
salt and freshly milled black pepper

You will also need a good solid baking tray 14 x 10 inches (35 x 25.5 cm).

Pre-heat the oven to gas mark 9, 475°F (240°C).

First, top, tail and peel the parsnips, then cut them in half through the centre. Cut the top half into 4 and the bottom half into 2 so that you have even-sized pieces. Cut out any woody stems from the centre, then place the parsnips in a steamer, sprinkle with salt, cover with a lid and steam over simmering water for 6 minutes. Meanwhile, put the baking tray containing the oil on the top shelf of the oven to pre-heat. When the parsnips are ready, use an oven glove to remove the tray carefully from the oven so as not to spill the oil, and place it over direct heat turned to low.

Now add the parsnips, rounded side up, to the sizzling oil. Then tilt the tray and use a large spoon to baste the parsnips, to make sure they are evenly coated with the oil. Give them a good grinding of pepper and return the tray to the oven. Bake for 25 minutes, by which time the parsnips should be nicely browned and crispy. Then using a brush, coat the parsnip pieces with a liberal coating of the mustard and maple mixture and return them to the oven for 8-10 minutes. Serve straightaway ■

Toasted Spinach with Pine Nuts, Raisins and Sherry Vinegar
Serves 4

You need to have everything weighed up and ready before you start this recipe as once the spinach is cooked, everything gets tossed together over a high heat.

1 lb (450 g) young leaf spinach
1½ oz (40 g) pine nuts
2 oz (50 g) raisins
3 tablespoons sherry vinegar
2 tablespoons olive oil
2 fat cloves garlic, peeled
and finely chopped
salt and freshly milled black pepper

You need to start this by cooking the spinach; place it in a large saucepan with a lid on, then place it over a medium heat. Just let it collapse into its own juices, timing it for 2-3 minutes and turning it halfway through. Drain the spinach in a colander, pressing with a saucer to extract every last bit of juice. Now separate the spinach so it is not in one big lump.

Next, heat a large frying pan over a medium heat and add the pine nuts. Toast the pine nuts until golden brown, then transfer to a plate. Now increase the heat to high and add the oil to the pan. When it is really hot, add the garlic and cook, stirring for 30 seconds. Then add the spinach, moving it around so that it is 'toasted' evenly in the hot oil.

Now, add the vinegar and raisins and let the liquid bubble for 30 seconds before stirring in the pine nuts and a seasoning of salt and freshly milled black pepper. Give everything one final toss together and then serve immediately ■

Barbecued Sweetcorn
Serves 4

I think this is the nicest way to eat sweetcorn. Even if you don't have a barbecue going, you can still cook it under a pre-heated grill.

2 cobs sweetcorn
1 dessertspoon olive oil
salt and freshly milled black pepper

Remove the husks and threads from the sweetcorn, then brush the kernels all over with the oil, seasoning them liberally with salt and pepper as you go. Place the corns on the grill over hot coals and watch them carefully, turning them around with tongs so that all the kernels get toasted to a golden-brown colour. The whole process will take about 5-10 minutes, depending on how far the corn is from the heat — test each one with a skewer to check that it is tender.

To serve, take your sharpest knife and cut the corns across into chunks. These are best eaten using your hands and just taking bites: delicious! ■

Clockwise from left: Stuffed Jacket Potatoes with Leeks,
Cheddar and Boursin; Quick-braised Celery; Oven-roasted Chunky Chips,
and Red Onion, Tomato and Chilli Relish

Quick-braised Celery
Serves 4-6

Celery has such a lot going for it as a raw ingredient in salads, and because of that, we rather forget how good it is cooked and served as a vegetable. This method is delightfully quick and easy, and tastes just wonderful.

1 head celery, trimmed, de-stringed and cut into 3 inch (7.5 cm) pieces
1 oz (25 g) butter
1 medium onion, peeled and thinly sliced
3 oz (75 g) carrot, peeled and thinly sliced
8 fl oz (225 ml) hot stock made with Marigold Swiss vegetable bouillon powder
1 tablespoon chopped fresh parsley
salt and freshly milled black pepper

You will also need a lidded frying pan with a diameter of 10 inches (25.5 cm).

First of all, melt the butter in the frying pan and begin to cook the onions for 3-4 minutes over a medium to high heat, until lightly golden, then add the carrots and cook for a further 2 minutes. Now add the celery and continue to fry for 5 minutes more, or until everything is slightly browned at the edges. Season with salt and freshly milled black pepper, then pour in the hot stock and place a lid on the pan.

Turn the heat down and simmer gently for 20 minutes, until the vegetables are almost tender, then take the lid off and increase the heat to medium and continue to simmer till the liquid has reduced and become slightly syrupy – about 5 minutes. Serve the celery with the juices poured over and sprinkled with the parsley ■

Stuffed Jacket Potatoes with Leeks, Cheddar and Boursin
Serves 2

In this recipe the potato is scooped out, mixed with soft cheese and topped with leeks and melted cheese.

2 large baked potatoes, 8-10 oz (225-275 g) each (see page 176)
1 leek, about 4 inches (10 cm) long, trimmed and cleaned
1½ oz (40 g) mature Cheddar, coarsely grated
1 x 80 g pack Ail & Fines Herbes Boursin, or same quantity Le Roulé herb cheese
1 tablespoon single cream
salt and freshly milled black pepper

You will also need a baking sheet measuring 10 x 14 inches (25.5 x 35 cm).

Pre-heat the oven to gas mark 4, 350°F (180°C).

To prepare the leek, slice it almost in half lengthways, then fan it out under a running tap to wash away any trapped dirt. Now slice each half into 4 lengthways, then into ¼ inch (5 mm) slices. After that, put the soft cheese into a medium-sized bowl and cut the potatoes in half lengthways. Protecting your hands with a clean cloth, scoop out the centres of the potatoes into the bowl, add the cream and season well with salt and freshly milled black pepper.

Next, quickly mash or whisk everything together, then pile the whole lot back into the potato skins. Now scatter the leeks on top, followed by the grated Cheddar – pressing it down lightly with your hand – then place on the baking sheet and bake in the oven for 20 minutes or until the leeks are golden brown at the edges and the cheese is bubbling ■

Oven-roasted Chunky Chips
Serves 4-6

These are, believe it or not, low fat – just one dessertspoon of oil between four to six people, so not quite as wicked as it would first seem.

2 lb (900 g) Desirée potatoes
1 dessertspoon olive oil
salt

You will also need a solid baking tray measuring approximately 16 x 11 inches (40 x 28 cm).

Pre-heat the oven to gas mark 8, 450°F (230°C).

First, wash the potatoes very thoroughly, then dry in a clean tea cloth – they need to be as dry as possible; if they're ready washed, just wipe them with kitchen paper. Leaving the peel on, slice them in half lengthways and then cut them again lengthways into chunky wedges, approximately 1 inch (2.5 cm) thick. Dry them again in a cloth, then place them in a large bowl with the oil and a sprinkling of salt.

Now toss them around a few times to get them well covered with the oil, then spread them out on the baking tray and place in the oven on a high shelf to roast for about 30 minutes. They should be golden brown and crisp after this time; if not, give them a few more minutes. Finally, sprinkle with a little more salt, then serve absolutely immediately. These are particularly good served with Red Onion, Tomato and Chilli Relish (see page 176) ■

Glazed Baby Turnips
Serves 4

Baby turnips about the size of golf balls are creamy white with leafy green tops, and usually sold in bunches in the summer when they are in season.

2 lb (900 g) young turnips
1-1½ pints (570-850 ml) light vegetable stock made with Marigold Swiss vegetable bouillon powder
1 teaspoon Dijon mustard
2 tablespoons dry white wine or dry cider
1 teaspoon sugar
2 tablespoons chopped fresh parsley
salt and freshly milled black pepper

First of all, prepare the turnips by peeling them carefully and thinly with a potato peeler, then put them into a large saucepan of boiling water and boil for 3 minutes. Next, drain in a colander and then return them to the saucepan. Now add just enough stock to cover the turnips, bring this to the boil and simmer (uncovered) for about 10 minutes, or until the turnips are tender. Use a draining spoon to remove the turnips, place them in a warmed serving dish and keep hot while you make the glaze.

Next, blend the mustard with a little of the white wine (or cider) and add to the stock in the saucepan with the remainder of the wine and the sugar. Re-heat, taste and season with salt and freshly milled black pepper. Simmer rapidly (without a lid) until the liquid has reduced to a syrupy consistency, then pour this syrup over the turnips, sprinkle with chopped parsley and serve ■

Baby Summer Vegetables with Lemon Vinaigrette
Serves 6-8

A truly beautiful combination of those first, tender vegetables of early summer – serve warm as a vegetable or cold as a salad.

12 oz (350 g) broad beans, shelled weight (about 4 lb/1.8 kg in shell)

8 oz (225 g) fresh tiny baby carrots

8 oz (225 g) fresh garden peas, shelled weight (about 1 lb 8 oz/700 g in shell)

10 bulbous spring onions, trimmed

For the lemon vinaigrette:

3 tablespoons lemon juice

grated zest 1 lemon

2 tablespoons white wine vinegar

8 tablespoons light olive oil

2 teaspoons mustard powder

1 tablespoon chopped fresh mint and chives, to garnish

To get the very best colour and texture (and if you have the patience), it's best to skin the broad beans. So shell them and then pour boiling water over them and when it has cooled sufficiently, simply slip off the outer skin, which will reveal the beautiful vivid green inner bean in two halves. As you do this, place them in a bowl. Next, put the carrots in a steamer fitted over a pan of simmering water, steam them for 4 minutes precisely, then add the peas and spring onion bulbs and steam for a further 3-4 minutes.

Meanwhile, make the vinaigrette by placing all the ingredients in a screw-top jar and shaking vigorously to combine everything. When the vegetables are tender but still retain their bite, remove the steamer, throw out the water and put the broad beans in the pan, along with the rest of the vegetables and the dressing, and toss everything around over a gentle heat for about 1 minute. Then transfer it to a warmed serving dish, sprinkle the herbs over as a garnish and serve ■

Gratin Dauphinois
Serves 3-4

This is so often served in restaurants as a gooey sludge that seems to have hung around too long. But home-made, straight from the oven, it is truly one of the great classics. I know it does seem extravagant to use 5 fl oz (150 ml) cream for 1 lb (450 g) potatoes, but I would forego a pudding with cream once in a while in order to justify it.

1 lb (450 g) potatoes (King Edward or Desirée)

1 small clove garlic, peeled and crushed

5 fl oz (150 ml) double cream

5 fl oz (150 ml) milk

freshly grated nutmeg

1 oz (25 g) butter

salt and freshly milled black pepper

You will also need an 8 inch (20 cm) oval, shallow gratin dish, well buttered.

Pre-heat the oven to gas mark 2, 300°F (150°C).

First, peel the potatoes and slice them very, very thinly (a wooden mandolin is excellent for this operation, if you have one), then plunge the potato slices into a bowl of cold water and swill them round and round to get rid of some of the starch. Now dry them very thoroughly in a clean tea cloth. Then, in the gratin dish, arrange a layer of potato slices, a sprinkling of crushed garlic, pepper and salt and then another layer of potatoes and seasoning.

Now mix the cream and milk together, pour it over the potatoes, sprinkle with a little freshly grated nutmeg, then add the butter in flecks over the surface and bake on the highest shelf in the oven for 1½ hours ■

Creamed Parsnips
Serves 4

Even people who think they don't like parsnips usually admit they like this.

1 lb (450 g) parsnips

5 fl oz (150 ml) single cream

freshly grated nutmeg

salt and freshly milled black pepper

Peel the parsnips and cut out the woody centre bits, then cut them up into small cubes. Then place them in a steamer over some simmering water, sprinkle with salt, and steam – covered – for approximately 10 minutes or until tender when tested with a skewer.

Now, either purée them with the cream in a blender or sieve them and beat in the cream a little at a time with a fork. Taste and season with freshly grated nutmeg, salt and pepper and, if you think the mixture is too dry, mix in 1 or 2 tablespoons of the steaming water. Serve piping hot ■

Potatoes Boulangères with Rosemary
Serves 6

These potatoes are so named because in France they were given to the local baker to place in a bread oven to cook slowly.

2 lb 8 oz (1.15kg) potatoes (Romano or Desirée), peeled

½ oz (10 g) fresh rosemary

2 medium onions, peeled

10 fl oz (275 ml) hot stock made with Marigold Swiss vegetable bouillon powder

5 fl oz (150 ml) milk

1½ oz (40 g) butter

salt and freshly milled black pepper

You will also need an ovenproof dish measuring 11 x 8 x 2 inches (28 x 20 x 5 cm), lightly buttered.

Pre-heat the oven to gas mark 4, 350°F (180°C).

Begin by preparing the rosemary, which should be stripped from the stalks, then bruised in a pestle and mortar. After that, take two-thirds of the leaves and chop them finely. Now cut the onions in half and then the halves into the thinnest slices possible; the potatoes should be sliced, but not too thinly.

All you do is arrange a layer of potatoes, then onions, in the dish, followed by a scattering of rosemary, then season. Continue layering in this way, alternating the potatoes and onions and finishing with a layer of potatoes that slightly overlap. Now mix the stock and milk together and pour it over the potatoes. Season the top layer, then scatter over the whole rosemary leaves.

Now put little flecks of the butter all over the potatoes and place the dish on the highest shelf of the oven for 50-60 minutes, until the top is crisp and golden and the underneath is creamy and tender ■

Potatoes Boulangères with Rosemary

Clockwise from left: Salt-crusted Mini Baked Potatoes with Cold Chive Hollandaise; Marinated Courgettes with a Herb Vinaigrette; Oriental Green Beans with Red Chillies and Toasted Sesame Seeds

Marinated Courgettes with a Herb Vinaigrette
Serves 4

If you grow courgettes then this recipe is superb for serving the ones that – if you don't keep a sharp eye on them – become baby marrows overnight. These still taste good after three days, so you can make them in advance if you prefer.

1 lb (450 g) courgettes

For the herb vinaigrette:
1 teaspoon snipped fresh chives
1 teaspoon each finely chopped fresh tarragon and fresh parsley
1 teaspoon fresh rosemary leaves, bruised and finely chopped
1 clove garlic, peeled
1 rounded teaspoon wholegrain mustard
2 tablespoons white wine vinegar
4 tablespoons olive oil
sea salt and freshly milled black pepper

To prepare the courgettes, trim off the stalky ends and, if they are small, simply slice them in half lengthways; if they are larger, cut them in 4 lengthways. Then place them in a steamer, pour in some boiling water, sprinkle with a little salt and let them cook, covered, for 10-14 minutes, depending on their size – they need to be firm but tender.

Meanwhile, prepare the dressing by pounding the garlic with a teaspoon of sea salt in a pestle and mortar until it becomes creamy. Now work in the mustard, then the vinegar and a generous amount of black pepper. Next add the oil and give everything a good whisk, then add the herbs. When the courgettes are ready, remove them to a shallow serving dish, then pour the dressing over. Allow them to get cold, then cover and leave in a cool place or in the fridge for several hours, turning them once or twice ■

Oriental Green Beans with Red Chillies and Toasted Sesame Seeds
Serves 4

This is a vegetable dish that will accompany any oriental recipe. Or, it can be served with a bowl of rice or noodles all on its own, in which case it will serve two.

8 oz (225 g) dwarf beans (or fine green beans, topped, but tails left on)

For the sauce:
1 small red chilli, deseeded and very finely chopped
1 heaped teaspoon sesame seeds
2 tablespoons Japanese soy sauce
2 tablespoons Shaosing (Chinese brown rice wine)

You will also need a steamer.

First, toast the sesame seeds. Place a small saucepan over a medium heat to warm through, then add the sesame seeds. Shake and keep them on the move until they have turned golden and begin to splutter – about a minute. Then remove the pan from the heat and allow it to cool. After that, add the rest of the sauce ingredients, return the pan to the heat and simmer for 5 minutes.

All this can be done well in advance, then, when you're ready to cook the beans, steam them over simmering water for about 6 minutes or until tender, then toss them quickly in the sauce just before serving ■

Salt-crusted Mini Baked Potatoes with Cold Chive Hollandaise
Serves 6

These are excellent to serve at a buffet. The topping can vary, and for those with rather less time to spare for preparation I would recommend a soft cheese mixed with garlic and herbs, or else a tub of ready-made herb and onion dip. For larger quantities, make a double quantity of hollandaise sauce.

20 small red potatoes, about the size of a very large egg
olive oil
1 tablespoon sea salt

For the hollandaise:
3 rounded tablespoons freshly snipped chives
6 oz (175 g) butter
1 tablespoon wine vinegar
2 tablespoon lemon juice
3 large egg yolks
generous pinch of salt

Pre-heat the oven to gas mark 5, 375°F (190°C).

First of all, make up the hollandaise: put the butter into a small saucepan and allow it to melt slowly. Place the wine vinegar and lemon juice in another pan and bring these to the boil.

Meanwhile, blend the egg yolks in a blender or food processor with the pinch of salt, then – with the motor still switched on – gradually add the hot lemon and vinegar. When the butter reaches the boil, start to pour this in very slowly in a thin trickle (with the motor running all the time) till it is all added and the sauce is thickened. Pour it into a small bowl and stir in the snipped chives. Cover the bowl with clingfilm and leave in the fridge until the sauce is cold and set. Next, scrub the potatoes thoroughly and dry them with a clean tea towel, then leave them aside

for the skins to dry completely (if you get ready-scrubbed potatoes, just wipe them with damp kitchen paper). When the skins are nice and dry, prick them with a fork, then moisten your hands with oil and rub the potatoes to oil them all over. Put about 1 tablespoon sea salt in a bowl and turn each potato in the salt to coat it lightly.

Place the potatoes on a baking sheet and bake for 1 hour, or until crisp and tender. Then, when you're ready to serve, cut a cross in the top of each potato and gently squeeze up from the base to open out the cut slightly (use a clean tea towel to protect your hands). Arrange the potatoes together on a warmed serving dish and quickly top each one with a spoonful of the chive hollandaise ■

Note: This recipe contains raw eggs.

Aligot (mashed potatoes with garlic and cheese)
Serves 2

I first ate this mashed potato with cheese in southwest France, in the Tarn region, and it was, quite simply, the best mashed potato I've ever eaten.

1 lb (450 g) potatoes (Desirée or King Edward), peeled and cut into even-sized chunks
2 fat cloves garlic, peeled and halved lengthways
1 oz (25 g) butter
8 oz (225 g) Lancashire cheese, grated
salt and freshly milled black pepper

Begin this by placing the garlic in a small saucepan with the butter, then leave it on the gentlest heat possible to melt and infuse for 30 minutes. Meanwhile, place the potatoes in a steamer, then pour some boiling water straight from the kettle into a saucepan. Fit the steamer over the saucepan, sprinkle the potatoes with 1 dessertspoon of salt, put a lid on and let them steam for 20-25 minutes, until tender in the centre when tested with a skewer. After this, transfer them to a large bowl (preferably a warm one) and cover with a cloth to absorb some steam.

Then with an electric hand whisk on slow, begin to break up the potatoes and add the butter and garlic, some black pepper and a handful of the grated cheese. Now switch the speed to high and add the cheese, a handful at a time, while you whisk. There's a lot of cheese, but as you whisk it in, the potatoes will turn translucent and glossy and, as you lift and whisk, it forms stiff, glossy peaks. As the cheese goes in, the mixture becomes stiff and clings to the whisk, but keep going and it will part company with the whisk eventually.

When all the cheese is in, serve very quickly, or to keep it warm, place the bowl over a pan of simmering water, but don't leave it too long ■

Courgettes and Tomatoes au Gratin
Serves 2-4

This is a very quick and easy vegetarian supper dish for two people, especially if you grow your own tomatoes and courgettes and have a glut to use up. You could also serve it as a starter for four people.

4 medium courgettes, trimmed and sliced into rounds but not peeled
2 tablespoons olive oil
1 large clove garlic, peeled and crushed
4 oz (110 g) mozzarella, or Cheddar, cut in slices
4 large tomatoes, skinned and sliced
4 tablespoons parmesan, grated
1 tablespoon fresh chopped basil, or 1 teaspoon dried oregano
salt and freshly milled black pepper

Pre-heat the oven to gas mark 5, 375°F (190°C).

If you have the time, salt, drain and dry the sliced courgettes. To do this, layer them in a colander, sprinkling each layer with salt. Then, put a plate on top and a heavy weight and leave for 30 minutes. Finally, dry the courgettes in a cloth. Either way, now heat the oil in a frying pan large enough to hold the courgettes in one layer (otherwise do them in 2 batches), add the crushed garlic and sauté the courgette slices to a nice golden colour on each side.

Next, arrange layers of courgettes, cheese slices and sliced tomatoes in a heatproof gratin dish so that they overlap each other slightly like slates on a roof.

Finally, sprinkle on the grated parmesan, basil (or oregano) and salt and freshly milled black pepper. Then bake on a high shelf in the oven for 30 minutes. Serve this with lots of crusty bread and a green salad with a sharp, lemony dressing ■

Parmesan-baked Parsnips
Serves 8

This is one of the nicest ways to serve parsnips or swede, baked crisp and golden brown in the oven with a parmesan coating. It also works well with sweet potatoes. They can be prepared well in advance, up to 24 hours, or they can even be prepared and frozen and will then cook perfectly if allowed to defrost first.

2 oz (50 g) freshly grated parmesan
2 lb 8 oz (1.15 kg) parsnips (or swede)
6 oz (175 g) plain flour
groundnut or other flavourless oil for baking
a knob of butter
salt and freshly milled black pepper

You will also need a large, solid roasting tin.

Pre-heat the oven to gas mark 6, 400°F (200°C).

Begin by combining the flour, parmesan, salt and freshly milled black pepper in a mixing bowl. Peel the parsnips using a potato peeler. Then halve and quarter them lengthways and cut each length in half across, so that you end up with smallish chunks. Cut out any tough, woody centres. Now pop the parsnips in a saucepan, pour in enough boiling water just to cover them and add salt. Put on a lid, bring them to the boil and boil for 3 minutes.

Meanwhile, have a large kitchen tray ready. Then, as soon as they are done, drain them in a colander and, whilst they are still steaming, drop a few at a time (with the aid of some kitchen tongs) into the flour and parmesan mixture, shaking the bowl and moving them around so that they get a good even coating. As they are coated, transfer them to the tray. Make sure you do them all fairly swiftly as the flour mixture will only coat them whilst they are still steamy! When they're all coated they are ready to cook or store in the fridge or freezer. Any leftover flour and parmesan can be kept (sifted) in the fridge or freezer for another time. What is important is to have plenty in order to coat the parsnips quickly.

To bake them, place a large solid roasting tin in the oven to pre-heat and in it put enough oil just to cover the base and a knob of butter for flavour. Then, when the oven is ready, remove the tin and place it over direct heat (turned fairly low) and, again using tongs, place the parsnips quickly, side by side, in the tin. Tilt it and baste all the parsnips with hot fat, place the tin in the oven and bake them for 20 minutes, then turn them over, drain off any surplus fat (a bulb baster is good for this) and continue to bake for a further 15-20 minutes or until they are crisp and golden ■

Parmesan-baked Parsnips

Purée of Potato and Celeriac
Serves 8

This is a beautiful combination of flavours and it can be made a couple of hours in advance and kept warm with no ill-effects whatsoever.

1 lb (450 g) potatoes

2 lb (900 g) celeriac

2 fat cloves garlic, peeled

2 oz (50 g) butter

5 fl oz (150 ml) double cream, or crème fraîche

salt and freshly milled black pepper

First, you need to tackle the celeriac. You will need to have a bowl of cold water ready in which to put the prepared pieces to prevent them browning. Peel the celeriac thickly with a knife. Then cut into approximately ¾ inch (2 cm) cubes. Leave these pieces in the water whilst preparing the potatoes. Peel and cut these into 1 inch (2.5 cm) cubes – i.e. slightly larger than the celeriac.

Now place the prepared vegetables in separate saucepans with 1 clove garlic in each saucepan. Pour enough boiling water over the vegetables just to cover them, add salt and simmer them for about 10 minutes or until they are tender.

Drain each vegetable in a colander, place them together in a large heatproof mixing bowl and add the butter and cream or crème fraîche and some freshly milled black pepper. Next, using an electric hand whisk, whisk them to a purée using the slow speed to break them up, then the fast one to whisk them till smooth. Now taste and season the purée, then place the bowl in a roasting tin half-filled with barely simmering water and it will keep warm quite happily until your guests arrive ■

Stir-fried Green Vegetables
Serves 4

This is the classic Chinese fry first, steam second, which results in a fragrant crunchiness.

4 oz (110 g) cauliflower

6 oz (175 g) broccoli

2 medium leeks

4 spring onions, trimmed

10 oz (275 g) pak choi

2 inch (5 cm) piece root ginger, peeled

2 tablespoons groundnut or other flavourless oil

2 cloves garlic, peeled and thickly sliced

3 tablespoons Japanese soy sauce

3 fl oz (75 ml) Shaosing brown rice wine, or dry sherry

1 dessertspoon golden caster sugar

To garnish:

2 spring onions, finely shredded

½ medium red chilli, deseeded and cut into fine shreds

First, prepare the vegetables: the cauliflower should be separated out and cut into tiny florets, and the same with the broccoli. Wash and trim the leeks, then halve and thinly slice them, while the spring onions should be sliced into matchsticks, as should the ginger. Finally, cut each head of pak choi into 6 wedges through the root. To cook, heat the oil over a high heat in a wok or large frying pan, add the the ginger and garlic and fry for 10 seconds, then add the cauliflower and broccoli and stir-fry for 1 minute. Next add the leeks and stir-fry for another minute. Add the spring onions and pak choi, toss it all together, then add the soy sauce, rice wine (or dry sherry), 3 fl oz (75 ml) water and the sugar. Reduce the heat to medium, put a lid on, and cook for 4 minutes, stirring occasionally. Serve the vegetables with the spring onions and chilli sprinkled over ■

Provençal Vegetable Stew (ratatouille)
Serves 4

This famous French recipe is best made in the autumn when the vegetables needed for it are cheap and plentiful. Don't cut the vegetables too small or they will end up mushy. They should retain their individuality. For roasted ratatouille, see page 163.

3 medium courgettes

2 large aubergines

2 medium onions, peeled and roughly chopped

2 red or green peppers, deseeded and roughly chopped

4 large tomatoes, skinned, and chopped, or a 14 oz (400 g) tin Italian tomatoes, well drained

2 cloves garlic, peeled and crushed

4 tablespoons olive oil

1 tablespoon chopped fresh basil

sea salt and freshly milled black pepper

First, you need to get rid of the excess moisture in the courgettes and aubergines. Begin, then, by wiping the aubergines and cutting them into 1 inch (2.5 cm) slices, then cut each slice in half; the courgettes should be wiped as well and cut into 1 inch (2.5 cm) slices. Now put the whole lot into a colander, sprinkle generously with salt, press them down with a suitably-sized plate and put weights (or other heavy objects) on top of the plate. Let them stand for about 1 hour – the salt will draw out any bitterness along with excess moisture.

Now gently fry the onions and garlic in the oil in a large saucepan for 10 minutes, then add the peppers. Dry the courgettes and aubergines with kitchen paper, then add them too. Next, add the basil and season with salt and pepper, stir once really well, then simmer very gently (covered) for 30 minutes. Now add the tomatoes, season to taste and cook for a further 15 minutes with the lid off ■

Pickled Beetroot with Shallots
Makes an 18 fl oz (510 ml) jar

Beetroot is vastly underestimated, in my opinion. Perhaps that's because the strong malt vinegar of the commercial pickling masks the true flavour of the beetroot, or maybe it's because of overboiling. But when prepared in the following way, it provides a wonderfully flavoured and textured accompaniment. To sterilise the jar, wash it thoroughly in warm, soapy water, rinse and heat in a moderate oven for 5 minutes.

1 lb (450 g) fresh beetroot

2 shallots

6 fl oz (175 ml) red wine vinegar

½ teaspoon mixed pepper berries

½ teaspoon crushed sea salt

You will also need an 18 fl oz (510 ml) jar, sterilised (as described above).

Pre-heat the oven to gas mark 5, 375°F (190°C).

Trim the beetroot and wipe them, but leave the skins on. Then wrap them all up together in a parcel of foil. Place the parcel on a baking sheet and bake them for about 3 hours or until they feel tender when pierced with a skewer. Now remove them from the oven and, as soon as they are cool enough to handle, peel off the skins and slice the beetroot thinly.

Peel and thinly slice the shallots, too, then layer the beetroot and shallots in the sterilised jar. Next, place the vinegar, berries and salt in a small saucepan, bring up to simmering point, and pour the whole lot straight over the beetroot and shallots to cover them completely. Seal the jar immediately, label it when cold, then store. The beetroot doesn't need to mature – it can be eaten within a day or two and will keep well, provided it is always totally immersed in the vinegar – so you may need to top it up after you use some ■

Braised Peas, Rocket and Spring Onions
Serves 6

This is a good recipe for slightly older peas, which, in my opinion, sometimes have more texture and flavour than the younger ones. However, if the peas you are using are very young, give them far less cooking time – 8 minutes at the most.

3 lb (1.35 kg) peas (unshelled weight), freshly shelled
2½ oz (60 g) fresh rocket
12 bulbous spring onions
1½ oz (40 g) butter
pinch golden caster sugar
1 rounded teaspoon salt

First, trim the spring onions: you need only the white bulbs (the rest can be chopped and saved for something such as a stir-fry). Pull off any thick, stalky bits from the rocket and tear the larger leaves in half.

Now all you do is put all the ingredients in a large saucepan, together with 3 tablespoons of water, cover with a lid, bring them up to simmering point and simmer gently for 8-15 minutes, depending on the age of the peas ■

Sauté Potatoes Niçoise
Serves 2

The secret of really crisp sauté potatoes is, first of all, to use olive oil, and secondly, to cook the potatoes in a single layer so they don't overlap each other.

1 lb (450 g) or 3 medium Desirée potatoes
2 tablespoons olive oil
1 small onion or shallot, peeled and finely chopped
¼ medium-sized green or red pepper, deseeded and finely chopped
1 small clove garlic, peeled and crushed
3 black olives, pitted and chopped
1 tablespoon chopped fresh parsley or other fresh herbs
sea salt and freshly milled black pepper

You will also need a warm serving dish with some crumpled greaseproof paper or kitchen paper placed in it.

First, thinly peel the potatoes and cut them in half. Then put them in a saucepan, cover them with boiling water, add some salt, bring to simmering point and cook for 8-10 minutes or until just tender when tested with a skewer. Now drain the potatoes and leave them to cool.

When the potatoes have cooled, arrange them on a wooden board and slice them thinly and evenly into slices about ¼ inch (5 mm) thick. For the next stage, you need a large frying pan, with a base diameter of approximately 10 inches (25.5 cm) and a small frying pan for the Niçoise mixture. Heat a dessertspoon of the olive oil in the small pan, add the onion and fry gently. Then when transparent, add the pepper and garlic and cook until soft. Then stir in the olives and set aside. Now heat the remaining oil in the large frying pan and when it begins to sizzle, add the potatoes, making sure they don't overlap. Fry them over a high heat, turning them after 5-7 minutes to cook on the other side until they are golden brown and crisp all over. Then, using a slotted spoon, transfer the cooked potatoes to the crumpled paper to drain, and scatter on the fried-onion mixture. Loosen the top of the pepper mill a little to get a really coarse grind and sprinkle over the potatoes; crush some sea salt between your finger and thumb and sprinkle on.

Lastly, pull out the paper from underneath, the potatoes and mix them with the pepper and olive mixture. Sprinkle with the chopped herbs over the top and serve at once – if you delay, the potatoes will go soggy ■

Oven-roasted Carrots with Coriander
Serves 4

This is a recipe for the large, chunky carrots of winter, which lack the sweet, delicate flavour of new carrots in summer. In the oven they turn slightly blackened and caramelised at the edges, which, together with the coriander seeds, gives an added flavour dimension. The carrots can be prepared well in advance and kept in a polythene bag in the fridge.

1 lb (450 g) winter carrots, wiped if dusty
1 dessertspoon coriander seeds
2 cloves garlic, peeled and crushed
½ teaspoon black peppercorns
½ teaspoon sea salt
1 dessertspoon olive oil

You will also need a baking tray measuring 10 x 14 inches (25.5 x 35 cm).

Pre-heat the oven to gas mark 8, 450°F (230°C).

Begin by cutting the carrots into 1½ inch (4 cm) chunks, but no smaller. Next, dry-roast the coriander seeds and peppercorns in a small frying pan or saucepan over a medium heat, stirring and tossing them around for 1-2 minutes, or until they begin to look toasted and start to jump in the pan. Now empty them into a pestle and mortar and crush them coarsely, then put the carrot chunks and crushed spices in a bowl.

Next, put the garlic cloves and salt in the mortar, crush to a purée, then whisk in the oil. Now toss this mixture around with the carrots and spices, then spread it out on the baking tray. Pop it into the oven on a high shelf and roast until the carrots are tender when tested with a skewer – 30 to 40 minutes ■

Oven-roasted Carrots with Coriander

Chapter Nine
Baking

Irish Seeded Soda Bread
Makes 1 large loaf

This excellent recipe comes from Avoca Café in Dublin. It keeps very well and makes great toast. The seed content can be altered and it is also delicious with the addition of 2 oz (50 g) each of sultanas and chopped semi-dried apricots.

12 oz (350 g) coarse plain wholemeal flour
6 oz (200 g) plain flour
2 oz (50 g) bran
1 oz (25 g) wheatgerm
2 heaped teaspoons baking powder
1 teaspoon salt
1 tablespoon sesame seeds
1 tablespoon poppy seeds
2 tablespoons sunflower seeds
1 tablespoon linseeds
2 tablespoons pumpkin seeds
1 tablespoon black treacle
1-1¼ pints (570-725 ml) milk

You will also need a 2 lb (900 g) loaf tin, lightly buttered.

Pre-heat the oven to gas mark 4, 350°F (180°C).

First of all, mix all the dry ingredients together in a large mixing bowl. Now add the treacle and enough milk to make a moist dough. Start by adding 1 pint (570 ml) milk and then add more if you need it – you are aiming for a mixture that has the consistency of stiff porridge.

Next, place the mixture in the prepared loaf tin and bake in the pre-heated oven for 1 hour, or until the loaf is well browned and sounds hollow when turned out of the tin and tapped underneath. Leave on a wire rack to cool ■

Feta, Olive and Sun-blush Tomato Scones
Makes 12

These are lovely served as a snack or savoury at tea-time. They also go very well as a companion to many soups for lunch.

For the scones:
3 oz (75 g) feta, cubed small, plus 2 oz (50 g) feta, crumbled for topping
10 black olives, pitted and roughly chopped
2 oz (50 g) sun-blush tomatoes in oil (or same quantity of mi-cuit tomatoes and a tablespoon of olive oil)
6 oz (175 g) self-raising flour, plus a little extra for dusting
2 oz (50 g) wholemeal flour
¼ teaspoon baking powder
¼ teaspoon cayenne pepper
¼ teaspoon mustard powder
2 tablespoons extra virgin olive oil
1½ teaspoons chopped fresh thyme
1 large egg
2 tablespoons milk

You will also need a 2 inch (5 cm) cutter (plain or fluted) and a baking tray measuring 10 x 14 inches (25.5 x 35 cm), lightly greased.

Pre-heat the oven to gas mark 7, 425°F (220°C).

First of all, drain the sun-blush tomatoes, reserving one tablespoon of oil. If you are using mi-cuit tomatoes, there will be no need to drain them. Either way, chop the tomatoes into small pieces.

Now sift the flours and baking powder into a large, roomy bowl, tip in any bran left in the sieve, then add the cayenne and mustard powder and, using a knife, work in the 2 tablespoons of olive oil, plus the reserved tablespoon of oil from the sun-blush tomatoes (or the extra tablespoon of oil, if using mi-cuit tomatoes). When the mixture

looks like lumpy breadcrumbs stir in the chopped thyme, cubed feta, olives and the tomatoes.

Now in a separate bowl beat the egg with the 2 tablespoons of milk and add half this mixture to the other ingredients. Using your hands, bring the mixture together to form a dough, adding more of the egg and milk as it needs it – what you should end up with is a dough that is soft but not sticky.

Now on a floured board, roll the dough out to a depth of 1 inch (2.5 cm). Then stamp out the scones using the cutter. Put the cut-out pieces on the baking tray and brush them with the remaining milk mixture.

Finally, top each scone with the crumbled feta, and put the tray on the highest shelf of the oven to bake for 12-15 minutes or until they've turned a golden colour. Then remove them to a wire rack until they are cool enough to eat ■

Parsnip, Parmesan and Sage Bread
Makes 1 loaf (serves 4-6)

I love to serve this with Curried Parsnip and Apple Soup with Parsnip Crisps (see page 23).

6 oz (175 g) parsnips (peeled weight)
2 oz (50 g) parmesan, cut into ¼ inch (5 mm) cubes
1 rounded tablespoon chopped fresh sage
8 oz (225 g) self-raising flour
1½ teaspoons salt
2 large eggs, lightly beaten with 1 tablespoon of milk

For the topping:
1 oz (25 g) parmesan shavings
a few whole small fresh sage leaves
a little extra flour for dusting
1 teaspoon olive oil

You will also need a small, solid baking sheet, very well greased.

Pre-heat the oven to gas mark 5, 375°F (190°C).

First of all, sift the flour and salt into a large, roomy bowl. Then put a grater in the bowl and coarsely grate the parsnips into the flour, then toss them around. After that, add the parmesan cubes and chopped sage and toss that in. Now add the egg mixture, a little at a time, mixing with a palette knife. You should end up with a rough, rather loose, sticky dough, so don't worry what it looks like.

Transfer this to the baking sheet and pat it gently into a 6 inch (15 cm) rough round, then make a cross with the blunt side of a knife. Now scatter the parmesan shavings over the surface, followed by a sprinkling of flour. Finally, dip each sage leaf in the oil and scatter them over the bread. Now it should go into the oven on a high shelf to bake for 45-50 minutes till golden and crusty. Cool on a wire rack, then serve it still warm or re-heat it later ■

Parsnip, Parmesan and Sage Bread

Left: Honey and Spice Cake. Top right: Poppy and Sesame Seed Rolls

Poppy and Sesame Seed Rolls
Makes 16

Basically, these are the familiar soft Vienna rolls – improved, I think, by a liberal sprinkling of poppy seeds.

1 lb 2 oz (500 g) strong white flour, warmed slightly, plus a little extra for dusting

11 fl oz (310 ml) hand-hot milk

1 teaspoon golden caster sugar

2 teaspoons easy-blend dried yeast

1½ teaspoons salt

4 oz (110 g) butter, at room temperature

For the topping:

1 tablespoon poppy seeds

1 tablespoon sesame seeds

1 large egg, beaten

You will also need a baking tray measuring 11 x 16 inches (28 x 40 cm), well greased.

Start by pouring 5 fl oz (150 ml) of the milk into a medium-sized bowl and whisk the sugar into it with a fork, followed by the dried yeast. Leave this on one side for 10 minutes to froth. Meanwhile, sift the flour and salt into a large bowl, make a well in the centre, and (when it's ready) pour in the frothed yeast and milk, and the rest of the milk. Mix to form a smooth dough, then turn out on to a working surface and knead for 10 minutes.

After that, put the dough back in the bowl, cover with clingfilm and leave it to rise until doubled in bulk (which will take 1½-2 hours at room temperature or 45-60 minutes in a warm place). Then punch the dough down in the bowl to knock the air out, and then gradually work in the soft butter. The dough will now be very sticky, but ignore this and carry on until the butter is evenly worked in. Next, turn it out on to a lightly floured work surface and knead and shape it into

roughly an 8 inch (20 cm) square. Now brush the top of the dough with the beaten egg. Next, combine the poppy and sesame seeds in a small bowl and sprinkle them evenly over the top of the dough. After that, take a large sharp knife and cut the dough into 16 squares, roughly measuring 2 inches (5 cm). Don't worry about getting perfect shapes – they can be quite haphazard.

Now transfer them to the baking tray, leaving a space between each one, as they will prove and rise before baking. Leave them for about 30 minutes in a warm place or an hour at room temperature. Meanwhile, pre-heat the oven to gas mark 5, 375°F (190°C).

Bake the rolls for 25-30 minutes or until crisp and golden brown. Cool on a wire cooling rack. If you're making them in advance, warm them through briefly in the oven before serving ■

Note: These rolls can also be made in a breadmaker. Use water instead of milk and there is no need to warm it. Just place all the ingredients in the breadmaker and set the machine to the dough-only setting. Then briefly knead the dough and shape into an 8 inch (20 cm) square and proceed as above.

Honey and Spice Cake
Serves 6-8

This cake has a tangy, citrus flavour and a sharp lemon icing, and tastes sensational, particularly when eaten outdoors.

3 oz (75 g) clear, runny honey

8 oz (225 g) plain flour

1 teaspoon ground ginger

1 teaspoon ground cinnamon

¼ teaspoon ground cloves

3 oz (75 g) golden caster sugar

finely grated zest 1 small orange

finely grated zest 1 small lemon

4 oz (110 g) butter, at room temperature

1 large egg, beaten

1 teaspoon bicarbonate of soda

2 oz (50 g) whole mixed candied peel, finely chopped

For the icing:

6 oz (175 g) icing sugar

1 tablespoon lemon juice

To decorate:

6 pieces crystallised ginger, chopped

Pre-heat the oven to gas mark 3, 325°F (170°C).

You will also need a 7 inch (18 cm) square tin or 8 inch (20 cm) round tin, lightly buttered.

First of all, weigh a cup or small basin on the scales, then weigh the 3 oz (75 g) of honey into it. Now place the basin into a saucepan containing barely simmering water and warm the honey a little, but be careful: it mustn't be too hot, just warm.

Next, sift the flour and spices into a large mixing bowl, then add the sugar and the orange and lemon zests. Now add the butter in small pieces, then rub it lightly into the flour, using your fingertips, until the mixture becomes crumbly. Next, lightly mix in the

beaten egg, using a large fork, followed by the warm honey. Then in a small basin, mix the bicarbonate of soda with 3 tablespoons of cold water, stir until dissolved, then add it to the cake mixture and beat, quite hard, until the mixture is smooth and soft. Finally, stir in the mixed peel and spoon the mixture into the prepared tin, spreading it out evenly.

Bake the cake just above the centre of the oven for about 50 minutes or until well risen and springy to the touch. Cool it for 10 minutes, then turn it out on to a wire rack to get quite cold.

Meanwhile, prepare the icing by sifting the icing sugar into a bowl, then add 2 tablespoons of warm water, along with the lemon juice, and mix to a thin consistency that will coat the back of a spoon. If you don't think it's thin enough, add a little more water.

Now place the cake on a wire rack, with a large plate underneath, and pour the icing all over, letting it run down and coat the sides a bit. Then decorate the top with chopped ginger and store in an airtight tin ■

Prune, Apple and Armagnac Cake with Almond Streusel Topping
Serves 6-8

This is a cake that borders on being a dessert, and it would be my choice for a celebration winter supper party, served warm with crème fraîche or whipped cream. If you are not a lover of Armagnac, the prunes are also good soaked in port or Amaretto liqueur. They are best soaked overnight.

For the prunes:

12 oz (350 g) ready-to-eat prunes (the ones without stones)

3 fl oz (75 ml) Armagnac

3 oz (75 g) golden caster sugar

For the streusel topping:

2 oz (50 g) whole untoasted almonds, halved lengthways and shredded very finely

3 oz (75 g) self-raising flour, sifted

1 oz (25 g) butter, at room temperature

3 oz (75 g) demerara sugar

For the cake:

2 oz (50 g) peeled and diced Bramley apple

3 oz (75 g) self-raising flour

½ teaspoon baking powder

2 oz (50 g) soft butter

1 oz (25 g) ground almonds

2 oz (50 g) golden caster sugar

1 large egg

2 tablespoons milk

icing sugar, to finish

You will also need an 8 inch (20 cm) tin with a loose base, greased and lined with greaseproof paper.

Pre-heat the oven to gas mark 4, 350°F (180°C).

Although the ready-to-eat prunes are not supposed to need soaking, I sometimes prefer to soak them just the same (the advantage is having them ready-stoned).

Start the recipe the night before you want to serve the cake by placing the prunes in a saucepan, along with the sugar and 5 fl oz (150 ml) water, and simmer them very gently for 15 minutes. After that, drain them, discarding the cooking liquid, then place them in a bowl. Add the Armagnac, stir well, then cover and leave overnight.

When you're ready to make the cake, begin with the streusel topping: place the sifted flour and the butter in a bowl and rub the butter in until the mixture becomes crumbly. Then add the sugar, mixing it in evenly, and after that, sprinkle in 1 dessertspoon of cold water and fork the mixture until it is coarse and lumpy. Now leave it to one side with the almonds.

The cake mixture is very simple indeed – all you do is sift the flour and baking powder into a bowl, add the rest of the ingredients (except for the apple and icing sugar), then, using an electric hand whisk or wooden spoon and some old-fashioned elbow grease, beat the mixture together until smooth. After that, fold in the apple, then spoon the mixture into the prepared tin.

Now arrange the prunes all over the mixture, then fork the streusel topping over them, and finally, sprinkle the shredded almonds evenly over the surface. Place the cake on the centre shelf of the oven, bake it for 1 hour, and remove it from the oven. Then leave it in the tin for 30 minutes before turning it out to cool on a wire rack. Just before serving, sift the icing sugar over the surface ■

The Ultimate Carrot Cake with Mascarpone, Fromage Frais and Cinnamon Icing
Serves 6-8

I have been making carrot cake for years, and each time it seems to improve with a little tinkering here and there. Now I think it has reached its all-time peak – this one has been unanimously voted the best ever!

7 oz (200 g) carrots, peeled and coarsely grated

6 oz (175 g) dark soft brown sugar

2 large eggs

5 fl oz (150 ml) sunflower oil

7 oz (200 g) wholemeal self-raising flour

3 teaspoons mixed spice

1 teaspoon bicarbonate of soda

grated zest 1 orange

4 oz (110 g) sultanas

2 oz (50 g) desiccated coconut

2 oz (50 g) pecan nuts

For the syrup glaze:

juice 1 small orange

1 tablespoon lemon juice

3 oz (75 g) dark brown soft sugar

For the cinnamon icing:

9 oz (250 g) mascarpone

7 oz (200 g) 8 per cent fat fromage frais

1 heaped teaspoon ground cinnamon

1 rounded tablespoon golden caster sugar

To finish:

2 oz (50 g) pecan nuts

You will also need two 8 inch (20 cm) x 1½ inches (4 cm) deep, sponge tins, bases lined with baking parchment.

Pre-heat the oven to gas mark 6, 400°F (200°C), then turn down to gas mark 3, 325°F (170°C), when you have toasted the pecan nuts.

First, place all the pecan nuts (4 oz/110 g) on a baking sheet and, using a timer, toast them in the oven for 8 minutes. Now chop one half

roughly for the cake, and the other more finely, for the topping later. Then don't forget to turn the oven down to gas mark 3, 325°F (170°C) for the cake.

To make the cake, whisk the sugar, eggs and oil together in a bowl with an electric hand whisk for 2-3 minutes, then check that there is no sugar left undissolved. Now sift the flour, mixed spice and bicarbonate of soda into the bowl, tipping in the bits of bran left in the sieve. Then stir all this in gently, followed by the remaining cake ingredients.

Divide the batter evenly between the prepared tins and bake the cakes on the centre shelf of the oven for 30 minutes. They should be nicely risen, feel firm and springy to the touch when lightly pressed in the centre, and show signs of shrinking away from the sides of the tin. If not, give them another 2-3 minutes and test again.

Meanwhile, make the topping by whisking all the ingredients together in a bowl until light and fluffy. Then cover with clingfilm and chill for 1-2 hours, until you are ready to ice the cakes.

To make the syrup glaze, whisk together the fruit juices and sugar in another bowl and then, when the cakes come out of the oven, stab them all over with a skewer and quickly spoon the syrup evenly over the hot cakes.

Now leave them on one side to cool in their tins, during which time the syrup will be absorbed. Then when the cakes are completely cold, remove them from the tins. Spread one-third of the icing over one of the cakes, place the other on top, then cover the top and sides with the remaining mixture. Scatter the remaining toasted pecan nuts over the top just before serving ■

The Ultimate Carrot Cake with Mascarpone, Fromage Frais and Cinnamon Icing

Chocolate Marbled Energy Bars

Chocolate Marbled Energy Bars
Makes 16

These little bars were originally invented to provide high-energy snack food for footballers or other sports enthusiasts doing hard training. But for strictly armchair sports enthusiasts like me, they go down a treat with a mug of cocoa and *Match of the Day*.

5 oz (150 g) dark chocolate (75 per cent cocoa solids), broken into small pieces
5 oz (150 g) luxury Belgian white chocolate, broken into small pieces
4 oz (110 g) pecan nuts
4 oz (110 g) ready-to-eat dried apricots
5 oz (150 g) organic porridge oats
1 oz (25 g) Rice Krispies
1 oz (25 g) Bran Flakes, lightly crushed
3 oz (75 g) raisins
1 teaspoon molasses syrup
5 fl oz (150 ml) whole condensed milk

You will also need a non-stick baking tin measuring 10 x 6 inches (25.5 x 15 cm) and 1 inch (2.5 cm) deep.

Pre-heat the oven to gas mark 4, 350°F, (180°C).

Begin by toasting the pecan nuts on a baking sheet on the top shelf of the oven for 7 minutes, using a timer, then chop them roughly. Next, chop the apricots to the same size as the pecans, and then in a large bowl mix together the oats, Rice Krispies, Bran Flakes, apricots, pecans and raisins.

Now in a small saucepan, heat the molasses syrup and condensed milk until they're warm and thoroughly blended, then pour this mixture into the bowl. Mix it well with a wooden spoon, then simply tip the mixture into the baking tin, press it down evenly all over and bake in the centre of the oven for about 25 minutes, or until golden brown. After that, leave it to get quite cold.

Meanwhile, melt the dark and white chocolate separately in heatproof bowls set over pans of barely simmering water, making sure the bowls don't touch the water. When the cereal mixture has cooled, loosen the edges with a palette knife and turn it out upside down on to a board.

Now, using a tablespoon, put spoonfuls of the plain chocolate all over the top of the cereal cake, leaving space in between. Then do the same with the white chocolate, but this time fill up the gaps. Next, take a small palette knife and, using a zigzag motion, swirl the two chocolates together to give a marbled effect. Then lift the board and gently tap it down on to the work surface to create a smooth finish. What you need to do now is chill it in the fridge for about 1 hour, then use a sharp knife to cut it into 16 bars ■

Banana and Walnut Loaf
Serves 8

This is a lovely, moist cake that keeps well and is perfect for picnics or packed lunches.

4 medium bananas, about 12 oz/350 g
6 oz (175 g) walnut pieces
pinch salt
1 rounded teaspoon baking powder
1 teaspoon ground cinnamon
4 oz (110 g) plain flour
4 oz (110 g) wholemeal flour
grated zest of an orange and a lemon
4 oz (110 g) butter, at room temperature
6 oz (175 g) soft dark brown sugar
2 large eggs, at room temperature
1 tablespoon demerara sugar for topping

You will also need a 2 lb (900 g) loaf tin, lightly buttered.

Pre-heat the oven to gas mark 4, 350°F (180°C).

Begin by lightly toasting the nuts on a baking tray in the oven for 7-9 minutes (use a timer). Then let them cool, before roughly chopping them. Now peel and mash 3 of the bananas to a purée, and peel and chop the other one into ½ inch (1 cm) chunks. Next, in a mixing bowl, sift the salt, baking powder, cinnamon and flours, holding the sieve up high to give it a good airing (adding any bran left in the sieve).

Now add the remaining ingredients (except the chopped banana, nuts and demerara sugar) and, using an electric hand whisk, beat until everything is well mixed. Then lightly fold in the chopped banana and walnuts. You may need to add a drop of milk to give a mixture that drops easily off a spoon when you give it a sharp tap. Now pile the mixture into the tin, level the top and sprinkle on the sugar. Then bake in the centre of the oven for 1¼-1½ hours, until the loaf feels springy in the centre. Let it cool for 5 minutes before serving ■

Pumpkin, Cheddar and Pumpkin Seed Bread
Makes 1 loaf (serves 4-6)

This is a great alternative to the Parsnip, Parmesan and Sage Bread (on page 202). It goes particularly well with the Pumpkin Soup with Toasted Sweetcorn (on page 19).

6 oz (175 g) pumpkin or butternut squash (peeled weight)
2 oz (50 g) mature Cheddar, cut into ¼ inch (5 mm) cubes
1 oz (25 g) pumpkin seeds
8 oz (225 g) self-raising flour
1½ teaspoons salt
2 large eggs, lightly beaten with
1 tablespoon of milk

For the topping:
a few extra pumpkin seeds
a little extra flour for dusting

You will also need a small, solid baking sheet, very well greased.

Pre-heat the oven to gas mark 5, 375°F (190°C).

First of all, sift the flour and salt into a large, roomy bowl. Then put a grater in the bowl and coarsely grate the pumpkin or butternut squash into the flour, then toss it all around.

After that, add the pumpkin seeds, and two-thirds of the Cheddar and toss that in. Now add the egg mixture, a little at a time, mixing with a palette knife. You should end up with a rough, rather loose, sticky dough, so don't worry what it looks like at this stage.

Transfer this to the baking sheet and pat it gently into a 6 inch (15 cm) rough round, then make a cross with the blunt side of a knife. Now lightly press the rest of the cheese over the surface, followed by a sprinkling of flour. Finally, scatter the extra pumpkin seeds over the bread. Bake on a high shelf for 45-50 minutes till golden and crusty. Cool on a rack, then serve warm or re-heat later ■

Left: A Classic Sponge Cake with Passion Fruit Cream
Top right: A Classic Sponge Cake with Raspberry and Mascarpone Cream

A Classic Sponge Cake with Raspberry and Mascarpone Cream
Serves 8

This sponge cake can also be made in a 7 inch (18 cm) tin (just use 2 eggs and 4 oz/110 g each of the flour, sugar and butter). It can then be filled with jam and the soft fruits of summer, or in winter, replace the raspberries and jam with passion fruit (see below).

For an 8 inch (20 cm) cake:

6 oz (175 g) self-raising flour

1 rounded teaspoon baking powder

3 large eggs, at room temperature

6 oz (175 g) very soft butter

6 oz (175 g) golden caster sugar

½ teaspoon pure vanilla extract

a little sifted icing sugar for dusting

For the filling:

8 oz (225 g) raspberries

3-4 tablespoons soft-set raspberry jam

9 oz (250 g) mascarpone

7 fl oz (200 ml) fromage frais

1 dessertspoon golden caster sugar

1 teaspoon pure vanilla extract

You will also need two 8 inch (20 cm) x 1½ inch (4 cm) deep sponge tins, lightly greased, and the bases lined with baking parchment.

Pre-heat the oven to gas mark 3, 325°F (170°C).

Take a very large mixing bowl, put the flour and baking powder in a sieve and sift it into the bowl, holding the sieve high to give it a good airing as it goes down. Now all you do is simply add all the other cake ingredients (except the icing sugar) to the bowl and, provided the butter is really soft, just go in with an electric hand whisk and whisk everything together until you have a smooth, well-combined mixture, which will take about 1 minute. If you don't have an electric hand whisk, you can use a wooden spoon, using a little bit more effort. What you will now end up with is a mixture that drops off a spoon when you give it a tap on the side of the bowl. If it seems a little too stiff, add a little water and mix again.

Now divide the mixture between the 2 tins, level it out and place the tins on the centre shelf of the oven. The cakes will take 30-35 minutes to cook, but don't open the oven door until 30 minutes have elapsed. To test whether the cakes are cooked or not, touch the centre of each lightly with a finger: if it leaves no impression and the sponges spring back, they are ready.

Next, remove them from the oven, then wait about 5 minutes before turning them out on to a wire cooling rack. Carefully peel off the base papers, which is easier if you make a fold in the paper first, then pull it gently away without trying to lift it off. Now leave the sponges to get completely cold, then add the filling.

For the filling, combine the mascarpone, fromage frais, sugar and vanilla extract, using a balloon whisk, which is the quickest way to blend them all together. Now spread 1 tablespoon of jam over one of the sponge cakes, follow this with the cream mixture, then scatter the raspberries all over that. Now drizzle the rest of the jam over the raspberries and place the other cake on top. Press very gently to sandwich everything together, then lightly dust the surface with a little sifted icing sugar ■

Passion Fruit Cream

Using the flesh of 6 passion fruit, fold about two-thirds of the passion fruit pulp into the cream mixture and drizzle the rest over the cream filling, placing the second half of the cake on top.

Lemon Curd Butterfly Cakes
Makes 12

These little butterfly sponge cakes are baked in small paper baking cases and filled with lemon curd. Lemon curd is never quite the same when shop bought, so I have given the recipe for it here. There is more than you will need for the cakes but it will keep for several weeks in a cool place.

For the cakes:

6 oz (175 g) self-raising flour, sifted

pinch salt

4 oz (110 g) butter, at room temperature

4 oz (110 g) golden caster sugar

2 large eggs, at room temperature

1 dessertspoon lemon juice

grated rind 1 lemon

For the filling:

about 4 oz (110 g) home-made (see recipe below) or good-quality bought lemon curd

For home-made lemon curd:

grated zest and juice 2 large juicy lemons

2 large eggs

6 oz (175 g) golden caster sugar

4 oz (110 g) unsalted butter, at room temperature, cut into small lumps

1 teaspoon cornflour

Pre-heat the oven to gas mark 5, 375°F (190°C).

You will also need a 12 hole patty tin with cups, each with a base measurement of 1¾ inches (4.5 cm) and depth of ¾ inch (2 cm), greased, and some paper baking cases.

To make the cakes, place all the ingredients together in a large mixing bowl and, using an electric hand whisk, whisk everything together until you have a smooth, well-combined mixture, which will take about 1 minute. Then, using a spoon, drop an equal quantity of the mixture into the paper cases, and sit the cases in the patty tin – giving it two or three light taps to settle the cake mixture.

Now bake on the shelf just above the centre of the oven for 20-25 minutes or until the cakes are well risen and golden. Then remove them to a wire rack and leave to cool.

If you are making your own lemon curd, begin by lightly whisking the eggs in a small saucepan, then add the rest of the ingredients and place the saucepan over a medium heat. Now whisk continuously, using a balloon whisk, until the mixture thickens – about 7-8 minutes. Next, lower the heat to its minimum setting and let the curd gently simmer for a further minute, continuing to whisk. After that, remove it from the heat and leave to cool.

When both the cakes and the lemon curd are cool, take a sharp knife and, leaving a ½ inch (1 cm) border around the edge, and cutting at an angle, remove a cone shape from the top of each cake. Cut each cone in half (top to bottom) and set aside.

Fill the cavity of each cake with lemon curd then sit the 2 cone-shaped pieces of cake on top like butterfly wings ■

Quick and Last-minute Christmas Sherry Mincemeat Cake
Serves 8-10

This Christmas cake is one of the nicest ever and can be made at the last minute. In fact, you could bake it on Christmas morning and it would be ready for tea in the afternoon. If time allows, some of the ingredients can be pre-soaked in sherry for three days, but if you have only three hours, that will do. It's an all-in-one cake, so everything can be mixed and baked with very little effort.

For the pre-soaking:

14 oz (400 g) good-quality bought or home-made vegetarian mincemeat

4 oz (110 g) ready-to-eat prunes, roughly chopped

2 oz (50 g) glacé cherries, quartered

6 oz (175 g) mixed dried fruits

2 oz (50 g) whole candied peel, chopped

5 fl oz (150 ml) Oloroso or other medium sherry

For the cake:

8 oz (225 g) wholemeal flour

3 teaspoons baking powder

5 oz (150 g) butter, at room temperature

5 oz (150 g) dark soft brown sugar

grated zest each 1 small orange and lemon

2 oz (50 g) brazil nuts, roughly chopped

2 oz (50 g) mixed chopped nuts

3 large eggs

For the topping:

approximately 7 walnut halves, 18 pecan halves, 26 almonds, 23 whole brazils (or any other mixture you like)

1 heaped tablespoon sieved apricot jam

1 tablespoon brandy

You will also need an 8 inch (20 cm) round cake tin, lightly oiled, the base and sides lined with baking parchment.

Pre-heat the oven to gas mark 3, 325°F (170°C).

If possible, begin the cake 3 days before you want to make it by simply placing all the pre-soaking ingredients into a bowl, stir really well, then cover with a cloth and leave in a cool place.

When you are ready to make the cake, take a roomy bowl and simply place the soaked ingredients, plus all the rest of the cake ingredients in it, all in one go. Now, preferably using an electric hand whisk (or a wooden spoon), beat everything together as thoroughly as possible, which will probably take about 1 minute.

Then pour it into the prepared tin, level the top and arrange the whole nuts in rows across the surface – one row of brazils, one of pecans, and so on.

Finally, cover the top of the cake with a double square of baking parchment, with a hole the size of a 50p piece cut in the centre. Then place the cake on the centre shelf of the oven and bake it for 2-2½ hours or until the centre springs back when lightly touched. Then let it cool in the tin for 30 minutes before turning it out to finish cooling on a wire rack.

The finishing touch is to heat the apricot jam and brandy together and brush the nuts with the mixture to give them a lovely glaze. Store the cake in an airtight tin – it will keep beautifully moist for 3 to 4 weeks ■

Spiced Apple Muffin Cake with Pecan Streusel Topping
Serves 10-12

I have included this because I still get letters from people saying they can't make muffins. My message to them is don't try too hard – undermixing is the golden rule and, once mastered, the American muffin mix makes the lightest cakes in the world. In the summer, you could always replace the apples with 12 oz (350 g) of fresh apricots, stoned and chopped, or, in the autumn, with 12 oz (350 g) of plums, stoned and chopped. In both cases, though, weigh after stoning. This recipe will also make 24 mini or 12 large muffins, cooking them for 20 and 30 minutes respectively.

12 oz (350 g) Bramley apples (weight after peeling and coring), chopped into ½ inch (1 cm) cubes

1 heaped teaspoon ground cinnamon

1 teaspoon ground cloves

½ whole nutmeg, grated

4 oz (110 g) butter

10 oz (275 g) plain flour

1 tablespoon, plus 1 teaspoon baking powder

½ teaspoon salt

2 large eggs, at room temperature

3 oz (75 g) golden caster sugar

6 fl oz (175 ml) milk

For the pecan streusel topping:

2 oz (50 g) pecan nuts, roughly chopped

3 oz (75 g) self-raising flour

3 oz (75 g) demerara sugar

1 rounded teaspoon ground cinnamon

1 oz (25 g) soft butter

You will also need a 9 inch (23 cm) springform cake tin, lightly greased and the base lined with baking parchment.

Pre-heat the oven to gas mark 5, 375°F (190°C).

First of all, place the butter in a small saucepan and put it on a gentle heat to melt. Then, as with all muffin mixtures, you need to sift the dry ingredients twice, so place the flour, all the baking powder, salt, cinnamon, cloves and grated nutmeg in a sieve and sift them into a bowl.

Then, in another large mixing bowl, whisk the eggs, sugar and milk together, pour the melted butter into the egg mixture and give it all another good whisk. Now sift the flour mixture again straight in on top of the egg mixture and fold it in, making as few folds as possible. Ignore the horrible lumpy mixture you're now faced with and don't be tempted to overmix. I think this is where people go wrong: they can't believe that what looks like a disaster can possibly turn into something so light and luscious. Now fold in the chopped apple and then spoon the whole lot into the tin, levelling off the surface.

Next, make the topping, and you can use the same bowl. Just add the flour, sugar and cinnamon and rub the butter in with your fingertips until crumbly. Finally, sprinkle in the nuts and 1 tablespoon cold water, then press the mixture loosely together. Again, it will be quite lumpy – no problem! Now spoon the topping over the surface of the cake, then bake on the centre shelf of the oven for about 1¼ hours, until it feels springy in the centre.

Allow the cake to cool in the tin for 30 minutes before removing the sides, then gently slide a palette knife under the base and transfer the cake to a wire rack to finish cooling. Serve this as fresh as possible, either on its own or warm as a dessert with whipped cream, crème fraîche or vanilla ice cream ■

Spiced Apple Muffin Cake with Pecan Streusel Topping

Richmond Maids of Honour

Richmond Maids of Honour
Makes 18

Rumour has it that these delectable little curd-cheese tarts were named after the maids of honour who served at Richmond Palace in the 16th century. True or not, they taste wonderful, made with crisp puff pastry and a filling of squidgy cheese and lemon curd.

9 oz (250 g) bought fresh puff pastry
flour for dusting
8 oz (225 g) curd cheese
1½ oz (40 g) golden caster sugar
grated zest 1 lemon
1 oz (25 g) ground almonds
1½ oz (40 g) whole candied lemon peel, finely chopped
1 large egg, plus 1 large egg yolk
about 2 tablespoons good-quality bought or home-made lemon curd (see page 213)
icing sugar for dusting (optional)

You will also need a 3¼ inch (8 cm) plain cutter and two 12 hole shallow bun trays.

Pre-heat the oven to gas mark 6, 400°F (200°C).

Begin by cutting the block of pastry in half so that you have 2 squares, and then sprinkle a surface with flour and roll each piece into a square of about 11 inches (28 cm). Then, using the cutter, cut out 9 circles from each piece. Be careful as you do this – just give the cutter a sharp tap and lift it, don't be tempted to twist it. Now line the tins with the pastry rounds; you should have 18 altogether.

Then, in a bowl, combine the curd cheese, sugar, lemon zest, ground almonds and chopped candied peel, then beat the egg and egg yolk together in a separate bowl, and add this to the rest of the ingredients. Mix very thoroughly with a large fork until everything is very evenly blended. Next, spoon half a teaspoon of lemon curd into the base of each pastry case – don't be tempted to add more, as it will bubble over during the cooking – then spoon a dessertspoon of the curd-cheese mixture on top of this.

Then, when all the mixture has been added, bake the tarts in 2 batches on the centre shelf of the oven for about 20-25 minutes, by which time the mixture will have puffed right up and turned a lovely golden brown colour.

Now take them out of the oven and transfer them to a wire rack to cool. Don't worry if you see them start to sink a little, that's absolutely normal. If you like, you can give them a faint dusting of icing sugar before you serve them ■

Quick Apricot, Apple and Pecan Loaf Cake
Serves 8

If you've never made a cake in your life before, I promise you that you can make this one – whether you're male, female, age six or 106, it really is dead simple, but tastes so divine you would think it took oodles of skill. The only important thing to remember (as with all cakes) is to use the right-sized tin.

6 oz (175 g) ready-to-eat dried apricots, each chopped in half
6 oz (175 g) cooking apple (medium size), cut into ½ inch (1 cm) chunks, with skin on
6 oz (175 g) pecan nuts
pinch salt
1½ teaspoons baking powder
2 rounded teaspoons ground cinnamon
4 oz (110 g) wholemeal flour
4 oz (110 g) plain flour
4 oz (110 g) butter, at room temperature
6 oz (175 g) soft brown sugar
2 large eggs, beaten
3 tablespoons milk, plus a little extra, if needed

For the topping:
4 cubes demerara sugar, roughly crushed
¼ teaspoon ground cinnamon

You will also need a 2 lb (900 g) loaf tin, lightly buttered.

Pre-heat the oven to gas mark 4, 350°F (180°C).

First of all, when the oven has pre-heated, spread the nuts out on a baking sheet and toast them lightly for about 8 minutes, using a timer so that you don't forget them. After that, remove them to a chopping board, let them cool a bit, then chop them roughly.

Meanwhile, take a large mixing bowl, sift the salt, baking powder, cinnamon and both flours into it, holding the sieve up high to give the flour a good airing and adding the bran from the sieve to the bowl as well. Then simply add all the rest of the ingredients except the fruit and nuts. Take an electric hand whisk, begin to beat the mixture on a slow speed, then increase the speed to mix everything thoroughly till smooth, before lightly folding in the apricots, apple and pecans.

When it's all folded in, add a drop more milk, if necessary, to give a mixture that drops easily off the spoon when you give it a sharp tap, then pile the mixture into the tin, level the top and sprinkle on the crushed sugar cubes and cinnamon. Bake in the centre of the oven for 1¼-1½ hours or until the cake feels springy in the centre.

After that, remove it from the oven, let it cool for about 5 minutes before turning it out on to a wire tray. Let it get completely cold before transferring it to a cake tin, which may not be needed if there are people around, as this cake tends to vanish very quickly! ■

Chocolate and Prune Brownies
Makes 15

Scottish Semolina Shortbread
Makes 12 wedges

Raisin Hazelnut Crunchies
Makes 18

Prunes with chocolate are, for me, a heavenly partnership, especially if soaked in Armagnac.

2 oz (50 g) dark chocolate (75 per cent cocoa solids), broken into pieces

2 oz (50 g) pitted pruneaux d'Agen, chopped and soaked overnight in 2 fl oz (55 ml) Armagnac

2 oz (50 g) almonds, skin on

4 oz (110 g) butter

2 large eggs, beaten

8 oz (225 g) demerara sugar

2 oz (50 g) plain flour

1 teaspoon baking powder

¼ teaspoon salt

You will also need a non-stick baking tin measuring 10 x 6 inches (25.5 x 15 cm) and 1 inch (2.5 cm) deep, lightly greased and lined with baking parchment.

Begin this the night before you are going to make the brownies by soaking the chopped prunes in the Armagnac. The next day, start by pre-heating the oven to gas mark 4, 350°F (180°C), then chop the almonds roughly, place them on a baking sheet and toast them in the oven for 8 minutes. Please use a timer here, or you'll be throwing burnt nuts away all day.

While the almonds are toasting, put the chocolate and butter together in a heatproof bowl fitted over a saucepan of barely simmering water, making sure the bowl doesn't touch the water. Allow the chocolate to melt – 4-5 minutes – remove it from the heat, then beat till smooth. Next, stir in all the other ingredients, including the prunes and Armagnac, until well blended. Now spread the mixture into the prepared tin and bake on the centre shelf for 30 minutes, or until slightly springy in the centre, then leave it to cool for 10 minutes before cutting into squares and transferring to a wire rack ■

This is the real thing. Using the fine semolina gives the shortbread a wonderful crunchy texture, and the flavour is extremely buttery.

6 oz (175 g) butter, at room temperature

3 oz (75 g) golden caster sugar, plus extra for dredging

6 oz (175 g) plain flour, sifted, plus extra for dusting

3 oz (75 g) fine semolina

You will also need an 8 inch (20 cm) diameter fluted flan tin, 1¼ inches (3 cm) deep with a loose base.

Pre-heat the oven to gas mark 2, 300°F (150°C).

First of all, beat the butter in a bowl with a wooden spoon to soften it, then beat in the sugar, followed by the sifted flour and semolina. Work the ingredients together with the spoon, pressing them to the side of the bowl, then finish off with your hands until you have a smooth mixture that doesn't leave any bits in the bowl.

Next, transfer the dough to a flat, lightly floured surface, and roll it out lightly to a round (giving it quarter turns as you roll) about the same diameter as the tin, then transfer the round to the tin. Now lightly press the mixture evenly into the tin right up to the fluted edges (to make sure it is even you can give it a final roll with a small glass tumbler). Finally, prick the shortbread all over with a fork – or it will rise up in the centre while it's baking. Bake for 60-70 minutes on the centre shelf – it should have turned pale gold and feel firm in the centre. Then remove it from the oven and, using a palette knife, mark out the surface into 12 wedges. Leave it to cool in the tin, then, when it's cold, cut it into wedges. Dredge with the sugar and store in an airtight polythene box or tin ■

You can almost imagine sneaking in to quickly grab one of these from under the cook's nose. This is one of the quickest, easiest and simplest recipes of all, and is supremely adaptable, so you can alter it to more or less any combination of nuts, fruits, and spices that you want. Other options are Cherry and Flaked Almond Crunchies, Apricot and Pecan Crunchies, or Chocolate Almond Crunchies.

2 oz (50 g) raisins

1½ oz (40 g) hazelnuts

4 oz (110 g) butter

3 oz (75 g) demerara sugar

1 dessertspoon golden syrup

4 oz (110 g) self-raising flour

pinch salt

4 oz (110 g) porridge oats

You will also need two baking sheets measuring 14 x 10 inches (35 x 25.5 cm), lightly greased with groundnut or other flavourless oil.

Preheat the oven to gas mark 3, 325°F (170°C).

First of all, put the butter, sugar and syrup in a saucepan, place it on the gentlest heat possible and let it all dissolve, which will take 2-3 minutes.

Meanwhile, chop the nuts into small chunks. When the butter mixture has dissolved, take it off the heat. Then, in a large mixing bowl, sift in the flour and salt and add the porridge oats and half the raisins and nuts, then give this a quick mix before pouring in the butter mixture. Now, using a wooden spoon, stir and mix everything together, then switch from a spoon to your hands to bring everything together to form a dough. If it seems a bit dry, add a few drops of cold water. Now take half the dough and divide it

into 9 lumps the size of a large walnut, then roll them into rounds, using the flat of your hand. Place them on a worktop and press gently to flatten them out into rounds approximately 2½ inches (6 cm) in diameter, then scatter half the remaining raisins and nuts on top of the biscuits, pressing them down lightly.

Once you have filled one tray (give them enough room to spread out during baking), bake them on the middle shelf of the oven for 15 minutes while you prepare the second tray. When they're all cooked, leave them to cool on the baking sheets for 10 minutes, then transfer them to a wire rack to finish cooling. You could store the biscuits in a sealed container, but I doubt you'll have any left! ■

Cherry and Flaked Almond Crunchies
Use 2 oz (50 g) of dried sour cherries and and 1½ oz (40 g) of flaked almonds instead of the raisins and hazelnuts.

Apricot and Pecan Crunchies
Use 2 oz (50 g) of ready-to-eat dried apricots and 1½ oz (40 g) of pecans.

Chocolate Almond Crunchies
Use 2 oz (50 g) dark continental chocolate and 1½ oz (40 g) whole unblanched almonds.

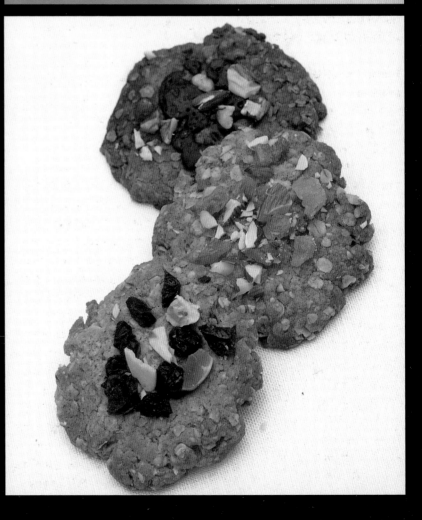

Clockwise from top left: Chocolate and Prune Brownies;
Scottish Semolina Shortbread; a selection of crunchies

Austrian Coffee and Walnut Cake with Coffee Cream

Austrian Coffee and Walnut Cake with Coffee Cream
Serves 8

This is unashamedly rich and luscious. Firstly, coffee and walnuts have a great affinity, secondly, so do coffee and creaminess, and thirdly, because the cake is soaked in coffee syrup, it's also meltingly moist.

For the sponge cake:
1½ tablespoons instant coffee mixed with 2 tablespoons boiling water
3 oz (75 g) walnut halves
6 oz (175 g) self-raising flour
1½ teaspoons baking powder
6 oz (175 g) butter, at room temperature
6 oz (175 g) golden caster sugar
3 large eggs, at room temperature

For the syrup:
1 tablespoon instant espresso coffee powder
2 oz (50 g) demerara sugar

For the filling and topping:
1 tablespoon instant espresso coffee powder
9 oz (250 g) mascarpone
7 fl oz (200 ml) 8 per cent fat fromage frais
1 rounded tablespoon golden caster sugar
10 walnut halves, reserved from the sponge cake

You will also need two 8 inch (20 cm) sandwich tins, 1½ inches (4 cm) deep, lightly greased, and the bases lined with baking parchment.

Pre-heat the oven to gas mark 3, 325°F (170°C).

First of all, you need to toast all the walnuts, so spread them on a baking sheet and place in the pre-heated oven for 7-8 minutes. After that, reserve 10 halves to use as decoration later and finely chop the rest. Take a very large mixing bowl, put the flour and baking powder in a sieve and sift it into the bowl, holding the sieve high to give it a good airing as it goes down.

Now all you do is simply add all the other cake ingredients (except the coffee and walnuts) to the bowl and, provided the butter is really soft, just go in with an electric hand whisk and whisk everything together until you have a smooth, well-combined mixture, then fold in the coffee and chopped walnuts. This will take about 1 minute but if you don't have an electric hand whisk, you can use a wooden spoon and a little bit more effort. What you should end up with is a soft mixture that drops off the spoon easily when you give it a sharp tap; if not, add a spot of water.

Divide the mixture between the prepared sandwich tins, spreading the mixture around evenly. Then place the tins on the centre shelf of the oven and bake them for 30 minutes.

While the cakes are cooking, you can make up the syrup and the filling and topping. For the syrup, first place the coffee and sugar in a heatproof jug, then measure 2 fl oz (55 ml) boiling water into it and stir briskly until the coffee and sugar have dissolved, which will take about 1 minute.

Next, the filling and topping, and all you do here is place all the ingredients, except the reserved walnuts, in a bowl and whisk them together till thoroughly blended. Then cover the bowl with clingfilm and chill till needed.

When the cakes are cooked, i.e. feel springy in the centre, remove them from the oven but leave them in their tins and prick them all over with a skewer while they are still hot. Now spoon the syrup as evenly as possible over each one and leave them to soak up the liquid as they cool in their tins. When they are absolutely cold, turn them out very carefully and peel off the base papers – it's a good idea to turn one out on to the plate you're going to serve it on. Then spread half the filling and topping mixture over the first cake, place the other cake carefully on top and spread the other half over.

Finally, arrange the reserved walnut halves in a circle all around. It's a good idea to chill the cake if you're not going to serve it immediately ▪

Green Peppercorn Bread
Makes 15 rolls or 50 breadsticks

This is a lovely, gutsy, spicy bread. Both the rolls and breadsticks freeze successfully in sealed polythene freezer bags

1 tablespoon dried green peppercorns, crushed in a pestle and mortar
1 lb (450 g) strong white bread flour, plus a little extra for dusting
2 teaspoons easy-blend yeast
2 teaspoons salt
3 tablespoons extra virgin olive oil

You will also need 2 solid baking sheets, lightly oiled.

Begin by sifting the flour into a large bowl, then sprinkle in the easy-blend yeast and the salt, make a well in the centre and pour in 10 fl oz (275 ml) of hand-hot water.

Begin to mix a little, then add the crushed peppercorns and olive oil and continue mixing until you have a smooth dough. Now knead the dough for 5 minutes or until it becomes springy and elastic, and after that, cover the bowl with clingfilm and leave it to prove till doubled in size – the length of time will depend on the kitchen temperature, but at all events, don't rush it because the longer the proving time, the better the bread.

When it has doubled in size, remove the dough from the bowl to a lightly floured surface, then punch it down to release the air. Now you can shape it either into rolls or breadsticks (in which case use ½ oz (10 g) quantities of the dough rolled into fat pencil shapes, then slashed diagonally with a knife to resemble miniature French sticks). Arrange them on the baking sheets, cover with clingfilm and leave to rise once more to double in size. Meanwhile, pre-heat the oven to gas mark 7, 425°F (220°C). Bake the rolls for 18-20 minutes, or the breadsticks for 10-12 minutes. Cool on a wire cooling tray ▪

Polenta and Ricotta Cake with Dates and Amaretto
Serves 8

This is a very unusual cake, quite different in flavour and texture from anything else. It's Italian in origin and polenta (cornmeal) gives it a sandy texture, while at the same time ricotta cheese and Amaretto liqueur give a wonderful moistness. It also freezes very well, but as you won't have any left over you might as well make two – it's so dead easy!

7 oz (200 g) polenta

9 oz (250 g) ricotta

6 oz (175 g) chopped dates

3 tablespoons Amaretto

2 oz (50 g) pecan nuts, roughly chopped

7 oz (200 g) self-raising flour

1 rounded teaspoon baking powder

1 heaped teaspoon ground cinnamon

8 oz (225 g) golden caster sugar

4 oz (110 g) butter, melted

1 tablespoon demerara sugar

You will also need an 8 inch
(20 cm) loose-based tin, lined with baking parchment.

Pre-heat the oven to gas mark 3, 325°F (170°C).

First of all, place the dates in a small bowl, pour the Amaretto over them and leave them to soak for 15 minutes. Then place the pecans on a baking tray and toast them for 8 minutes – use a timer so they don't get over-cooked.

Now to make the cake, take a large mixing bowl and first sift the polenta, flour, baking powder and cinnamon. Keep the sieve held high to give the flour a good airing, then tip the grains from the polenta in to join the rest.

Next, add the caster sugar, ricotta, melted butter and 7 fl oz (200 ml) tepid water, and whisk with an electric hand whisk until everything is thoroughly blended (about

1 minute. After that, fold in the nuts, dates and the liqueur in which they were soaking.

Fold everything in thoroughly, spoon the mixture into the prepared tin and smooth the top with the back of a spoon. Now scatter the demerara sugar evenly over the surface, then pop the cake into a pre-heated oven on the middle shelf, where it will take between 1¾ and 2 hours to cook. When it's cooked, it will feel springy in the centre when you make a very light depression with your little finger. If it's not cooked, give it another 10 minutes and then do another test.

When the cake is ready, remove it from the oven, allow it to cook in the tin for 15 minutes, then remove it from the tin and leave it to cool completely on a wire rack. Store in an airtight tin ■

Coconut Lime Cake
Serves 8

This is a summery, fairly simple cake that is particularly great for summer baking.

2 oz (50 g) desiccated coconut

2 limes

6 oz (175 g) self-raising flour

6 oz (175 g) golden caster sugar

6 oz (175 g) very soft butter

3 large eggs, lightly beaten

2 tablespoons dried coconut milk powder

1 rounded teaspoon baking powder

For the icing:

3 limes

8 oz (225 g) icing sugar

You will also need two 8 inch (20 cm), 1½ inch (4 cm) deep sponge tins, the bases lined with baking parchment.

Pre-heat the oven to gas mark 3, 325°F (170°C).

For the cake, start off by grating the zest of the 2 limes on to a small saucer, then cover that with clingfilm and set on one side. Next, measure the desiccated coconut into a small bowl, then squeeze the juice of the limes and pour this over the coconut to allow it to soften and soak up the juice for an hour or so.

To make the cake, just take a large, roomy bowl and sift in the flour, lifting the sieve up high to give the flour a good airing. Then simply throw in all the other cake ingredients, including the lime zest and soaked coconut, and with an electric hand whisk, switched to high speed, whisk everything till thoroughly blended – about 2-3 minutes.

Now divide the mixture equally between the two prepared tins, smooth to level off the tops and bake on a middle shelf of the oven for 30-35 minutes, or until the centres feel springy to the touch. Allow the cakes to cool

in the tins for 5 minutes, then turn them out on to a wire rack to cool completely, carefully peeling off the base papers. They must be completely cold before the icing goes on.

To make the icing, begin by removing the zest from the remaining 3 limes – this is best done with a zester, as you need long, thin, curly strips that look pretty. Then, with your sharpest knife, remove all the outer pith from the limes, then carefully remove each segment (holding the limes over a bowl to catch any juice), sliding the knife in between the membrane so that you have the flesh of the segments only. This is much easier to do with limes than it is with other citrus fruits. Drop the segments into the bowl and squeeze the last drops of juice from the pith.

Now sift the icing sugar in on top of the lime segments, a little at a time, carefully folding it in with a tablespoon in order not to break up the lime segments too much. When all the sugar is incorporated, allow the mixture to stand for 5 minutes, then spread half of it on to the surface of one of the cakes and scatter with half the lime zest.

Place the other cake on top, spread the rest of the icing on top of that and scatter the rest of the zest over. Then place the cake in the fridge for 30 minutes to firm up the icing before serving ■

Fresh Coconut Layer Cake

Fresh Coconut Layer Cake
Serves 8

The optimum word here is 'fresh'. Fresh coconut (you'll only need one) is very moist and has a fragrant, slightly sour, sweet flesh that is perfect for this cake.

For the cake:
3 oz (75 g) finely grated fresh coconut (see below)
6 oz (175 g) self-raising flour
1 rounded teaspoon baking powder
3 large eggs, at room temperature
6 oz (175 g) very soft butter
6 oz (175 g) golden caster sugar
1 teaspoon pure vanilla extract

For the coconut frosting:
1½ oz (40 g) finely grated fresh coconut
9 oz (250 g) mascarpone
7 fl oz (200 ml) fromage frais
1 teaspoon pure vanilla extract
1 dessertspoon golden caster sugar

For the topping and sides:
2 oz (50 g) coarsely grated fresh coconut

You will also need two 8 inch (20 cm), 1½ inch (4 cm) deep sandwich tins, lightly greased, the bases lined with baking parchment.

Pre-heat the oven to gas mark 3, 325°F (170°C).

Before you start this cake, you'll first have to deal with the coconut. Not half as impenetrable as it might seem, as all you do is first push a skewer into the 3 holes in the top of the coconut and drain out the milk.

Then place the coconut in a polythene bag and sit it on a hard surface – a stone floor or an outside paving stone. Then give it a hefty whack with a hammer – it won't be that difficult to break. Now remove the pieces from the bag and, using a cloth to protect your hands, prise the top of a knife between the nut and the shell. You should find that you can force the whole piece out in one go. Now discard the shell and take off the inner skin, using a potato peeler. The coconut is now ready to use.

The best way to grate coconut flesh is with the grating disc of a food processor, but a hand grater will do just as well.

To make the cake, sift the flour and baking powder into a large bowl, holding the sieve high to give them a good airing. Now just add all the other ingredients, except the grated coconut, to the bowl and go in with an electric hand whisk and combine everything until you have a smooth mixture, which will take about 1 minute. If you don't have an electric hand whisk, use a wooden spoon, using a little more effort.

What you should now have is a mixture that drops off a spoon when you give it a tap on the side of the bowl. If it seems a little stiff, add a drop of water and mix again. Finally, stir in the 3 oz (75 g) finely grated coconut and divide the mixture between the tins.

Now place them on the centre shelf of the oven for 30-35 minutes. To test whether the cakes are cooked, lightly touch the centre of each with a finger: if it leaves no impression and the sponges spring back, they are ready.

Next, remove them from the oven, then wait about 5 minutes before turning them out on to a wire cooling rack. Gently peel off the base papers, and when the cakes are absolutely cold, carefully divide each one horizontally into two halves using a very sharp serrated knife.

Now make up the frosting by simply whisking all the ingredients together in a bowl to combine them. Next, select the plate or stand you want to serve the cake on – you'll also need a palette knife – then simply place one cake layer on first, followed by a thin layer of frosting (about a fifth), followed by the next layer of cake and frosting, and so on.

After that, use the rest of the frosting to coat the sides and top of the cake. Don't worry how it looks: the good thing is that it's all going to be covered with the rest of the grated coconut next. And that's it! ■

Celeriac and Lancashire Cheese Bread
Makes 1 loaf
(serves 4-6)

This is yet another favourite and blissfully easy bread, which is crunchy and crusty on the outside and soft and squidgy within.

6 oz (175 g) celeriac (peeled weight)
4 oz (110 g) Lancashire cheese, roughly crumbled into ½ inch (1 cm) pieces
6 oz (175 g) self-raising flour, plus a little extra for the top of the loaf
4 spring onions, finely chopped (including the green parts)
pinch cayenne pepper
1 teaspoon salt
1 large egg
2 tablespoons milk

You will also need a small baking tray, very well greased.

Pre-heat the oven to gas mark 5, 375°F (190°C).

All you do is sift the flour into a large mixing bowl, add the spring onions, two-thirds of the crumbled cheese, the cayenne pepper and the salt. Then, using the coarse side of a grater, grate in the celeriac as well.

Now give everything a really good mix. Beat the egg and milk together and, using a palette knife to mix, gradually add it all to the mixture until you have a loose, rough dough.

Now transfer it to the baking tray and, still keeping the rough texture, shape it into a round with your hands. Next, lightly press the rest of the cheese over the surface, sprinkle with a little flour and bake the bread on the middle shelf of the oven for 45-50 minutes, or until golden brown. Cool on a wire rack and eat as fresh as possible. This is lovely served still warm, and if you have any left over, it's really good toasted ■

Irish Tea Bread
Makes 2 loaves
(each serves 4-6)

It's always hard for me to believe that this simple little fruit loaf can taste so good.

8 oz (225 g) raisins

8 oz (225 g) currants

8 oz (225 g) sultanas

4 oz (110 g) whole candied peel cut into ¼ inch (5 mm) pieces

8 oz (225 g) demerara sugar

10 fl oz (275 ml) Lapsang Souchong, Earl Grey or any other hot tea

4 oz (110 g) pecan nuts

1 large egg, at room temperature, lightly beaten with 2 tablespoons milk

1 lb (450 g) self-raising flour

You will also need two 1 lb (450 g) loaf tins, bases lined with baking parchment.

Begin this the evening before by placing all the fruits, including the candied peel, in a bowl, then dissolve the sugar in the hot tea, pour this over the fruits, cover the bowl and leave it overnight so the fruits become plump and juicy.

The next day, pre-heat the oven to gas mark 3, 325°F (170°C), then place the nuts on a baking sheet and pop them into the oven for 6-8 minutes (use a timer, as they burn easily). Then, when they're cool, roughly chop them. Next, add the beaten egg mixture to the bowl containing the fruits. Then sift in the flour, add the toasted nuts and give everything a really good mixing. Now divide the mixture between the prepared loaf tins and bake them in the centre of the oven for 1¼-1½ hours, until they feel springy in the centre. Then straightaway, loosen them with a palette knife and turn them out on to a wire rack to cool. Then have patience – it won't be long before you can taste some ■

Buttermilk Scones
with Cheshire Cheese and Chives
Makes 6

I'm convinced cheese scones were invented to use up the last remnants of some wonderful cheese – in this case, Cheshire. When you're down to the last bit, that is the time to make these meltingly light, squidgy cheese scones. Serve them for tea on Sunday, warm from the oven and spread with butter.

about 2½-3 tablespoons buttermilk

3 oz (75 g) Cheshire cheese, grated

1 rounded tablespoon freshly snipped chives

6 oz (175 g) self-raising flour

½ teaspoon mustard powder

½ teaspoon salt

a good pinch cayenne

1 oz (25 g) butter

1 large egg

For the tops:

1 oz (25 g) Cheshire cheese, grated

a little milk for brushing

a good pinch cayenne

You will also need a well-greased baking sheet measuring 10 x 12 inches (25.5 x 30 cm), and a 2 ½ inch (6 cm) fluted cutter.

Pre-heat the oven to gas mark 7, 425°F (220°C).

Start by sifting the flour into a bowl, holding the sieve up quite high to give the flour an airing, then add the mustard, salt and one really good pinch of cayenne. Mix them in thoroughly, then rub the butter in, using your fingertips, until it's all crumbly.

Now mix in the 3 oz (75 g) grated cheese, along with the freshly snipped chives. Next, beat the egg with 2½ tablespoons buttermilk and gradually add it to the dry ingredients, mixing first with a knife, then with your hands

to make a soft dough – if it seems a little dry add another ½ tablespoon of buttermilk, or enough to make a smooth dough that will leave the bowl clean. It's important not to overwork the dough or the scones will be heavy.

Now roll it out as evenly as possible to around 1 inch (2.5 cm) thick – be very careful not to roll the dough out too thinly. The secret of well-risen scones is to start off with a thickness no less than an inch. Then, using the fluted cutter, cut out 6 scones. You may need to re-roll the dough to cut out all 6.

Now place them on the well-greased baking sheet, brush the tops with milk, then sprinkle the grated cheese on top of each scone, along with a faint sprinkling of cayenne.

Bake them on a high shelf for about 15-20 minutes until the scones are risen and golden brown. Then cool a little on a wire rack, but serve warm, spread with lots of butter ■

Chocolate Chip Ginger Nuts
Makes 16

I don't know who invented the expression 'that takes the biscuit', but home-made ginger nuts with cocoa *and* chocolate are, I think, precisely what that expression is trying to convey.

2 oz (50 g) dark chocolate (75 per cent cocoa solids), chopped into little chunks

1 slightly rounded teaspoon ground ginger

4 oz (110 g) self-raising flour

½ oz (10 g) cocoa

1 teaspoon bicarbonate of soda

2 oz (50 g) butter, cut into cubes

1½ oz (40 g) golden granulated sugar

2 oz (50 g) golden syrup

Pre-heat the oven to gas mark 4, 350°F (180°C).

You will also need a 11 x 16 inch (28 x 40 cm) baking tray, lined with baking parchment.

Begin this by sifting the self-raising flour, cocoa, ginger and bicarbonate of soda into a mixing bowl. Then, using your fingertips, rub in the butter until the mixture resembles breadcrumbs and next, stir in the sugar and chopped chocolate. Now add the golden syrup, then mix everything together with a wooden spoon and finish off by squeezing the mixture together with your hands.

After that, divide the mixture into 16, and roll each portion into a ball. Place them on the lined baking tray, leaving plenty of room between them as they spread out while they're cooking. Flatten each ball slightly and bake on the centre of the oven for 15-20 minutes or until they have spread out and cracked rather attractively. Cool on the baking tray for a few minutes, then using a palette knife, transfer to a wire rack to finish cooling, and store in an airtight tin ■

Clockwise from above: Chocolate Chip Ginger Nuts; Buttermilk Scones
with Cheshire Cheese and Chives; Irish Tea Bread

Chapter Ten
Puddings

Strawberry Hazelnut Shortcakes with Strawberry Purée
Serves 8

Strawberry shortcakes have long been a favourite, adding a bit of sweet crunch and texture to complement the acidity of the fruit. Any nuts can be used in the shortcakes but hazelnuts are particularly good.

For the hazelnut shortcakes:

4 oz (110 g) hazelnuts

5 oz (150 g) softened butter

2½ oz (60 g) golden icing sugar, plus a little extra to garnish

2½ oz (60 g) ground rice or rice flour, sifted

5 oz (150 g) plain flour, sifted

For the strawberry purée:

8 oz (225 g) fresh strawberries, hulled

1 tablespoon golden caster sugar

For the strawberry filling:

1 lb (450 g) fresh strawberries, hulled, reserving 8 small strawberries with leaves and stalks intact, to garnish

7 fl oz (200 ml) crème fraîche

5 fl oz (150 ml) ready-made fresh custard

2 drops pure vanilla extract

You will also need 2 baking trays measuring 11 x 16 inches (28 x 40 cm), lightly greased, and a 3½ inch (9 cm) round pastry cutter.

Pre-heat the oven to gas mark 4, 350°F (180°C).

To begin, you'll need to toast the hazelnuts by spreading them out on a baking tray and popping them in the oven for 5 minutes. It's important to use a timer here as they burn very easily. After that, cool and place them in a processor to grind them down until they look rather like ground almonds.

Now, in a mixing bowl, cream the butter and icing sugar together until light and fluffy, then gradually work in the sifted flours, followed by the ground hazelnuts, bringing the mixture together into a stiff ball. Then, place the dough in a polythene bag and leave it in the fridge to rest for about 30 minutes.

After that, roll it out to a thickness of about ¼ inch (5 mm), then stamp out 16 rounds by placing the cutter on the shortcake and giving it a sharp tap, then simply lift the cutter and the piece will drop out.

Now arrange the biscuits on the baking trays and lightly prick each one with a fork. Bake them for 10-12 minutes, then leave them on the baking trays for about 10 minutes, before removing them to a wire rack to cool completely. While the shortcakes are cooling, place the strawberries for the purée in a bowl, sprinkle them with the sugar and leave for 30 minutes. After that, purée them in a processor and press them through a nylon sieve to remove the seeds. Cover with clingfilm till needed.

For the strawberry filling, whisk the crème fraîche in a mixing bowl with an electric hand whisk until it becomes really stiff, then add the custard and vanilla extract and whisk again, also until thick. Then this also needs to be covered and chilled till you are ready to serve.

Slice or roughly chop the strawberries, not forgetting to reserve 8. Spread equal quantities of the cream mixture over 8 of the biscuits, then arrange the strawberries on top. Spoon some purée over, then sandwich with the remaining shortcakes. Now place a reserved strawberry on top of each one, and finish off with a light dusting of icing sugar ■

Plum and Almond Buttermilk Cobbler
Serves 6

I have a small Victoria plum tree but so laden is it every year that Richard, who helps us with our garden, has to put a stake under one of the branches. This is one of our favourite family puddings, which allows the plums to cook in their own luscious juice and provides a cloud of crisp fluffy topping. Damsons are a lovely alternative (you may need a little extra sugar). Either way, serve it with some chilled Jersey cream or vanilla ice cream.

2½ lb (1.15 kg) medium-sized plums

2 oz (50 g) golden caster sugar

For the topping:

2 tablespoons flaked almonds

6 fl oz (170 ml) buttermilk

8 oz (225 g) plain flour, sifted

½ teaspoon salt

3 teaspoons baking powder

1 teaspoon ground cinnamon

4 oz (110 g) cold, hard butter, cut into pieces

1 tablespoon demerara sugar, mixed with 1 teaspoon ground cinnamon

You will also need a baking dish about 9 inches (23 cm) in diameter and 2 inches (5 cm) deep.

Pre-heat the oven to gas mark 7, 425°F (220°C).

To prepare the plums, slide the tip of a sharp knife, following the natural line of the fruit, all around each plum through to the stone. Then, using both hands, give it a twist and divide it in half. Remove the stone and cut into quarters. Now all you do is arrange the fruit in the baking dish, scattering the caster sugar as you go.

To make the topping, place the sifted flour, salt, baking powder, cinnamon and butter into the bowl of a food processor. Then switch on and give it a pulse (on/off) action several times until the mixture resembles fine breadcrumbs. Then pour in the buttermilk and switch on again briefly until you have a thick, very sticky dough.

Now spoon tablespoons of the mixture over the fruit in rocky mounds – the more haphazardly you do this, the better.

Lastly, sprinkle the sugar and cinnamon all over, followed by the flaked almonds, then pop the dish on to a high shelf in the oven for 30 minutes or until it is a crusty golden brown. Serve the cobbler warm from the oven ■

Right: Plum and Almond Buttermilk Cobbler
Top left: Strawberry Hazelnut Shortcakes with Strawberry Purée

Deep Lemon Tart

Deep Lemon Tart
Serves 6-8

I once spent a great deal of time trying every sort of lemon tart imaginable in order to come up with the definitive version. And here it is – thicker than is usual, which, quite rightly I think, includes much more filling than pastry. If you want to serve it warm you can prepare everything in advance – and pour the filling in just before you bake it.

For the pastry:
6 oz (175 g) plain flour
1½ oz (40 g) icing sugar
3 oz (75 g) softened butter
pinch salt
1 large egg yolk (reserve the white for later)

For the filling:
zest 6 lemons and 10 fl oz (275 ml) juice (about 6-8 lemons)
6 large eggs
6 oz (175 g) golden caster sugar
7 fl oz (200 ml) whipping cream

To serve:
a little icing sugar and crème fraîche

You will also need a deep, fluted quiche tin with a loose base 9 inches (23 cm) round and 1½ inches (4 cm) deep, lightly oiled, and a solid baking sheet.

The best way to make the pastry is in a food processor. To do this add all the pastry ingredients (reserving the egg white for later), together with 1 tablespoon of water, to the bowl and process until it forms a firm dough. Then turn it out and knead lightly before placing in a polythene bag and leaving in the fridge for 30 minutes to rest.

To cook the pastry base, pre-heat the oven to gas mark 6, 400°F (200°C) and place the baking sheet inside to pre-heat as well. Now roll out the pastry as thinly as possible and carefully line the flan tin, pressing the pastry around the base and sides so that it comes about ¼ inch (5 mm) above the edge of the tin. Then prick the base with a fork and brush it all over with the spare egg white, which you should lightly beat first.

Bake on the baking sheet on the middle shelf for 20 minutes, then, as you remove it, turn the temperature down to gas mark 4, 350°F (180°C).

To make the filling, grate the zest from 6 of the lemons, and squeeze enough juice to give 10 fl oz (275 ml). Now break the eggs into a bowl, add the sugar and whisk to combine, but don't overdo it or the eggs will thicken. Next, add the lemon juice and zest, followed by the cream, and whisk lightly. Now pour it all into a 2 pint (1.2 litre) jug.

The easiest way to fill the tart is to place the pastry case on the baking sheet in the oven, and then pour the filling straight into the pastry (this avoids having to carry the tart to the oven and spilling it). Bake for about 30 minutes or until the tart is set and feels springy in the centre. Let it cool for about half an hour if you want to serve it warm. It's also extremely good served chilled. Either way, dust it with icing sugar just before serving and serve with well-chilled crème fraîche ■

A Very Easy One-crust Blackcurrant Pie
Serves 6

This American idea for making a pie is blissfully easy – no baking tins and no lids to be cut, fitted and fluted. It looks very attractive because you can see the fruit inside and, because there is less pastry, it's a little easier on the waistline. This can also be made with raspberries and redcurrants; instead of blackcurrants, use 1¼ lb (675 g) raspberries and 4 oz (110 g) redcurrants.

For the shortcrust pastry:
6 oz (175 g) plain flour, plus a little extra for dusting
1½ oz (40 g) pure vegetable fat
1½ oz (40 g) butter, at room temperature
1 small egg yolk
2 rounded tablespoons semolina

For the filling:
1lb 8 oz (700 g) blackcurrants, topped and tailed
2 oz (50 g) golden caster sugar

For the glaze:
1 small egg white
6 sugar cubes

To serve:
crème fraîche or ice cream

You will also need a solid baking sheet, lightly greased.

Make up the pastry by sifting the flour into a large mixing bowl, then rubbing the fats into it lightly with your fingertips, lifting everything up and letting it fall back into the bowl to give it a good airing.

When the mixture reaches the crumb stage, sprinkle in enough cold water (1-2 tablespoons) to bring it together to a smooth dough that leaves the bowl absolutely clean, with no crumbs left. Give it a little light knead to bring it fully together, then place the pastry in a polythene bag in the fridge for 30 minutes. After that, pre-heat the oven to gas mark 6, 400°F (200°C). Then roll the pastry out on a lightly floured, flat surface to a round of approximately 14 inches (35 cm) – as you roll, give it quarter turns so that it ends up as round as you can make it (don't worry, though, about ragged edges – they're fine). Now carefully roll the pastry round the rolling pin and transfer it to the centre of the lightly greased baking sheet.

To prevent the pastry getting soggy from any excess juice, paint the base with egg yolk (you'll need to cover approximately a 10 inch /25.5 cm circle in the centre), then sprinkle the semolina lightly over this. The semolina is there to absorb the juices and the egg provides a waterproof coating.

Now simply pile the blackcurrants in the centre of the pastry, sprinkling them with sugar as you go. Then all you do is turn in the edges of the pastry: if any breaks, just patch it back on again – it's all meant to be ragged and interesting.

Next, brush the pastry surface all round with the egg white, then crush the sugar cubes with a rolling pin and sprinkle over the pastry (the idea of using crushed cubes is to get a less uniform look than with granulated).

Now pop the pie on to the highest shelf of the oven and bake for approximately 35 minutes or until the crust is golden brown. Remove from the oven and serve warm with chilled crème fraîche or ice cream ■

Crème Brûlée
Serves 6

Crème brûlée has its origins in England – it was invented at Trinity College, Cambridge, where it was known as Burnt Cream. Here the caramel is made separately and simply poured over. Alternatively, use golden caster sugar and a cook's blowtorch; just sprinkle the sugar over the surface of the ramekins, very lightly spray it with water, using a plastic spray bottle, and then aim the tip of the blowtorch flame at the sugar and caramelise the sugar.

1 pint (570 ml) double cream
6 large egg yolks
4 teaspoons cornflour
2 tablespoons golden caster sugar
a few drops pure vanilla essence

For the caramel:
4 oz (110 g) granulated sugar

You need also need six 1½ inches (4 cm) deep ramekins with a base diameter of 3 inches (7.5 cm).

You need to start the recipe the day before, so that the custard can be well chilled and firm. First of all, heat the cream in a saucepan until it reaches boiling point, and while it's heating, blend the egg yolks, cornflour, caster sugar and vanilla essence in a bowl. Then pour the hot cream in, stirring all the time with a wooden spoon, and return the mixture to the saucepan.

Heat very gently, still stirring, until the sauce has thickened – which should only take a minute or two. (If it does overheat, don't worry – if you remove it from the heat and continue to beat, the custard will become smooth again as soon as it cools.) Now divide the custard between the ramekins and leave to cool. Then cover each dish with clingfilm and refrigerate overnight.

About an hour before serving, make the caramel. Place the granulated sugar in a heavy-based pan, then place the pan over a very low heat to dissolve the sugar gently and caramelise it (to get all the sugar to melt, just shake and tilt the pan from side to side, but don't stir). When all the sugar has dissolved and you have a clear syrup (about 10-15 minutes), remove the pan from the heat and pour immediately over the custards, covering the surface of each one.

Now just leave them for a few minutes for the caramel to harden. Before eating the crème brûlée, tap the surface of the caramel with a spoon to crack and break it up. To remove any hardened caramel from your pan, fill it with hot water and bring it to the boil ■

Old-fashioned Rhubarb Trifle
Serves 6

Old-fashioned because when I was a child – a very long time ago – I used to love jelly trifles, and my mother would always make one for my birthday. This is a much more adult version, and the sharp, fragrant acidity of the rhubarb makes it a very light and refreshing dessert for spring and early summer.

1 lb 8 oz (700 g) fresh rhubarb
4 oz (110 g) golden caster sugar, plus a little extra, if needed
grated zest and juice 1 orange
2 oz (50 g) pecans
6 trifle sponges
3 tablespoons marmalade
4 fl oz (120 ml) Sercial (dry) Madeira
about 10 fl oz (275 ml) freshly squeezed orange juice
2 x 6 g packets vegetarian gelatine powder
12 oz (350 g) ready-made fresh custard
7 oz (200 g) Greek yoghurt
a little pouring cream (optional), to serve

You will also need an ovenproof baking dish measuring 7½ inches (19 cm) square and 2 inches (5 cm) deep, and 6 individual serving bowls or 1 large trifle bowl with a capacity of 3½ pints (2 litres).

Pre-heat the oven to gas mark 4, 350°F (180°C).

To prepare the rhubarb, cut it into 1 inch (2.5 cm) chunks and add these to the baking dish. Then sprinkle in the caster sugar, together with the zest and juice of the orange.

Now pop the whole lot in the oven without covering and let it cook for 30-40 minutes, until the rhubarb is tender but still retains its shape. At the same time, place the pecans in the oven and put a timer on for 7 minutes to toast them lightly, then you can either leave them whole or chop them roughly. While the rhubarb is cooking, slice the trifle sponges in half lengthways, spread each half with the marmalade, then re-form them and cut each one into 3 little sandwiches. Now arrange them either in the individual serving bowls or the large trifle bowl. Then make a few stabs in the sponges and sprinkle the Madeira carefully over them, then leave it all aside so it can soak in.

When the rhubarb is cooked and has become completely cold, taste it – if it is a bit sharp, add a little more sugar. Take a draining spoon and carefully remove the chunks of rhubarb, placing them amongst the sponges. Now pour all the juices from the dish into a measuring jug and make this up to 18 fl oz (510 ml) with the orange juice.

Next, pour 8 fl oz (225 ml) of this into a small saucepan, scatter the gelatine over, whisk it and leave it to soak for 5 minutes. Then place the pan over a gentle heat and whisk everything until all the gelatine has completely dissolved – about 2 minutes. Bring the mixture to boiling point, then return it to the remaining juice in the jug and give it all another good whisk.

Now pour it over the sponges and rhubarb. When it is completely cold, cover it with clingfilm and leave in the fridge till completely set. The last thing you need to do is whisk the custard and Greek yoghurt together in a mixing bowl, then spoon this mixture over the set jelly. Now cover with clingfilm again and chill until you're ready to serve.

Don't forget to sprinkle the toasted pecan nuts over just before serving, and, although it doesn't strictly need it, a little chilled pouring cream is a nice addition ■

Old-fashioned Rhubarb Trifle

Left: Meringues with Summer Fruit. Top right: Petits Monts Blancs

Petits Monts Blancs
Serves 8

When I first worked in a restaurant kitchen in the early 1960s, this recipe was on the menu and I became totally addicted to the sweetened chestnut purée. Chestnut has an amazing affinity with meringue and whipped cream, but in this modern version I have replaced the cream with mascarpone and fromage frais; this way you get the flavour and creamy richness of the mascarpone but lightened by the fromage frais.

For the meringues:
2 large egg whites
4 oz (110 g) white caster sugar

For the filling:
2 x 250 g tins crème de marrons de l'Ardèche (sweetened chestnut purée), chilled

For the mascarpone cream:
9 oz (250 g) mascarpone
7 fl oz (200 ml) 8 per cent fat fromage frais
1 rounded dessertspoon caster sugar
1 teaspoon pure vanilla extract
a little icing sugar for dusting

You will also need a 16 x 12 inch (40 x 30 cm) baking sheet, lined with baking parchment.

Pre-heat the oven to gas mark 2, 300°F (150°C).

To make the meringues, place the egg whites in a large spanking clean bowl and, using an electric hand whisk on a low speed, begin whisking.

Continue for about 2 minutes, until the whites are foamy, then switch the speed to medium and carry on whisking for 1 more minute. Now turn the speed to high and continue whisking until the egg whites reach the stiff-peak stage. Next, whisk the sugar in on fast speed, a little at a time (about a

dessertspoon), until you have a stiff and glossy mixture.

Now all you do is spoon 8 heaped dessertspoons of the mixture on to the prepared baking sheet, spacing them evenly. Then, using the back of the spoon or a small palette knife, hollow out the centres. Don't worry if they are not all the same shape – random and rocky is how I would describe them.

Next, pop them on the centre shelf of the oven, immediately reduce the heat to gas mark 1, 275°F (140°C) and leave them for 30 minutes. After that, turn the oven off and leave the meringues to dry out in the warmth of the oven until it is completely cold (usually about 4 hours) or overnight. The meringues will store well in a tin or plastic box, and will even freeze extremely well.

To assemble the Monts Blancs, spoon equal quantities of the crème de marrons into each meringue, whisk the mascarpone cream ingredients together (except the icing sugar) and then spoon equal amounts on top of the chestnut purée. A light dusting of icing sugar is good for a snowcapped-mountain image ▪

Meringues with Passion Fruit
This is a variation of the Petits Monts Blancs recipe, and all you need is the same amount of meringue and mascarpone filling, together with 6 passion fruit and a little icing sugar.

To assemble the 8 meringues, spoon the seeds from half a passion fruit into the bottom of each meringue. Then, mix the seeds from the other 2 passion fruit into the mascarpone mixture. Spoon this mixture on top of the nests, dust with a little icing sugar and serve.

Meringues with Summer Fruit
The two previous meringue fillings are perfect for winter months, but in the summer, soft fruits make the perfect filling, as their sharp acidity contrasts beautifully with the sweetness of the meringue.

For 8 meringue nests, use the same quantity of mascarpone cream as for the Petits Monts Blancs, together with 1 lb (450 g) of strawberries, raspberries or, my favourite, a mixture of redcurrants, raspberries, blueberries and strawberries. Then dust the fruit with icing sugar before serving. Nice with a sauce made of puréed raspberries, sweetened with a little icing sugar.

Apple and Orange Crunch
Serves 4

I like this crunchy pudding, served with proper custard sauce or, failing that, a thick pouring cream.

3 medium cooking apples, peeled and sliced thinly
½ the zest and all the juice of 1 small orange
4 oz (110 g) butter
approximately 12 thinnish slices bread from a small brown wholemeal or white day-old loaf
3 oz (75 g) demerara sugar

Pre-heat the oven to gas mark 4, 350°F (180°C).

You will also need a baking dish measuring 8 x 6 inches (20 x 15 cm), and 2 inches (5 cm) deep, well buttered.

Melt the butter in a saucepan over a low heat. Cut the crusts off the bread slices, and, using a pastry brush, spread 6 or 7 on both sides with melted butter (reserving some for the rest). Place them in the baking dish, covering the base and sides as a lining. Press them down firmly, then sprinkle in a layer of sliced apple, a little grated orange zest and juice, and a layer of sugar. Carry on like this until all the apple is used, but keep back a tablespoon of sugar.

Brush melted butter on the other slices of bread and press them on top. Sprinkle on the remaining sugar and add any melted butter that's left over.

Bake the pudding for 50-55 minutes or until the top is crisp, golden and crunchy and the apples inside are soft ▪

Caribbean Bananas Baked in Rum Served with Rum Syllabub
Serves 6

The ease and simplicity of this recipe belies its excellent depth and flavour – definitely one of those recipes that tastes infinitely better than it sounds. Serve it straight from the oven with the chilled syllabub, or it tastes every bit as good served cold.

6 bananas, thickly sliced
(1½ inches/4 cm) on the diagonal
3 tablespoons dark rum
3 oz (75 g) large raisins
3 tablespoons molasses sugar
1 dessertspoon freshly grated orange zest
1 teaspoon freshly grated lime zest
2 tablespoons freshly squeezed orange juice
1 tablespoon freshly squeezed lime juice

For the syllabub:
2 tablespoons dark rum
2 tablespoons lime juice
1 tablespoon molasses sugar
5 fl oz (150 ml) double cream
whole nutmeg

You will also need a large, shallow gratin dish measuring 8 x 11 inches (20 x 28 cm), buttered

You need to start this off about half an hour before you intend to cook the bananas by placing the raisins in a small basin, along with the rum, then leave them aside to soak for about 30 minutes to plump up.

Next, make the syllabub. Measure the rum and lime juice into a medium-sized bowl, add the sugar, give it a whisk and leave aside for 10 minutes to allow the sugar to dissolve. Next, pour in the cream and, using an electric hand whisk, beat until it stands in soft peaks. Then cover with clingfilm and chill until needed. When you're ready to cook the bananas,

pre-heat the oven to gas mark 4, 350°F (180°C). Then sprinkle half the sugar over the base of the gratin dish and arrange the bananas on top. Now sprinkle the rum and raisins over them, followed by the orange and lime zests and juice, and then finally, sprinkle over the remaining sugar.

Now cover the dish with foil and then place it on the top shelf of the oven and cook the bananas for about 20-25 minutes. After that, remove the foil, and then give them a further 5 minutes.

Just before serving, re-whisk the syllabub and spoon it on top of the bananas and lastly, grate a little nutmeg over the top ■

Spiced Apple and Pecan Crumble with Mascarpone Vanilla Cream
Serves 6-8

This recipe is great for windfalls and I love the combination of fluffy Bramleys and the wonderful flavour of Cox's. You could serve it with an ice cream or pouring cream, but I think this mascarpone vanilla cream is extra special.

1 lb 8 oz (700 g) Bramley apples
8 oz (225 g) Cox's apples
1 oz (25 g) light muscovado sugar
1 slightly rounded teaspoon ground cinnamon
½ teaspoon ground cloves
⅓ whole nutmeg, grated
4 oz (110 g) raisins

For the crumble:
4 oz (110 g) pecans
3 oz (75 g) chilled butter, cut into small dice
175 g (6 oz) self-raising flour, sifted
2 teaspoons ground cinnamon
4 oz (110 g) demerara sugar

For the mascarpone cream:
9 oz (250 g) mascarpone, at room temperature
7 fl oz (200 ml) 8 per cent fat fromage frais
1 rounded dessertspoon golden caster sugar
1 teaspoon pure vanilla extract

You will also need a round, ovenproof baking dish with a diameter of 9½ inches (24 cm) and 1¾ inches (4.5 cm) deep.

Pre-heat the oven to gas mark 6, 400°F (200°C).

Begin by preparing the apples. I always find the best way to do this is to cut them first in quarters and slice out the cores. You can peel the apples or I like to leave the peel on for extra flavour. Either way, now cut them into thickish slices and toss them in a bowl

with the sugar, cinnamon, ground cloves, nutmeg and raisins, then place them in the baking dish.

Next, make the crumble, which couldn't be simpler, as it is all made in a processor. All you do is place the butter, sifted flour, cinnamon and sugar in the processor and give it a whiz till it resembles crumbs. Next, add the pecans and process again until they are fairly finely chopped but so there are still a few chunky bits left. If you don't have a processor, in a large bowl, rub the butter into the sifted flour until it resembles crumbs, then stir in the cinnamon, sugar and pecans, which should be fairly finely chopped by hand.

Now simply sprinkle the crumble mixture all over the apples, spreading it right up to the edges of the dish, and, using the flat of your hands, press it down quite firmly all over: the more tightly it is packed together the crisper it will be.

Now bake the crumble on the centre shelf of the oven for 35-40 minutes, by which time the apples will be soft and the topping golden brown and crisp. Meanwhile, mix together all the ingredients for the mascarpone vanilla cream until smooth and chill until needed

Leave the crumble to rest for 10-15 minutes before serving, then serve it warm with the mascarpone cream ■

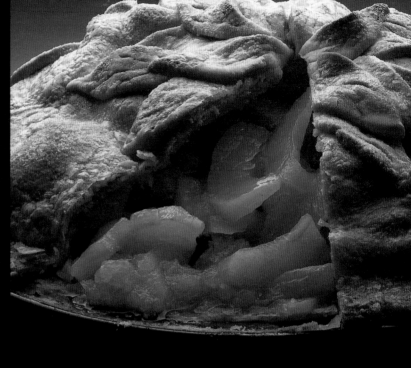

Left: Lemon and Lime Refrigerator Cake
Top right: Traditional Apple Pie with a Cheddar Crust

Lemon and Lime Refrigerator Cake
Serves 6

I hadn't made one of these cakes for years until it was recently requested on the deliaonline website, and I had forgotten how good it is. Don't forget to start the night before you want it though.

finely grated zest and juice 1 large lemon

finely grated zest and juice 1 lime

4 digestive biscuits, crushed to crumbs

1 oz (25 g) Grape-Nuts cereal

2 tablespoons soft light brown sugar

1 oz (25 g) butter, melted

5 fl oz (150 ml) double cream

3 large eggs, separated

2½ oz (60 g) golden caster sugar

1 x 6 g packet vegetarian gelatine powder

You will also need a 2 lb (900 g) loaf tin, lightly oiled with groundnut or other flavourless oil.

In a small basin combine the biscuit crumbs with the Grape-Nuts and brown sugar, then pour in the melted butter and mix thoroughly. Sprinkle a third of this mixture over the base of the loaf tin. Now using an electric hand whisk, beat the cream until floppy but not too thick, then clean the whisks.

Next, put the egg yolks, grated zests, strained lemon and lime juice and caster sugar into a bowl. Sprinkle the gelatine over the top and then place the bowl over a pan of barely simmering water and whisk for about 8-10 minutes or until the mixture thickens. Then remove the bowl from the heat and fold in the cream.

Now clean and dry the whisks thoroughly again and beat the egg whites till stiff. Next, working quickly, take a metal spoon and carefully fold the egg whites into the lemon and lime mixture. Now pour the mixture into the tin, sprinkle the remaining crumbs over

the top, cover with foil and transfer it to the freezer and freeze overnight.

Two hours before serving transfer the tin to the main body of the fridge, then turn it out on to a serving dish and serve cut into slices. If you have any left over, there is no need to re-freeze it; just leave it in the fridge where it will become more like a mousse ▪

Note: This recipe contains raw eggs.

Traditional Apple Pie with a Cheddar Crust
Serves 8

This is a huge family apple pie, which I often call 'More Apple Than Pie' as it has four pounds of apples in it. Putting Cheddar cheese in the crust gives it a lovely crisp, flaky texture without a strong cheese flavour.

For the pastry:

3 oz (75 g) mild Cheddar, coarsely grated

8 oz (225 g) plain flour, plus a little extra for rolling

2 oz (50 g) softened butter

2 oz (50 g) pure vegetable fat

For the filling:

2 lb (900 g) Bramley apples

2 lb (900 g) Cox's apples

1 tablespoon fine semolina

3 oz (75 g) golden caster sugar

12 whole cloves

1 large egg, beaten, to glaze

You will also need a rimmed metal pie dish, 9 inches (23 cm) in diameter and 1¼ inches (3 cm) deep, with sloping sides, and a solid baking sheet.

First, make the pastry. Sift the flour into a roomy bowl, holding the sieve up high to give it a good airing, then add the butter and vegetable fat cut into small pieces, rubbing the fat into the flour with your fingertips until it reaches the crumbly stage. Now add the grated Cheddar and about 3 tablespoons of water, enough to make a soft dough that leaves the bowl clean. Then turn it out on to a board, knead it briefly and lightly, then wrap it in clingfilm and leave it to rest in the fridge for about 30 minutes.

Meanwhile, peel, quarter and core the apples and then cut them into very thin slices straight into a bowl, mixing the two varieties together. Now pre-heat the oven to gas mark 7, 425°F (220°C). Next, take a little less than half of the pastry and roll it out very

thinly on a lightly floured surface to about 12 inches (30 cm) in diameter, to line the base and sides of the pie dish. Trim the edges and leave the unused pastry aside for the trimming. Then scatter the semolina over the base of the pastry and after that, pile in the apple slices, building up the layers closely and scattering in the sugar and cloves as you go. Then press and pack the apples tightly.

Now roll the remaining pastry out, again very thinly, to make the lid, this time 16 inches (40 cm) in diameter. Brush the rim of the base pastry with a little beaten egg and carefully lift the lid over the top. Press the edges together to get a good seal all round, then trim, using a knife.

Next, gather up the trimmings and re-roll them to cut out into leaf shapes. Make a small hole in the centre the size of a 10p piece (to allow the steam to escape) and arrange the leaves on top. Press the edges together to get a good seal all round, then trim, using a knife. Now, with the back of a small knife, 'knock up' the edges, then flute them, using your thumb and the back of the knife.

Finally, brush the whole lot with beaten egg, then place the pie on the baking sheet and bake on a high shelf for 10 minutes. After that, reduce the temperature to gas mark 5, 375°F (190°C) and cook for a further 45 minutes, or until it has turned a deep golden brown. Then remove the pie and allow it to stand for at least 20 minutes before serving ▪

Chocolate Mascarpone Cheesecake with Fruit and Nuts served with Crème Fraîche

Serves 6-8

This is quite simply a chocolate cheesecake to die for. If you like chocolate, if you like dark chocolate with fruit and nuts, and if you like luscious, velvet-textured mascarpone – need I say more? Before embarking on a baked cheesecake remember that, to prevent cracking, it's best cooled slowly in a switched-off oven. So you will need to make it well ahead.

For the filling:

3½ oz (95 g) dark chocolate (75 per cent cocoa solids)

9 oz (250 g) mascarpone, at room temperature

2 oz (50 g) raisins

4 oz (110 g) whole hazelnuts

7 oz (200 g) 8 per cent fat fromage frais, at room temperature

2 large eggs, at room temperature, lightly beaten

1½ oz (40 g) golden caster sugar

For the base:

2 oz (50 g) whole hazelnuts

4 oz (110 g) sweet oat biscuits

1 oz (25 g) butter, melted

For the chocolate curls, to decorate:

3½ oz (95 g) dark chocolate (75 per cent cocoa solids)

To serve:

crème fraîche or pouring cream

1 teaspoon cocoa powder

You will also need a 7 inch (18 cm) springform cake tin, with a depth of 3 inches (7.5 cm), the base lightly oiled, and if the tin is shallower than 3 inches (7.5 cm), line the sides with baking parchment.

Pre-heat the oven to gas mark 6, 400°F (200°C).

First of all, place all of the hazelnuts for the base and the filling into the oven and toast to a golden brown; use a timer and have a look after 5 minutes, giving them extra if they need it. Then remove them from the hot tray to cool. Set aside 4 oz (110 g) for the filling. Meanwhile, make the base of the cheesecake by crushing the biscuits in a polythene bag with a rolling pin – not too finely, though, as it's nice to have a fairly uneven texture, then chop the remaining 2 oz (50 g) toasted hazelnuts.

Tip all the crushed biscuit crumbs into a bowl, then add the chopped nuts and melted butter and mix everything very thoroughly before packing into the base of the cake tin, pressing it very firmly all over. Now place the tin in the oven and pre-bake the crust for 20 minutes. Then remove it and let it cool while you make the filling. Reduce the oven temperature to gas mark 2, 300°F (150°C).

To make the filling, first place 2 inches (5 cm) of water into a saucepan, then put the saucepan on to heat and meanwhile, break the chocolate into small squares and place this into a basin. As soon as the water is boiling, remove the pan from the heat and place the bowl on top until everything melts. Don't be tempted to put the bowl on top of the saucepan while the water is still boiling – because of the high cocoa-solids content – the chocolate mustn't get overheated or it will separate.

Now spoon the mascarpone and fromage frais into a large bowl and whisk them together until smooth, preferably with an electric hand whisk. Then add the eggs and sugar and give it another good whisking before adding the melted chocolate – use a rubber spatula so that you get every last bit of chocolate from the basin – and then lightly whisk the chocolate into the egg mixture. Finally, fold in the raisins and toasted hazelnuts.

Now pour the mixture into the tin, smoothing it out with the back of a spoon, then place it on the centre shelf of the oven and bake for 1¼ hours. After that, turn the oven off but leave the cheesecake inside until it's completely cold.

To make the chocolate curls: melt the chocolate, as before, then pour it on to a flat, smooth surface. The underside of a large plate will do. It should form a circle of about 6 inches diameter (15 cm) and ¼ inch (5 mm) thick. Place the plate into the fridge to chill for 45 minutes. What you want is the chocolate to be set hard enough so that if you press the surface of the chocolate it doesn't leave an indentation.

Now take it from the fridge and use a cheese slicer, otherwise a sharp knife will do if you hold the blade in both hands. Just pull it all along the chocolate towards you and it should curl up. What is very important to know here is that if it doesn't curl and you end up with a pile of chocolate shavings they'll look just as nice – either way, place them in a rigid plastic container and then put this in the fridge until you need them.

To serve the cheesecake, sprinkle the surface with chocolate curls, dust with a sprinkling of cocoa powder and serve in slices with crème fraîche or cream, handed round separately ▪

Compote of Fresh Figs in Muscat Wine with Vanilla Custard

Serves 4

This is a good way to serve imported figs which are rarely ripe and ready to eat.

8 fresh figs

½ bottle (37.5 cl) Muscat wine

1 vanilla pod

1 strip lemon zest

10 fl oz (275 ml) milk

3 large egg yolks

1 rounded teaspoon cornflour

1 tablespoon mild runny honey

First, select a lidded saucepan or frying pan, large enough to hold the figs in a single layer. Pour in the wine, add the lemon zest and vanilla pod and bring it up to simmering point. Now stab each fig two or three times with a skewer, then, using a long-handled spoon, lower them into the liquid, stalk side up. Cover and cook gently for 5-10 minutes or until they are tender. Now use a draining spoon to transfer them to a shallow serving dish where they can sit in a single layer. Then scoop out the lemon zest and the vanilla pod (reserving this for use later) and boil the liquid rapidly until it has reduced to half its original volume. Pour it over the figs, leave to cool and chill until needed.

To make the custard, wipe the vanilla pod, split it lengthways and place it in a saucepan along with the milk. Heat it very gently and meanwhile, whisk the egg yolks, cornflour and honey together in a basin. When the milk has come to boiling point, remove the vanilla pod and pour on to the egg mixture, whisking it in as you pour. Then return the whole mixture to the pan and put it back on the heat, whisking gently, until it has thickened. Now pour the custard into a jug, cover with clingfilm, leave to cool and then chill. Remove from the fridge 1 hour before serving with the figs ▪

Left: Pears Baked in Marsala Wine
Top right: Chocolate Blancmange with Cappuccino Sauce

Chocolate Blancmange with Cappuccino Sauce
Serves 8

I have had a long association with chocolate blancmange: I've always wanted it desperately but never been able to make it successfully. This time, eureka! The result – absolute perfection, a good texture, the right amount of wobble and a lovely frothy coffee sauce to pour over.

7 oz (200 g) dark chocolate (75 per cent cocoa solids)

10 fl oz (275 ml) double cream

10 fl oz (275 ml) milk

5 large egg yolks

3 oz (75 g) golden caster sugar

1 dessertspoon cornflour

2 level teaspoons vegetarian gelatine powder (measure carefully)

For the cappuccino sauce:

6 slightly rounded teaspoons instant espresso powder

2 fl oz (55 ml) milk

1 rounded tablespoon golden caster sugar

10 fl oz (275 ml) whipping cream

cocoa powder, to dust

You will also need 8 small pudding basins of 5 fl oz (150 ml) capacity, brushed with groundnut oil or other flavourless oil.

First of all, break up the chocolate: this is easiest to do by bashing the pack with a rolling pin before you unwrap it. Then pour the double cream and milk into a medium saucepan and heat it to just below simmering point.

Meanwhile, using an electric hand whisk, beat the egg yolks, sugar and cornflour together in a mixing bowl. Then, sprinkle the gelatine over the top and whisk again. When the cream mixture is hot, remove from the heat and whisk in the broken chocolate, beating vigorously until the chocolate has

melted and the mixture is smooth. Now gradually pour the hot chocolate over the egg yolk mixture, whisking as you go and then continue to whisk for a further 2 minutes to make sure everything is thoroughly mixed. Then return this chocolate custard mixture to the saucepan and place it back over a gentle heat, stirring all the time, until the mixture has thickened, this takes 3-4 minutes (don't panic, the small amount of cornflour will keep the mixture stable and prevent it from curdling).

Now immediately divide the chocolate mixture between the oiled pudding basins, filling them to around three-quarters full – you need to work quickly as the mixture will soon thicken. Smooth the tops and then place the basins on a tray, cover with clingfilm and chill in the fridge for at least 4 hours.

To make the cappuccino sauce, heat the milk and sugar in a small saucepan, then whisk the espresso powder once the mixture is hot. Then remove it from the heat and allow it to cool before pouring it into a mixing bowl, then add the cream. Now beat the mixture until slightly frothy and beginning to thicken, then leave it to stand for about 5 minutes while you unmould the chocolate creams. (You can make the sauce up to 4 hours ahead and store it, covered, in the fridge.)

To unmould, ease the cream away from the edge of the basin with your little finger, then invert the basin on to a plate and give it a really hefty shaking. Using a draining spoon, lift some of the cappuccino 'froth' off the top of the sauce and place a spoonful on the top of each cream, then pour the remaining thinner sauce around each plate. Finish with a light dusting of cocoa and serve ■

Pears Baked in Marsala Wine
Serves 8

The rich, dark flavour of Marsala combined with fragrant pear juices is quite a stunning combination. When you shop for the pears, looks are important: a good pear shape and a long stalk intact are essential, and the fruit needs to be hard and not ripe – which is perhaps fortunate as ripe pears always seem difficult to find. This recipe can also be made with red wine or strong dry cider – each version has its own particular charm.

For the pears:

8 large hard pears

1 pint (570 ml) Marsala

2 oz (50 g) golden caster sugar

2 whole cinnamon sticks

1 vanilla pod

1 rounded dessertspoon arrowroot

1 x 500 ml tub crème fraîche, to serve (optional)

You will also need a large flameproof casserole with a tight-fitting lid.

Pre-heat the oven to gas mark ½, 250°F (130°C). (If you have a post-1992 oven, gas mark ½ will be gas mark 1. Please refer to the manufacturer's instruction booklet for further information.)

Using a potato peeler, thinly pare off the outer skin of the pears, but leave the stalks intact. Then slice off a thin little disc from each pear base so they can sit upright. Now lay the pears on their side in the casserole. Pour in the Marsala, then sprinkle over the sugar and add the cinnamon sticks and vanilla pod.

Now bring everything up to simmering point, then cover the casserole and bake the pears on a low shelf in the oven for about 1½ hours. After that, remove the casserole from the oven, turn the pears over on to their

other side, then replace the lid and return them to the oven for a further 1½ hours. When the pears are cooked, transfer them to a serving bowl to cool, leaving the liquid in the casserole. Then remove the cinnamon sticks and vanilla pod. Place the casserole over direct heat and then, in a cup, mix the arrowroot with a little cold water until you have a smooth paste. Add this to the casserole, whisking with a balloon whisk as you add it. Bring the syrup just up to simmering point, by which time it will have thickened sightly. Then remove from the heat and when the syrup is cool, spoon it over the pears, basting them well.

Now cover the pears with foil or clingfilm and place them in the fridge to chill thoroughly. Serve the pears sitting upright in individual dishes with the sauce spooned over and, if using, the crème fraîche handed round separately ■

Fresh Peaches Baked in Marsala Wine

In the summer months peaches make a perfect alternative to pears. Pre-heat the oven to gas mark 4, 350°F (180°C). For 6, use 6 firm, ripe peaches that have been stoned, halved and peeled (cover them with boiling water, leave for 30 seconds, then drain and slip off their skins). Poach the peach halves in a shallow baking dish in 10 fl oz (275 ml) Marsala with 1½ oz (40 g) golden caster sugar, uncovered, for 35-40 minutes. Then drain the juices into a small saucepan and thicken the liquid as described above with 1 rounded teaspoon of arrowroot. Pour the syrup back over the peaches and leave to cool. Cover and refrigerate for 24 hours before serving with crème fraîche or mascarpone cream (see page 240).

Apricot Hazelnut Meringue
Serves 6

A light and delicious – and rather special – pudding. The sharpness of the apricots counteracts the sweetness of the meringue, which has a lovely nutty flavour. You can buy ready-ground hazelnuts at wholefood shops and delicatessens, or if you're grinding your own, brown them first in the oven gas mark 4, 350°F (180°C) for 8 minutes and grind them in a food processor or blender.

For the meringue:

3 oz (75 g) ground hazelnuts

3 large egg whites

6 oz (175 g) white caster sugar

For the filling:

4 oz (110 g) dried apricots, soaked overnight

juice 1 small orange

1 small strip orange rind

½ inch (1 cm) cinnamon stick

1 tablespoon soft brown sugar

2 teaspoons arrowroot

To finish:

10 fl oz (275 ml) double cream

a few whole toasted hazelnuts

Pre-heat the oven to gas mark 5, 375°F (190°C).

You will also need two 7 inch (18 cm), 1½ inch (4 cm) deep sponge tins, lightly greased, and the base lined with baking parchment.

First, whisk the egg whites in a large scrupulously clean bowl until they form stiff peaks, then whisk in the caster sugar, a little at a time. Then, using a metal spoon, lightly fold in the ground hazelnuts. Now divide the mixture equally between the two tins and level them out.

Bake the meringues on the centre shelf of the oven for 20-30 minutes. Leave them in the tins to cool for 30 minutes before turning out (the surface will look uneven, but don't worry). When they're cooled, loosen round the edges, turn them out on to wire racks and strip off the base papers.

While the meringues are cooking, you can prepare the apricot filling. Drain the soaked apricots in a sieve over a bowl, then transfer the apricots to a small saucepan and add the orange juice, rind, cinnamon stick and sugar, plus 2 tablespoons of the soaking water. Simmer gently for 10-15 minutes or until they are tender when tested with a skewer, then remove the cinnamon stick and orange rind. Mix the arrowroot with a little cold water and add this to the apricot mixture, stirring over a fairly low heat, until the mixture has thickened. Then leave it to get quite cold.

To serve the meringue: whip the cream, then carefully spread the cold apricot mixture over one meringue, followed by half the whipped cream. Place the other meringue on top, spread the remaining cream over that and decorate the top with some whole toasted hazelnuts ■

Christmas Pud
(without the pudding), served with Marsala Syllabub
Serves 8

What I've done is to take all the essential ingredients – the fruit, nuts, spices and so on – and make them into a very slowly cooked compote in Marsala wine, so that the wonderful flavours can develop and mingle together. The result is quite sublime.

For the compote:

6 oz (175 g) dried apricots, quartered

6 oz (175 g) dried figs, chopped the same size as the apricots

6 oz (175 g) dried Agen prunes, pitted and chopped the same size as the apricots

6 oz (175 g) large raisins

1 oz (25 g) whole candied peel, finely chopped

¼ teaspoon mixed spice

a few good gratings of nutmeg

1 small Cox's apple, chopped (peel left on)

grated zest and juice ½ orange

grated zest and juice ½ lemon

1 pint (570 ml) Marsala

1 oz (25 g) whole blanched almonds

For the Marsala syllabub:

3 fl oz (75 ml) Marsala

1 dessertspoon molasses sugar

5 fl oz (150 ml) double cream

whole nutmeg

You will also need a flameproof casserole with a capacity of about 4 pints (2.25 litres).

All you do to start off with is place all the Christmas-pudding compote ingredients (except the almonds) in a bowl, cover with a cloth and leave in a cool place overnight.

The next day, preheat the oven to gas mark ½, 250°F (130°C). (If you have a post-1992 oven, gas mark ½ will be gas mark 1. Please refer to the manufacturer's instruction booklet for further information.)

Pour everything from the bowl into the casserole. Place it over direct heat and bring it up to a gentle simmer. After that, cover with a lid and place the casserole in the oven to cook very slowly for 3 hours. Leave the compote to cool, then cover and chill in the fridge until needed. (This will keep for up to 10 days in the fridge.)

Meanwhile, toast the almonds: to do this, cut them finely into thin slivers and place them on a piece of foil, then pop them under a hot grill. Don't leave them, but watch them like a hawk until they're nice and golden brown. Then cool and wrap them in foil until needed.

When you are ready to make the syllabub, pour the Marsala into a bowl, add the sugar and leave aside for about 10 minutes to allow the sugar to dissolve. Then pour in the cream and whisk with an electric hand whisk until it stands in soft peaks. Cover and chill until needed.

To serve, stir the nuts into the fruit, then spoon the compote into stemmed glasses. After that, re-whisk the syllabub and spoon it on top of the fruits and lastly, grate a little nutmeg over the top ■

Christmas Pud (without the pudding)
served with Marsala Syllabub

Left: Strawberry and Balsamic Ice Cream with Sweet Strawberry and Mint Salsa
Top right: Rhubarb, Almond and Ginger Crumble

Strawberry and Balsamic Ice Cream with Sweet Strawberry and Mint Salsa
Serves 8-10

The addition of balsamic vinegar to dairy products like cream and ice cream tempers the richness and adds a subtle flavour. Couple this with its affinity with strawberries and you have something exquisite and unique.

1 lb (450 g) strawberries

2 fl oz (55 ml) balsamic vinegar

4 oz (110 g) granulated sugar

15 fl oz (425 ml) whipping cream

For the salsa:

9 oz (250 g) strawberries

¾ oz (20 g) fresh mint – 1 tablespoon chopped and the rest left whole for decoration

1 tablespoon balsamic vinegar

1 tablespoon molasses sugar

You will also need a 2 lb (900 g) loaf tin, lined with clingfilm.

First of all, roughly chop 12 oz (350 g) of the strawberries and place them in a bowl, sprinkle in the balsamic vinegar, stir well and leave them to marinate for about 30 minutes.

Meanwhile, you need to make a sugar syrup. To do this, place the granulated sugar and 2 fl oz (55 ml) of water in a small saucepan. Then put it on a gentle heat and allow the sugar to dissolve completely, stirring from time to time – this should take about 5-6 minutes. When there are no granules left, let the syrup come up to simmering point and simmer very gently for a further 5 minutes.

Now whiz the prepared strawberries and the sugar syrup together in a food processor until you have a smooth purée. Then you need to strain the purée through a nylon sieve (metal tends to discolour) into a bowl to extract the seeds.

Next, mix the purée with the whipping cream and either put the whole lot into an ice-cream maker to freeze-churn, or if you don't have an ice-cream maker, you need to pour the mixture into a shallow polythene box measuring 8 x 8 x 2½ inches (20 x 20 x 6 cm), cover with a lid and pop it into the freezer for about 3 hours. It's impossible to be precise because freezers vary. What you need is a mixture that is half frozen; the particles around the edge will be frozen and the centre will be soft.

At this stage, you remove it from the freezer and, using an electric hand whisk, beat the frozen bit into the soft bits until you get a uniform texture. Then cover and freeze again, by which time it will be almost completely frozen. Now you need to give it a second whisk and the ice cream is ready.

Whether you are using an ice-cream maker or the hand-whisk method, the next stage is to fold in the rest of the strawberries by hand (first cut in slices), then pack the ice cream into the loaf tin. Then cover and freeze till needed.

Before serving the ice cream, you need to remove it from the freezer to the main body of the fridge for about 2 hours.

To make the salsa, all you do is chop the strawberries into tiny, even-sized pieces. Then gently heat the balsamic vinegar in a small pan, add the molasses sugar and just heat it gently until all the sugar is dissolved. Then remove the pan from the heat, allow it to cool, then combine the strawberries, chopped mint and balsamic mixture.

Then, to serve the ice cream, turn it out on to a flat board, remove the clingfilm and cut it into slices, garnishing each slice with some of the salsa and a sprig of mint ■

Rhubarb, Almond and Ginger Crumble
Serves 6

Rhubarb is never better than in this most English of puddings. On Sundays, we serve it with proper custard, an extra luxurious addition. One of my other favourite accompaniments is stem ginger ice cream. This recipe also works well with topped-and-tailed gooseberries.

2 lb (900 g) rhubarb

1 rounded teaspoon grated fresh root ginger

4 oz (110 g) golden caster sugar

For the crumble:

4 oz (110 g) whole almonds, skin on

1 teaspoon ground ginger

3 oz (75 g) chilled butter, cut into small dice

6 oz (175 g) self-raising flour, sifted

2 teaspoons ground cinnamon

4 oz (110 g) demerara sugar

You will also need a round, ovenproof baking dish with a diameter of 9½ inches (24 cm) and 1¾ inches (4.5 cm) deep.

To serve:

custard, ice cream or pouring cream

Pre-heat the oven to gas mark 6, 400°F (200°C).

Begin by preparing the rhubarb. First of all, wash it, then trim off the leaves and cut the stalks roughly into 1 inch (2.5 cm) chunks. Next, toss them in a bowl with the sugar and freshly grated root ginger, then place them in the baking dish and keep on one side.

Now make the crumble, which couldn't be simpler, as it is all made in a food processor. All you do is place the butter, sifted flour, cinnamon, ground ginger and sugar in the processor and give it a whiz till it resembles crumbs. Next, add the almonds and process again, not too fast – they should be fairly finely chopped but still with a few chunky bits. If you don't have a processor, in a large bowl, rub the butter into the sifted flour until it resembles crumbs, then stir in the almonds (which should be fairly finely chopped by hand), the cinnamon, ginger and sugar.

Now you need to press the rhubarb very firmly with your hands all over the base of the dish to spread it evenly without too many large lumps sticking out. Then simply sprinkle the crumble mixture all over the rhubarb, spreading it right up to the edges of the dish, and, using the flat of your hands, press it down quite firmly all over; the more tightly it is packed together, the crisper it will be. Then finish off by lightly running a fork all over the surface.

Now bake the crumble on the centre shelf of the oven for 35-40 minutes, by which time the rhubarb will be soft and the topping golden brown and crisp. Leave it to rest for 10-15 minutes before serving, then serve it warm with custard, ice cream or pouring cream ■

Baked Apple and Almond Pudding
Serves 4-6

Classic Crepes Suzette
Serves 6

Since this recipe was given to me many years ago by the proprietor of the Sign of the Angel in Laycock, it has become really popular with readers, as I know from their many letters.

1 lb (450 g) cooking apples, peeled, cored and sliced

2 oz (50 g) soft brown sugar

4 oz (110 g) butter, at room temperature

4 oz (110 g) golden caster sugar

2 large eggs, beaten

4 oz (110 g) ground almonds

Pre-heat the oven to gas mark 4, 350°F (180°C).

You will also need a round, ovenproof baking dish with a diameter of 8 inches (20 cm), and 1¾ inches (4.5 cm) deep, buttered.

Place the apples in a saucepan with the brown sugar and approximately 2 tablespoons of water, simmer gently until soft, and then arrange them in the bottom of the prepared pie dish.

In a mixing bowl, cream the butter and caster sugar until pale and fluffy and then beat in the eggs a little at a time. When all the egg is in, carefully and lightly fold in the ground almonds. Now spread this mixture over the apples, and even out the surface with the back of a tablespoon. Then bake on a 'highish' shelf in the oven for exactly 1 hour.

This pudding is equally good served warm or cold – either way, it's nice with some chilled pouring cream. It will keep in the fridge for 3 or 4 days ▪

This is a qualifier for my 1960s recipe revival. There was a time when this recipe was certainly overexposed, but now that it has become a forgotten rarity, we can all re-appreciate its undoubted charm, which remains in spite of changes in fashion.

For the crepes:
4 oz (110 g) plain flour

pinch salt

2 large eggs

7 fl oz (200 ml) milk, mixed with 3 fl oz (75 ml) water

grated zest 1 medium orange

1 tablespoon golden caster sugar

2 oz (50 g) butter, melted

For the sauce:
5 fl oz (150 ml) orange juice (from 3-4 medium oranges)

grated zest 1 medium orange

grated zest and juice 1 small lemon

1 tablespoon golden caster sugar

3 tablespoons Grand Marnier, Cointreau or brandy, plus a little extra, if you are going to flame the pancakes

2 oz (50 g) unsalted butter

You will also need two solid-based frying pans, one with a 7 inch (18 cm) base diameter and the other with a 10 inch (25.5 cm) base, some kitchen paper, greaseproof paper, a palette knife or flexible pan slice, and a ladle.

First of all, to make the crepes, sift the flour and salt into a large mixing bowl with the sieve held high above the bowl so the flour gets an airing.

Now make a well in the centre of the flour and break the eggs into it. Then begin whisking the eggs – any sort of whisk or even a fork will do – incorporating any bits of flour from around the edge of the bowl as you do so. Next, gradually add small quantities of the milk and water mixture, still whisking (don't worry about any lumps – they will eventually disappear as you whisk). When all the liquid has been added, use a rubber spatula to scrape any elusive bits of flour from around the edge into the centre. Then, add the orange zest and caster sugar and whisk once more until the batter is smooth, with the consistency of thin cream.

Now spoon 2 tablespoons of the melted butter into the batter and whisk it in, then pour the rest into a bowl and use it when needed to lubricate the pan, using a wodge of kitchen paper to smear it round.

Next, get the 7 inch (18 cm) pan really hot, then turn the heat down to medium and to start with, do a test crepe to see if you're using the correct amount of batter. I find 1½ tablespoons about right. It's also helpful if you spoon the batter into a ladle so it can be poured into the hot pan in one go. As soon as the batter hits the hot pan, tip it around from side to side to get the base evenly coated with batter. It should take only half a minute or so to cook; you can lift the edge with a palette knife to see if it's tinged gold as it should be.

Flip the crepe over with a pan slice or palette knife – the other side will need a few seconds only – then simply slide it out of the pan on to a plate. If they look a bit ragged in the pan, no matter, because they are going to be folded anyway. You should end up with 15-16 crepes, and as you make them, stack them between sheets of greaseproof paper.

For the sauce, mix all the ingredients – with the exception of the butter – in a bowl. At the same time warm the plates on which the crepes are going to be served. Now melt the butter in the larger frying pan, pour in the sauce and allow it to heat very gently. Then place the first crepe in the pan and give it time to warm through before folding it in half and then half again to make a triangular shape. Slide this on to the very edge of the pan, tilt the pan slightly so the sauce runs back into the centre, then add the next crepe. Continue like this until they're all re-heated, folded and well soaked with the sauce.

You can flame them at this point if you like. Heat a ladle by holding it over a gas flame or by resting it on the edge of a hotplate, then, away from the heat, pour a little liqueur or brandy into it, return it to the heat to warm the spirit, then set light to it. Carry the flaming ladle to the table over the pan and pour the flames over the crepes before serving on the warmed plates ▪

Basic Pancakes with Sugar and Lemon
Omit the grated orange zest and tablespoon of caster sugar from the pancake mixture and use 2 tablespoons of batter at a time in a 7 inch (18 cm) pan, as basic pancakes should be a little thicker than crepes. You should end up with 12-14 pancakes. Stack the pancakes as you make them between sheets of greaseproof paper on a plate fitted over simmering water, to keep them warm while you make the rest.

To serve, sprinkle each pancake with freshly squeezed lemon juice and caster sugar, fold in half, then in half again to form triangles, or else simply roll them up. Serve, sprinkled with a little more sugar and lemon juice and extra sections of lemon.

Basic Pancakes with Sugar and Lemon

Chocolate Hazelnut Meringue Roulade
Serves 10-12

When we first put this on the menu at Delia's City Brasserie at the football club, it was one of the fastest-selling desserts ever. Please don't worry about rolling it up – if it cracks, it's quite normal. It's lovely having the layers of meringue and filling providing a contrast to each other.

7 oz (200 g) dark chocolate (75 per cent cocoa solids), broken into small pieces
4 oz (110 g) hazelnuts
4 large egg whites
8 oz (225 g) golden caster sugar
1 pint (570 ml) double cream

You will also need a baking tray measuring 10 x 14 inches (25.5 x 35 cm), ¾ inch (2 cm) deep, lightly oiled, and lined with baking parchment, to stand 2.5 cm (1 in) proud of the tray.

Preheat the oven to gas mark 5, 375°F (190°C).

Toast the hazelnuts on a baking sheet on the top shelf of the oven for 8 minutes, cool and grind in a food processor until very finely chopped, but do not over-process or they will turn oily. Whisk the egg whites in a large, clean bowl, until they form soft peaks, then whisk in the caster sugar a little at a time. Using a metal spoon, fold the ground hazelnuts into the meringue and spread the mixture evenly in the prepared tin. Bake in the centre of the oven for 20 minutes, cool and then turn out on to a piece of baking parchment, slightly larger than the roulade, on a clean surface. Gently ease away the lining paper.

Melt the chocolate in a heatproof bowl over simmering water, making sure the bowl doesn't touch the water. Then remove the bowl from the heat and leave the chocolate to cool. Whip the cream and divide between 2 bowls. Reserving 4 tablespoons of the melted chocolate for decoration, quickly but gently fold the rest of the melted chocolate into one bowl of whipped cream until it looks evenly mixed and mousse-like. Spread this mixture evenly over the roulade to within ½ inch (1 cm) of the edge. Spread the remaining whipped cream over the chocolate mixture.

Now, with the meringue placed long side towards you, and using the paper to assist you, roll up the meringue to form a long log shape (don't worry about the roulade cracking – it's quite normal).

Make sure the seam is at the base of the roulade and, using a spoon, drizzle the reserved chocolate all over the top, using a zigzag movement. Lift on to a long serving dish and chill in the fridge. Remove from the fridge about 15 minutes before serving ▪

Fromage Frais Cheesecake with Strawberry Sauce
Serves 8

Whenever I see cheesecake on a menu I'm filled with longing – there's something awfully comforting about cheesecake – but the question always arises as to whether it will or will not be cloying (and if it is, what a waste of calories!). This version is definitely not cloying: it's light in texture and, made with fromage frais, a bit lighter on the calories, too.

For the filling:
12 oz (350 g) 8 per cent fat fromage frais at room temperature
12 oz (350 g) full-fat curd cheese at room temperature
3 large eggs
6 oz (175 g) golden caster sugar
1 teaspoon pure vanilla extract

For the topping:
1 lb 8 oz (700 g) strawberries, hulled
2 tablespoons golden caster sugar

For the base:
6 oz (175 g) sweet oat biscuits
2 oz (50 g) butter, melted
2 oz (50 g) coarsely chopped toasted hazelnuts

You will also need a 9 inch (23 cm) springform cake tin, the sides and base lightly oiled.

Pre-heat the oven to gas mark 6, 400°F (200°C).

Begin by crushing the biscuits in a food processor, or by putting them in a plastic bag and rolling them with a rolling pin, then mix them with the melted butter and stir in the hazelnuts.

Now press the mixture into the base of the tin and pre-bake for 15 minutes, then lower the temperature to gas mark 2, 300°F (150°C).

For the filling, in a large bowl combine the curd cheese, fromage frais, eggs, sugar and vanilla, using an electric hand whisk to beat everything together until silky smooth.

Now pour this mixture over the biscuit base and place on the centre shelf of the oven to cook for 30 minutes. At the end of the cooking time, turn off the oven, but leave the cheesecake in the cooling oven to set until it's completely cold (I find that this is the best method, as it prevents cracking).

Remove the cheesecake from the oven and from the tin, transfer it to a plate, cover and chill till needed.

For the topping, weigh out 8 oz (225 g) of the strawberries into a bowl, sprinkle them with the golden caster sugar and leave to soak for 30 minutes. After that, pile these strawberries and the sugar into a food processor and purée, then pass the purée through a nylon sieve to remove the seeds.

To serve the cheesecake, arrange the remaining strawberries all over the surface, then spoon some of the purée over them and hand the rest of the purée round separately ▪

Recipes for vegans

Roasted Tomato Soup with a Purée of Basil
and Olive Croutons

Ajo Blanco (chilled almond soup)

Globe Artichokes with Shallot Vinaigrette

Roasted Tomato Salad

Roasted Red Peppers Stuffed with Fennel

Belarussian Carrot Salad

Anya Potato Salad
with Shallots and Vinaigrette

Pitta Bread Salad

Brown and Wild Rice Salad
with Dried Cranberries

Bruschetta with Tomato and Basil

Mexican Guacamole

Chinese Beansprout Salad
with Soy Dressing

Sweet and Sour Red Onion Salad

Fresh Mexican Tomato Salsa

Tomato and Balsamic Jam

Pears in Balsamic Vinaigrette

Spaghetti with Olive Oil, Garlic and Chilli

Singapore Stir-fried Noodles

Pasta with Pepper Relish

Lemon Pasta with Herbs
and Cracked Pepper

Soba Noodles with Soy and Citrus Dressing

Aduki Bean and Brown Rice Salad
Perfect Rice

Dolmades (stuffed vine leaves)

Thai Bean Salad with Pink Grapefruit
and Grapes

Stuffed Cabbage Leaves
with Toasted Pistachios and Pine Nuts

Mixed Vegetable Salad à la Grècque
Spiced Pilau Rice with Nuts

Three Bean Salad with Cider Dressing

Hummus bi Tahina

Mashed Black-Eyed Beancakes
with Ginger Onion Marmalade

Stuffed Yellow Peppers with Pilau Rice,
Currants and Toasted Pine Nuts

Turkish Stuffed Tomatoes

Stir-fried Tofu with Oyster Mushrooms

Thai Green Vegetable Curry

Silken Tofu with Chilli, Spring Onion
and Frizzled Leek

Fresh Date and Apple Chutney

Sweet Pepper and Coriander Relish

Spiced Pickled Pears

Red Onion, Tomato and Chilli Relish

Oven-Roasted Cauliflower and Broccoli
with Garlic

Oven-roasted Winter Vegetables

Purple Sprouting Broccoli
with Chilli, Lime and Sesame Dressing

Sliced Potatoes Baked with Tomatoes
and Basil

Mashed Potato with Garlic-infused Olive Oil

Oven-roasted Red Potatoes
with Red Onion and Red Wine Vinegar

Compote of Glazed Shallots

Compote of Garlic and Sweet Peppers

Parsnips with a Mustard and Maple Glaze

Toasted Spinach with Pine Nuts, Raisins
and Sherry Vinegar

Barbecued Sweetcorn

Glazed Baby Turnips

Oven-roasted Chunky Chips

Baby Summer Vegetables
with Lemon Vinaigrette

Marinated Courgettes
with a Herb Vinaigrette

Oriental Green Beans with Red Chillies
and Toasted Sesame Seeds

Stir-fried Green Vegetables

Sauté Potatoes Niçoise

Oven-roasted Carrots with Coriander

Pickled Beetroot with Shallots

Provençal Vegetable Stew (ratatouille)

Green Peppercorn Bread

Pears Baked in Marsala Wine

Picture credits

Jean Cazals 82, 161, 166, 204, 227.

Miki Duisterhof 6, 14, 17, 18, 22, 26, 29, 31, 32, 40, 43, 47, 48, 51, 55, 56, 57, 59, 60, 63, 64, 67, 71, 72, 74, 75, 77, 78, 82, 90, 94, 97, 101, 102, 105, 106, 110, 113, 114, 119, 133, 134, 138, 141, 143, 146, 150, 154, 166, 173, 177, 180, 184, 188, 191, 192, 199, 200, 203, 204, 212, 215, 219, 220, 224, 227, 238, 246, 258.

Ken Field 78, 82, 137, 157, 173.

Jared Fowler 210/211.

Norman Hollands 68, 183.

Peter Knab 11, 28, 35, 36, 40, 43, 44, 51, 63, 71, 78, 82, 84/5, 86, 89, 90, 93, 108/9, 110, 114, 120, 123, 124, 128, 141, 146, 153, 157, 161, 166, 180, 184, 192, 201, 204, 207, 208, 212, 216, 223, 227, 229, 231, 232, 238, 241, 242, 246, 250, 254, 258.

Jonathan Lovekin 6, 14, 35, 38/9, 71, 150, 184, 196, 228, 234/5, 258.

David Munns 161, 231.

James Murphy 35, 192, 195.

Michael Paul 258.

Simon Smith 145, 253.

Dan Stevens 231.

Kevin Summers 6, 20/21, 35, 149, 162, 164/5, 178/9, 204, 242.

Patrice de Villiers 10.

Ian Wallace 169.

Simon Walton 81.

Cameron Watt 3, 6, 8, 13, 14, 18, 51, 52, 63, 78, 90, 95, 110, 116, 117, 126/7, 137, 141, 142, 146, 166, 170, 173, 174, 175, 180, 187, 212, 219, 242, 245, 249, 250, 258.

Rob White 6, 204.

Peter Williams 98.

Useful suppliers and stockists

Cheese

Twineham Grange Farms
Bob Lane
Twineham
Haywards Heath
Sussex RH17 5NH
Telephone 01444 881394
enquiries@twinehamgrangefarms.co.uk
Italian creamery products, including a
vegetarian parmesan-style cheese
and ricotta

Neal's Yard Dairy
17 Short's Gardens
London WC2H 9UP
Telephone 020 7045 0555
mailorder@nealsyarddairy.co.uk
British and Irish cheeses
by mail order, including a selection of
cheeses made without animal rennet

Ingredients

Japanese
Clearspring Ltd
www.clearspring.co.uk
Telephone 020 8746 0152
Mail order available

Thai
Thai Taste
www.thaitaste.co.uk
Telephone 0870 241 1960
Mail order available

Italian
Fratelli Camisa Ltd
www.camisa.co.uk
Telephone 01992 763076
Mail order available

Esperya
www.esperya.com
info@esperya.com
Mail order available

Spanish
PataNegra
www.patanegra.net
info@patanegra.net
Mail order available

Spices
The Spice Shop
www.thespicesshop.co.uk
1 Blenheim Crescent
London
W11 2EE
Telephone 020 7221 4448
Mail order available

Kitchen Equipment

Cucina Direct
www.cucinadirect.co.uk
Telephone 020 8246 4311
Sales@cucinadirect.co.uk
Mail order available

David Mellor
www.devidmellordesign.com
4 Sloane Square
London SW1 8EE
Telephone 020 7730 4259
Mail order available

Divertimenti
www.divertimenti.co.uk
33/34 Marylebone High Street
London W1U 4PT
Telephone 020 7935 0689
Sales@divertimenti.co.uk
Mail order available

Lakeland Limited
www.lakelandlimited.co.uk
Telephone 015394 88100
Mail order available
and outlets nationwide

Catering

*For more information on Delia's restaurant
and Canary Catering:*
Norwich City Football Club
Carrow Road
Norwich NR1 1JE
Telephone 01603 218704
Reception@ncfc-canaries.co.uk

Index